RESTORING
OUR
LOST
LEGACY

Restoration Foundation

Understanding the Jewish roots of our faith is a golden key that unlocks the treasures of Holy Scripture and enables us to enrich our Christian lives. This fundamental concept is the focus of Restoration Foundation, an international, transdenominational, multi-cultural, and interracial educational and publishing resource to the body of Christ.

Restoration Foundation features a network of scholars, church leaders, and laypersons who share the vision for restoring to the church the Hebrew foundations of our Christian faith and returning the church to a biblical relationship of love and support for the international Jewish community and the nation of Israel.

We are pleased to make available to all denominations and fellowships the teaching of the gifted scholars and Christian leaders in our network. Conferences, seminars, and other instructional forums are available on a wide range of topics that can be tailored to each individual setting. We also teach these concepts throughout the world with our International Institutes.

We publish *Restore!* magazine, a high-quality journal featuring theological balance and scholarly documentation which helps Christians recover their Hebrew heritage while strengthening their faith in Jesus.

Restoration Foundation also publishes and distributes Golden Key Books in order to disseminate teaching about Christianity's Judaic foundations.

The ministry of Restoration Foundation is made possible by our many partners around the world who share in our Golden Key Partnership program. If you would like to join us, you will have the satisfaction of knowing that you are a partner in an organization that is making a difference in the world by restoring Christians to their biblical Hebrew heritage, by eradicating Judaeophobia and anti-Semitism, by supporting Israel and the international Jewish community, and by encouraging collaborative efforts among those who share this vision.

For information about Restoration Foundation, *Restore!* magazine, Golden Key Books, and Golden Key Partnerships, contact us at the address below.

Restoration Foundation
P. O. Box 421218
Atlanta, Georgia 30342, U.S.A.

RESTORING
OUR
LOST
LEGACY

Christianity's Hebrew Heritage

Selected Essays and Lectures
By Dr. John D. Garr

GOLDEN KEY BOOKS
Restoration Foundation
P. O. Box 421218
Atlanta, Georgia 30342, U.S.A.

To my wife Pat, whose faithful love and support has made this book possible.

TABLE OF CONTENTS

FOREWORD

As a child, I heard the late Grady R. Kent minister on the Jewishness of Jesus and of the gospel. The pure and simple truth taught by this man of keen understanding and insight made a deep impact on my life and has since brought me to a full appreciation of the heritage of my Christian faith in the ancient religion of the Jewish people.

I have devoted much of my academic and spiritual life to research, writing, teaching, and preaching the truth about Christianity's historical and theological emergence from the matrix of biblical Judaism. I have come to realize that the church has been robbed of its rightful heritage with and among the Jewish people. As a result of the Judaeophobia, anti-Judaism, and anti-Semitism that have characterized Christianity for some nineteen centuries, the church and individual believers have been denied the rich relationship with God that should have been theirs if the church's inherent Jewishness had not been either outright denied or benignly neglected by Christian leaders.

Surely it is time to restore the church's lost legacy. As we prepare for the coming of Messiah, Peter's teaching in the earliest days of the church echo in our ears: "And that he may send Jesus Christ, who was preached to you before, whom heaven must receive until the times of restoration of all things, which God has spoken by the mouth of all his holy prophets since the world began." (Acts 3:20, 21). To understand what is to be restored, we must make a careful, detailed search of Scripture and history to determine what has been lost, damaged, or covered over. Then, restoration can begin.

For forty years, I have studied and written extensively on various aspects of this theme, analyzing the historical and scriptural Jewishness of earliest Christianity and the need for restoring the church's ancient heritage. At the urging of many of my colleagues, I have endeavored to collate some of my essays and lectures on Christianity's Hebrew foundations and publish them in this book.

DEFINITION OF TERMS

When we use the term *Judaism*, we speak of biblical Judaism, a Judaism that is grounded in the Torah, the written Word of God, in contrast with Rabbinic Judaism, which is based both in Scripture and in the traditions of the sages and rabbis. While much can be learned from the Talmud and from rabbinics to expand our understanding of God's Word and of Judaism, our faith must ever be established in the Hebrew Scriptures, both the first and the second testaments, which are able to make us "wise for salvation through faith which is in Christ Jesus" (2 Timothy 3:15). Our use of the term *Judaism*, then, connotes the system of praise, worship, and service that was manifest among the Hebrew prophets, kings, and sages from the time of Genesis to Malachi and perfected and extended to all mankind by Jesus the Messiah.

When we speak of the *Jewish roots* of Christian faith, we are talking about the biblical foundations of Christianity, which happen to have been from and of the Jews (John 4:22). We could perhaps more accurately use the term *biblical roots*; however, the term *biblical* does not convey our meaning clearly, for virtually all the diverse cultural manifestations of Christianity consider their doctrines and practices to be *biblical.* To be truly *biblical* is to think and act Hebraically, as Jesus did during his incarnation. We, therefore, emphasize the biblical roots of our faith as they were cultivated in the soil of Judaism and among the Jewish people.

Many practices in modern Judaism are biblical; however, others are merely cultural additions to biblical faith. We do not encourage Christians, therefore, to become culturally Jewish, to adopt the appearance or lifestyles normative among contemporary Jews. We do urge Christians to allow their faith in Jesus to manifest Judaic principles in their lives, to cause them to become Jewish in heart, and to help them support the international Jewish community.

MAINTAINING OUR EQUILIBRIUM

The quest to restore the church's biblically Judaic heritage is an exciting effort that draws clear lines between scriptural truth and the accretions of human tradition. This effort represents the ultimate reforming and restorative work, perhaps the final restoration in preparation for the coming of Messiah. Because of the momentous and historic nature of this work of restoration, it is imperative that those who share the vision–and work toward its fulfillment–maintain their equilibrium both theologically, spiritually, and practically. We simply cannot afford the luxury of extremism. This effort is so important to the health and renewal of the body of Messiah that we cannot allow it to be marginalized by losing our balance. We cannot allow the pendulum to swing from the extreme of the antinomianism of the Christian past to the other extreme of legalism, where we seek to acquire or maintain status before God by obedience to the law rather than by or in addition to grace through faith only in the shed blood of Jesus Christ.

Many Christians lose their balance and find themselves falling for everything, being blown away by every wind of teaching (Ephesians 4:14).

They like the comforts of their "ego trip" or their "holier-than-thou" status. They are like the Corinthians who simply delighted in hearing some new thing and indulging in spiritual excess. In 1 Corinthians 14:26, 40, Paul gave a lesson on balance to this Gentile church, addressing its history of extremism, flights of fancy, and immaturity. His fear was that they would be "corrupted from the simplicity that is in Christ"(2 Corinthians 11:3). He appealed to their familiar Olympic tradition, urging them to be like athletes who strive for mastery–"*temperate in all things*" (1 Corinthians 9:24, 25). Temperance is the art of maintaining the balance between extremities. Neither abstinence nor indulgence is the answer. Temperance finds a happy medium, a safe position that is both reasonable and practical and does not bring offense to others. Temperance in all things is *the law of the New Covenant.*

Balance is maintained in our physical bodies by two small organs in the inner ear. In like manner, it can be said that our spiritual balance is effected to a large degree by the still small voice in our inner spiritual ear that seeks to maintain our equilibrium and keep us on track. It is the Spirit of God that gently woos us and keeps us centered in God's will. When we hear his voice, he will never lead us into the dangers of excess.

There is one surefire way to avoid the extremes of legalism *and* antinomianism. The New Testament must always be for us the lens through which the "shadows" found in the Old Testament Scriptures are brought into picture-perfect focus (Colossians 2:17). Our faith must always remain Christocentric, grounded in the person of Jesus Christ. To deviate either to the left or to the right is to lose our equilibrium and our effectiveness in sharing this restoration truth with our fellow believers in Messiah.

The restoration of the Jewish roots of our faith has the potential to be one of the greatest blessings that we have experienced since the church lost its "Jewish connection" some nineteen centuries ago. Extremism and unbalanced approaches to this restoration, however, can do much damage not only to the restoration itself but also to the spiritual condition of those who are so engaged.

I encourage you, therefore, to read carefully chapters 6, 7, and 8: "A Perfect Sacrifice," "Christ, Our Righteousness," and "Raised Again for Our Justification." Without a clear understanding of New Testament foundations, one treads dangerous ground in exploring Judaism and can easily be enticed by his own immaturity into legalism, elitism, and judgmentalism. The church's one foundation is Jesus Christ, the risen Lord, and believers are justified before God only by grace through faith in him. As we build upon the bedrock-firm foundation of his teachings, we will find ourselves enriched by God's system of praise, worship, and service that was revealed in Judaism and perfected by Messiah Yeshua.

ACKNOWLEDGMENTS

The publication of this book would not have been possible without considerable input from many close personal friends and colleagues. I would like to honor and offer my deepest gratitude to those who have shared their lives, minds, and spirits with me over the years.

Foremost among these was my mentor, the late Bishop Grady R. Kent, a devout man of pioneering insight who developed many of the fundamental ideas contained in this book in the 1940's and 1950's, at a time when there was little understanding in the church about its biblical Hebrew foundations. His teaching kindled a fire in my heart that has burned incessantly for over thirty-five years.

I am deeply indebted to my late father, Rev. D. E. Garr, a faithful pastor and overseer with over 65 years of service to the body of Christ, for his balanced and rock-solid theological perspectives and his dignified, unassuming approach to every aspect of life.

Other scholars, teachers, and ministers who have shared insights that have helped develop and polish many of the concepts contained in this book include Dr. Marvin Wilson, Dr. Karl Coke, Dr. Howard Morgan, Dr. Clifford Denton, Dwight Pryor, Rev. Isaac Rottenberg, Rev. Robert Somerville, Dr. John Looper, Dr. Terril Littrell, Dr. Leon Mohammed, Dr. Doug Wheeler, Randy Felton, David Bivin, Dr. Brad Young, Dr. Bill Bean, Clarence Wagner, Rev. David Andrew, and Dr. Ron Moseley. Each of these has not only supported me intellectually but has also undergirded me with their prayers, love, and sound advice.

I am also indebted to Dot McCoy and Lynn Ray, two ladies like Dorcas and Phoebe in Bible times who have a burden for biblical insight and the gift of giving to support cutting-edge ministries. Their generous contributions have largely made possible the publication of this book.

Finally, and perhaps most importantly, my family has given me their unwavering love and support, sacrificing time and comforts to facilitate my research, writing, teaching, and ministry. My wife, Pat, and my sons, David, Tim, and Steve always insist that I can do more.

I salute all these and countless others who have significantly impacted my life for Christ. May God grant each of you his eternal *shalom*.

Fraternally in Messiah

John D. Garr

Passover, 1998,

Revised, Tabernacles, 2001

INTRODUCTION

The New Testament, the will that was sealed in the blood of Messiah Yeshua (Jesus Christ), provided a profound legacy to all those who would be begotten again unto the hope of life through his resurrection (Hebrews 9:15-18; 1 Peter 1:2-5). This irrevocable testament guaranteed its provisions to all those who would come under the aegis of the kingdom of God through faith in the completed work of Calvary (Colossians 1:12). Unfortunately, however, the vast majority of those who have become heirs of God through Jesus Christ have been deprived of much of the inheritance that was provided for them in the last will and testament of our Lord. The legacy of Jesus has been lost to much of the church, covered over by centuries of human tradition.

The provision of the will was simple and clear. Through the death and resurrection of Jesus Christ, the faith of father Abraham that had been reserved to his progeny alone was extended to all mankind. What had once been held exclusively by and for the Jews as the fleshly descendants of Abraham was then made available to Jew and Gentile alike as the spiritual children of Abraham. This is the truth set forth by the apostle Paul in Galatians 3:14, 29: "that the blessing of Abraham might come upon the Gentiles in Christ Jesus, that we might receive the promise of the Spirit through faith . . . And if you are Christ's, then you are Abraham's seed, and heirs according to the promise." Simply stated, Abraham is "the father of all them that believe. . ." (Romans 4:11).

A RICH LEGACY FOR THE GENTILES

This is also the apostle's thesis in Romans 11:7, 11, 12, 33: "Israel has not obtained what it seeks; but the elect have obtained it, and the rest were blinded. . . . So I ask, have they stumbled so as to fall? By no means! But through their stumbling salvation has come to the Gentiles, so as to make Israel jealous.Now if their stumbling means riches for the world, and if their defeat means riches for Gentiles, how much more will their full inclusion mean! . . . O the depth of the riches and wisdom and knowledge of God! How unsearchable are his judgments and how inscrutable his ways!" The failure of the collective Jewish nation to recognize in Jesus of Nazareth the coming of their Messiah was a part of God's plan to bring salvation and the wealth of his knowledge and wisdom to the Gentile peoples of the world. This is what Paul meant in Romans 3:1, 2 when he posed the questions, "Then what advantage has the Jew? Or what is the value of circumcision?", and gave his own conclusion, "Much, in every way. For in the first place the Jews were entrusted with the oracles of God [the Word of God]." The advantages of being Jewish or of practicing the Hebrew faith of the Bible are many, but the chief advantage is the wealth of knowledge about God and his Word that is gained by being and doing so.

With God there is no respect of persons; therefore, he gives "glory, honor, and peace to everyone who works what is good, to the Jew first and also to the Greek" (Romans 2:10). Fundamentally, then, everything that God had given to the Jews was to be extended through the New Covenant to the Gentiles. This was the wealth of God's inheritance of good things that was enjoyed by the joint heirs with Jesus Christ through the New Will that Jesus sealed with his own blood. The Gentiles, who were "once not a people," came to be included in the people of God as a "chosen race, a royal priesthood, a holy nation, a people for God's own" (1 Peter 2:9, 10). They did not replace the Jews as the people of God, but they did come alongside them as "fellow citizens" of the "commonwealth" of Israel with all the rights and privileges extended therein (Ephesians 2:12, 19). Through the New Covenant, the Gentiles entered into the household of God, which Israel had been for centuries (Ephesians 2:19). They were cut out of their wild, unproductive olive tree and were grafted into the cultivated, productive olive tree of salvation (Romans 11:17). They who had been no people became a part of the people of God (1 Peter 2:10), when they became a part of God's family tree of covenant relationship. They partook of the rich sap from the root of the olive tree and were subjected to the pruning hook of God's Word that made them even more productive.

From the time of the resurrection and ascension of Jesus around 30 C.E. and of the inclusion of the converted Gentiles shortly thereafter, the church continued to function as a sect of Judaism which was struggling to make its understanding of the Messiahship of Jesus normative for all of their brethren according to the flesh. The church did not seek to break away from the rest of Judaism, despite the fact that its leaders were engaged in an ongoing dialogue with the leaders of Israel, a dialogue that was often vitriolic and occasionally violent. The apostles, however, maintained their loyalty to the faith of their fathers (Acts 24:14) and continued to worship in both the temple, in the synagogues of their ancestors, and finally in their own synagogues (cf. James 2:2 where the word translated *assembly* in the Authorized Version is literally συναγωγή [synagogue]).

LOSING THE LEGACY

By the end of the first century C.E., however, as the church became increasingly Gentile in demographics and leadership, the fierce loyalty to the Holy Scriptures and to the Judaic faith which Jesus and the apostles taught and practiced was replaced by an inclination toward traditions of the Gentile cultures and religions of the Greco-Roman world. As the church spread rapidly in obedience to the Great Commission to "go into all the world," it was increasingly influenced by the cultures into which it expanded. Gradually, various elements of the first century Christian Judaism were replaced by Gentile customs and traditions. The faith of Jesus was very rapidly Hellenized, influenced through and through with neo-Platonism and other Gentile philosophies.

Finally, even Palestinian Christianity became Gentilized when Hadrian's armies crushed the Bar Kochba rebellion, expelled all Jews from Jerusalem, and built the Roman city *Aelia Capitolina* upon its ruins in 135 C.E. Since the Roman Empire then persecuted the Jews and proscribed things Jewish, the church in Israel rapidly distanced itself from both Jewish believers and Jewish practices. Tragedy was occurring, for the church's beautiful, rich legacy from Judaism was being buried by the winds of false doctrine under the sands of human tradition.

Since the law and its symbolic ritual were not necessary as means of establishing righteousness before God, the value of the principles of Old Testament worship was gradually diminished until it reached the point of insignificance. Other concepts of worship were considered of equal value at first and, then, of superior value to those of Judaism. The Gentiles were simply more comfortable with forms of worship employed in the temples of the Hellenistic world's pantheon of gods. They felt more at home with the reason and logic of neo-Platonic philosophy than they did with the faith and trust of the nascent church's Judaism. They functioned better with their own calendars than they did with Judaism's biblical liturgical calendar.

When the New Testament order of Judaism became detestable in the eyes of the ecclesiastical and political authorities, it was finally forbidden upon penalty of death. The transition was completed in 321 C.E. when Constantine the Great issued the imperial edict which prescribed Sunday as the day of rest for the Roman empire and in 325 C.E. when he effectively outlawed the Christian observance of communion on the day of Passover.

DEPRIVED

Since the time when these tragic events occurred, millions of believers in the Jewish Messiah have been deprived of their rightful heritage in biblical Judaism as a part of the faith race of Abraham. A vast legacy of knowledge of the eternal God and the opportunity to worship and praise him in the manner which best pleases him have been lost to them, buried under nearly two millennia of Gentile tradition. Countless believers have not even understood that their Lord Jesus himself was Jewish, much less that the reformed faith which he commissioned his apostles to teach among all nations remained itself inherently Jewish. The church has been torn from its moorings and set adrift in the maelstrom of human tradition and doctrines of demons. Its history bears witness to its lost identity; for, instead of being the body of the suffering Jewish Messiah, it became little more than a whip of political imperialism, enslaving the souls of millions of people in superstition and darkness and wreaking havoc in the lives of millions of Jewish people.

Lately, however, spiritual archaeologists have been digging in the Word of God and have begun to uncover bits and pieces of this lost legacy. Scholars of various denominations have awakened to the realization that our over-Hellenized, over-Latinized Christian faith needs to be restored to its original context. Since Christianity is inherently Jewish, many theologians are calling for a reevaluation of traditional Christian attitudes toward Judaism. Some are calling for a full restoration of the Hebrew foundations of Christian faith, reattaching church to its Jewish roots. Due to the extensive Gentilization of the church, this call to reclaim Christianity's Judaic heritage seems radical and even revolutionary to some; however, it is both scriptural and prophetic, for everything biblical is to be restored at the time of the Messianic age (Acts 3:20, 21).

Many Christian believers today are daring to demand that the rights and privileges provided for them under the will of the New Testament of Jesus be restored in full. They are claiming their Christian heritage in biblical Judaism, the faith of Jesus and the apostles. They are finding in the legacy of the children of Abraham a manner of praise, worship, and service that more scripturally honors the Heavenly Father. Entitlements of which the church had no knowledge until recently are being claimed and enjoyed by believers from all backgrounds, denominations, nationalities, and ethnic groups. In what can only be described as a work of the Holy Spirit (since no single earthly source can be identified), God is leading Christians into ancient truths long obscured by human tradition.

We invite you to join the growing numbers of those who are rediscovering and claiming their long-lost spiritual legacy, Christianity's heritage in biblical Judaism.

Biblical Judaism– The Root of Christian Faith

Chapter 1
BIBLICAL JUDAISM–THE ROOT OF CHRISTIAN FAITH

"They were all together part of the Jewish community, which included all sorts of movements. The Christians, as they eventually were called, didn't have a uniform approach to Jewish law, but they were not trying to break away from Judaism. They were a group within it, trying to make their views normative. First-generation Christianity was a part of Judaism, but the next generation read us out of it." This is Presbyterian theologian Harry Gaylord's enlightening observation concerning the first century Christian church. Bible scholar Morton Scott Enslin noted that the scattering of the Jerusalem church, together with the destruction of its records when Jerusalem was conquered by the Romans in 70 C.E., was "the last blow which separated mother [*Judaism*] from child [*Christianity*]."

These two scholars of religious history have discovered a truth that more and more believers in the Christian community are learning today: Christianity's roots are in Judaism. Without Judaism, there would be no Christianity, for biblical Judaism is the parent of Christianity. One of history's most ironic aberrations is the fact that Christianity, the child, has for the most part risen up in antipathy toward Judaism, the parent, so that Judaeophobia, anti-Judaism, and anti-Semitism have come to characterize Christianity for more than nineteen centuries.

JESUS, THE JEW

Let's face it, Jesus was a Jew! He was proud of his Jewish heritage. His own genealogy, outlined in both Matthew and Luke, was founded in the great patriarchs of Israel, Abraham, Isaac, and Jacob, and included Israel's great kings, David and Solomon. Jesus was called the son of David, the son of Abraham, and the Son of God (Matthew 1:1; Luke 3:38).

The physical seal of his faith was placed in him on his eighth day when his devoutly Jewish parents had him circumcised, initiating him physically into God's covenant with Abraham and incorporating him into Israel's ancient covenant, making him an heir of God's promises to Abraham and his natural, linear descendants.

From the time of his birth until he reached adulthood, his parents "performed everything according to the law" (Luke 2:39), fulfilling their parental responsibility to the faith of Abraham (Genesis 18:19). They dedicated him at the temple and trained him in their home, in the synagogue, and in the temple, teaching him Judaism's Scriptures, history, culture, and tradition. When he was twelve, they introduced him to Yahweh's pilgrimage festivals, a custom that he continued throughout his life.

By his own admission, Jesus came not to abolish the law and religion that God himself had given to Israel but to complete or perfect that "one faith" forever (Matthew 5:17-19). He came as a reformer, but his reformation was actually a restoration in which he sought to return Judaism to the original principles upon which it had been founded in Abraham and at Sinai (Hebrews 9:10, 11; 12:2). As a result of tradition, Judaism had drifted from its inherent ideal; therefore, Jesus promoted restoration of the pure faith of God grounded solely in the authority of the Hebrew Scriptures (Matthew 5:21, 22, 27-32; 38-41, 43-44). Naturally, his reforming ideas often brought the charge that he was a destroyer of Judaism's law; however, he immediately countered such charges with the affirmation that he had come only to fulfill (or complete) the law. The record of the gospels is clear: our Lord never undermined but always strengthened the law (Torah) of God, which was the foundation of the many sects of Judaism in his day, including the emerging Christian faith (Matthew 19:16-19).

A REFORMED MOVEMENT

When Jesus established the church by ordaining the twelve apostles, he did so to maintain the order that had been unique to Israel since the days of Jacob. When he introduced new methods for observing Passover and the Sabbath, he did so to perpetuate eternal ordinances of God in a new and living way. When he offered up his own blood for the sins of mankind, he did so to continue the divine law of atonement, unique to Judaism, by dying once and for all.

No, Jesus was not a renegade. He was not a disrespectful rebel. He was a Jew who declared that he was "not sent except unto the lost sheep of the house of Israel" (Matthew 15:24) and who initially instructed his disciples, "Go nowhere among the Gentiles, and enter no town of the Samaritans, but go rather to the lost sheep of the house of Israel" (Matthew 10:5, 6). He was a Jew who hesitated to give the children's bread (healing) to the Gentiles (Matthew 15:26). He was a Jew who wept bitterly over the fact that his fellow Jews had not embraced the reformation that he brought to Judaism (Matthew 23:37).

The church which Jesus established was altogether a reform movement within Judaism. Since there was no such thing as a monolithic Judaism in the first century, the Jesus movement was in fact one of the many Judaisms, albeit a reformed Judaism that differed in many ways from the Sadducean, Pharisaic, and Essene Judaisms that were dominant in first century Israeli society. Its leaders were Jews who still honored God's only religion while at the same time seeking to cause their fellow Jews to understand that their religious faith had been perfected by Jesus of Nazareth, whom they recognized as Israel's long-awaited Messiah.

When the Gentiles came into the church, they were not required to carry out all the ritual of Judaism; however, they were not at liberty to maintain practices adopted from pagan rituals, mystery religions, or Greco-Roman philosophy, and they were not at liberty to ignore the eternal principles of Judaism that were to be applied to their lives in new and living ways. In the earliest times, these Gentiles continued to observe this "Jesus-reformed" Judaism, God's appointed system of praise, worship, and service in its New Testament order.

THE APOSTASY

After the death of the apostles of Jesus, and according to their predictions, grievous wolves entered into God's religion, not sparing the flock or the sheepfold (Acts 20:29). Various theological and Christological heresies challenged the very existence of the church, and though the church survived these challenges, it was, nevertheless, persuaded to deny much of its Judaic heritage in favor of concepts from the Greco-Roman world in which it functioned.

Earliest and greatest of these challenges against the church was Gnosticism, a form of which was championed in the early second century by Marcion, who taught that Jesus was the good God who had replaced and cast into hell Yahweh, the God of the Old Testament, whom he recognized as the Demiurge of Greek philosophy. Marcion introduced the first canon of Scripture, a truncated and self-edited version that included parts of Luke and some of Paul's letters. He declared that Jesus was not really a man, and he maintained that Jesus was most certainly not the Jewish Messiah predicted by the Hebrew prophets. While Marcion was branded a heretic and excommunicated from the church, the influence of his teachings has remained to this day, particularly his efforts at de-Judaizing the Scriptures and the church.

From this time, some church leaders began well-intended and sincere efforts at introducing the intelligentsia of the Greco-Roman world to Christian faith. Since some of them were converted neo-Platonists (so named because they were disciples of Plato's philosophy), they thought that Platonic philosophy could be reconciled with biblical teaching. Some even declared that Plato was really a Christian despite the fact that he had been unaware of it! Others said that the same God who revealed himself through Moses also spoke through Plato. Unfortunately, this line of reasoning that was an attempt to indiginize or contextualize the gospel in order to make it relevant to Greek society resulted in the sacrifice of the Judaic world view and mind-set of biblical times in favor of Platonic dualism which has pervaded subsequent Christian thought.

In an effort of self-preservation, many leaders of the church sought to syncretize Greco-Roman philosophy and polytheistic religion with the purity of their Judaic heritage. As had happened numerous times throughout Old Testament history, Yahwism (the religion of the God of the Jews) was overcome by concepts which were, in fact, based in the traditions of ancient Babylon. Century after century of Babylonian accretions were added from peoples, religions, and philosophies that were foreign to the religion of Moses, Samuel, Elijah, Isaiah, Daniel, Jesus, and the apostles. The result is what we know as Christianity today, a far cry from the faith which Jesus and the apostles practiced in the first century.

SEVERED FROM THE ROOT

Christianity was systematically excised from its Jewish roots, as one by one the church transplanted the teachings of Jesus into the foreign soil of human tradition. The final blow of the Greco-Roman axe which severed Christianity from the tap root of Judaism was wielded by Constantine the Great, *pontifex maximus* of Roman polytheism, when he arrogated to himself the headship of the church, enjoined the observance of Sunday as a day of worship in the Roman Empire, and outlawed any practice in the church which was obviously rooted in Judaism. Constantine's impact upon the church was summed up in his own words: "Let us, then, have nothing in common with the Jews, who are our adversaries . . . therefore this irregularity [Passover celebration] must be corrected, in order that we may no more have anything in common with [the Jews] the parricides and murderers of our Lord."

If some of the Jewish branches had been broken off from the life-giving sap of the olive tree because of their unbelief, the Roman axe struck at the very root of the tree itself because of the continuing anti-Judaism–if not outright anti-Semitism–of both Greek and Latin church fathers and finally of the "Christian" emperor himself. Is it any wonder, then, that the tree of faith in the God of Israel was replaced by the rationalistic sacramentalism of an imperialistic church and that the church took on a totally different appearance from what it had when Jesus and the apostles led it in reforming Judaism and restoring its inherent biblical ideals?

REAWAKENING TO OUR JEWISH HERITAGE

Today, after many convulsive efforts at shaking off the Babylonian traditions of men that have been heaped on the faith of Jesus through the centuries, thousands of believers are coming to recognize the fact that they are deeply indebted to Judaism and that Christianity is far more Jewish than they had ever dared to imagine. As more and more people get back to the Bible, they find that the parts of modern Christianity that are founded on the Word of God are deeply rooted in Judaism. When you read the Bible, you get the picture: true Christianity is a New Covenant Judaism. Every theological and ethical concept in Christianity that is authentic is based in Judaism, as is the vast majority of Christian practices.

Look at what Christians have received from Judaism. The four greatest and most important things in Christianity–the one true God, the Bible, the Messiah, and salvation–are direct products of the Jewish faith. The Christian understanding of God is purely Judaic. Though some primitive cultures believed in the existence of one God, there was simply no concept of ethical monotheism in the ancient world except in Judaism. The understanding that God is a person who interacts with his people was totally unique to Judaism. (Gentile religions, on the other hand, recognized polytheism's pantheon of capricious gods, or they conceived of God as an impersonal cosmic force, much as they still maintain to this day.)

The Bible is a Jewish book from Genesis to maps. All of the authors were Jews (with the possible exception of Luke, a proselyte to Judaism). The message of the Bible is uniquely Judaic and can be found in no other religion in the world (except, of course, in Christianity, which came from Judaism).

Jesus, himself, was a Jew. "According to he flesh" he was called an "Israelite" (Romans 9:3-5). He calls himself the "root and offspring of David" in Revelation 22:16, and Hebrews 7:14 tells us that it is "evident that our Lord arose from Judah," the Israelite tribe that was first called "Jews," a contracted form of their tribal identity.

Salvation, both as a person (Jesus) and as a concept, comes to us from Israel and Judaism (John 4:22). Indeed, no other religion in the world conceives of the doctrine of sin and atonement except Judaism and Christianity which sprang from its matrix; therefore, no other religion espouses the idea of salvation, much less the person of salvation, Jesus, himself.

Numerous Christian practices have their roots in Judaism. Believers practice water baptism because proselytes were initiated into Judaism by circumcision and immersion in the waters of the *mikveh*, the ritual bath and because transitions in status were also confirmed in the *mikveh*. The church celebrates communion because Israel had the Passover, the elements of which our Lord used to celebrate the first New Testament Passover with communion. Christians tithe their income because Israel tithed and give offerings because Israel offered sacrifices. Believers gather for public worship because Israel of old had the temple and because they gathered in homes for prayer, study, and worship in a system that became synagogal Judaism.

So, to one extent or another, we recognize Judaism in our worship of God. Some are more obedient to the faith of God than others, carrying out the ordinances of the New Testament order of Judaism. But, to one degree or another, all Christians are Jewish, for every believer in Christ Jesus is rightly called spiritually Jewish by the apostle Paul (Romans 2:28). Judaeo-Christianity, then, is an all-inclusive faith. Every believer in Messiah Jesus has a part, for every believer is a spiritual Jew and as such is entitled to the rights of Judaism. Having been grafted into God's family tree of salvation (Romans 11:17), they have become naturalized citizens of the commonwealth of Israel (Ephesians 2:12-16), and as such, they have all the rights of citizenship. They have not superseded or supplanted the natural Jews in God's plans, nor have they received citizenship in the modern nation of Israel; however, they have come alongside the Jews in the economy of salvation.

If you are a Christian looking for your roots, look into Judaism. Many who have been searching for their roots have found themselves "on the Canterbury trail" and have embraced Anglicanism. Others have returned to Roman Catholicism, and still more have accepted Greek Orthodoxy. Why stop at Canterbury or Rome or Constantinople? Why not go all the way back to Jerusalem, where Christianity began? The answer to the search for roots is in your Bible, which proves that your Christian faith was birthed from biblical Judaism. Let us join Edward H. Flannery in affirming that an over-Hellenized, over-Latinized Christianity needs a "re-Judaizing process" to restore it to its founding Jewish roots and renew it in its own inherent ideal. Let us reconnect with the roots of our faith and begin again to draw from Judaism and the Jewish people the rich and nourishing sap that healthy, productive believers need.

Chapter 2

Hold to God's Unchanging Hand

HOLD TO GOD'S
UNCHANGING HAND

"Build your hope on things eternal: hold to God's unchanging hand." This refrain from an old, familiar hymn contains perhaps the single most important truth that the believer can use to understand the Eternal God. Comprehension of God's unchanging nature is the most fundamental of all keys for understanding the Bible. Without this master key, we can only hope to stumble blindly about in the Scriptures, spasmodically achieving a limited knowledge of truth. With this key understanding of the unchanging nature of God, however, we can undertake a progressive, systematic search of the Holy Writ from Genesis to Revelation and thereby arrive at eternal, unchanging truth, the principles which apply in any situation or time.

God never changes! We have his word on it: "I am the Lord, I do not change . . ." (Malachi 3:6). If we can fully grasp the impact of this statement, we can begin to fathom the depths of the revelation of God's will and plan for the ages. We can recognize that though men change, God is ever consistent, and we can understand that his plan for mankind is and has been an ever-unfolding manifestation of his will that is forever unchanged and unchanging.

The concept of the unchangeable nature of God could best be described as divine law, the one law which Yahweh, the God of the Bible, established to govern his own actions. It is, quite simply, the governing element of all that pertains to or proceeds from the nature of God. It is foundational to all that God does, for he is eternally consistent, unchanging.

The unchangeable nature of God is encapsulated in the word *immutability*. Immutability is that principle of God which remains perpetual regardless of time, people, or circumstance. The manifestation and/or application of a divine law may change, but the principles which govern those manifestations never change. They always remain consistent and are irrevocable.

AN IMMUTABLE GOD

The immutability of God is summed up very succinctly in this passage of Scripture: "I know that whatever God does, it shall be forever . . . that which is has already been, and what is to be has already been; and God requires an account of what is past" (Ecclesiastes 3:14,15). No, God is not subject to change. Though his fundamental and basic plan for the ages may be developed for the purpose of bringing perfection, it is not subject to revocation or abrogation and the introduction of another totally different plan and will.

Even the name that God chose to be his memorial forever (Exodus 3:15) is a revelation of his immutable nature. Contrary to popular practice in the Western world, names in Hebrew culture were chosen to reflect the nature of the bearer. So it was with God's personal name, Yahweh, which is associated with other forms of the name and translated as, "I Am That I Am" or "I Will Be What I Will Be" (Exodus 3:14). This name stands first as a statement of its Bearer's aseity, his condition of underived existence. God is because he is: he is the source of his own existence. It also reveals his eternity. There was never a time when he did not exist, nor will there ever be a time when he will not exist. The name *Yahweh* also reveals God's quality of immutability. Yahweh is eternally the same. He lives in the eternal now, outside the envelope of the space-energy-time continuum that we call the universe. There is no past for him, and there is no future, only the present. Though this principle is incomprehensible to finite beings like ourselves, it helps us to understand why and how God can always be the same, immutable.

God never changes in two senses: he always remains consistent in the principles by which he operates, and he is forever constant in the fulfillment of his promises and decrees. We can have perfect confidence that the promises of God are sure to the believer because they are founded on the same principle of immutability on which the very existence of God is based. He cannot lie (Hebrews 6:18). He cannot fail (Deuteronomy 31:6). God is ever the same: the immutable one, and his Word is ever the same: incontrovertible.

God does not change because he cannot change. If he were ever to change, either what he was or what he would be must, of necessity, be imperfect. And, if he ever were or ever should be imperfect, then he would not be God. There was never a time when he was not perfect, and there will never be a time when he will not be perfect; therefore, there was never a time when he changed, nor will there ever be a time when he will change.

UNDERSTANDING THROUGH MATERIAL THINGS

Romans 1:20 tells us that we can understand God, even his eternal power and deity, by observing the things that he has made. We can know, therefore, that we are serving an unchanging God by looking at the universe which he created. Orderly existence on our planet and in the rest of the universe would be impossible if it were not for the existence of immutable laws of physics. Without the physical laws which Sir Isaac Newton discovered (what goes up must come down and for every action there is an equal and opposite reaction), everything would be flying apart in every direction with resultant cataclysm and self-destruction. Electricity could not possibly bless us all if it were not for the fact that Ohm's law of resistance charts an unchangeable course of action for its flow. Albert Einstein's General Theory of Relativity has led to the discovery of the interconnection between matter and energy. All of the amazing technology of our day would be impossible if certain immutable principles were not operating in the universe to maintain consistency and order.

ISRAEL: GOD'S SURE SIGN

One of the surest indications that God never changes is found in the nation of Israel. God related his immutability to the perpetual existence of the Jews in Malachi 3:6: "For I am the Lord, I do not change; therefore, you are not consumed, O sons of Jacob." For nearly four thousand years, the Jews have stood as a memorial to the unchanging nature of the Almighty, and they remain such even today. They have defied all the historical norms for the assimilation of conquered peoples, and they persist as an identifiable entity despite centuries of unrelenting and systematic persecution, torture, and murder directed against them wherever they have lived. Satan has continually plotted their destruction, and he has had ready volunteers to carry out his plans. If only they could be eradicated, the Word of God would fail, and God would be defeated. But, despite the best (or worst) efforts of tyrants, despots, and megalomaniacs to destroy the Jewish people, *Am Yisrael Chai*! (The people of Israel live!).

The vicissitudes of Israel's continuing failures and lack of faithfulness to Yahweh, her husband, have never been grounds for his denial of his own immutability. God's covenant with Abraham and his physical descendants was a unilateral commitment from God himself and was not contingent upon Abraham's performance or Israel's actions; therefore, the calling of God upon Israel is irrevocable (Romans 11:29). It could also be said that the unrelenting unfaithfulness of the church to Jesus, her husband (Romans 7:4), has not been cause for him to deny the immutability of his own deity. Jesus, like the Eternal Father, remains unchangeable: "Jesus Christ the same yesterday, today, and forever" (Hebrews 13:8). He is ever like his Father in continuing to give good gifts to his people, both Israel and the church: "Every good gift and every perfect gift is from above, and comes down from the Father of lights, with whom there is no variation or shadow of turning" (James 1:17). The High Priest who now offers gifts to men (Ephesians 4:8) is an immutable Mediator between an immutable God and man. This is why Jesus could say, "Before Abraham was, I am," because his goings forth were "from everlasting" (Micah 5:2). He, with the Father, has always been and will always be. And, even "unto everlasting" he will remain the same.

HISTORY REPEATS ITSELF

This common, well-known saying very accurately states the overriding application of the immutability of God in the affairs of men. World history is replete with examples of the repetition of circumstances and events governed by the same laws. The birth, rise, decline, and fall of empires in succeeding generations have followed a strikingly similar pattern as though a given set of circumstances applied to the frailties of human nature always produces the same results. Just as God is immutable, sin remains unchanged, so that there is no such thing as a new morality—just the same old immorality in the society of man.

This truth of the repetitive nature of history is clearly encapsulated in Ecclesiastes 1:9: "The thing that hath been, it is that which shall be; and that which is done is that which shall be done: and there is no new thing under the sun." The eternal, immutable principles of God's Word continue to be manifest in every generation of man's existence upon planet earth.

This is not to say that history is, as Eastern Monism would have us believe, purely fatalistic, an unending, mindless cycle of cause and effect, with every effect becoming the cause of the next effect *ad infinitum* and the ideal being escape from existence. Nor is it to say that history is cyclical, as the Greek philosophers believed, with everything returning to its source and the ideal condition's being escape from time itself. History is linear, not cyclical. It is covenantal, not causal. It began somewhere (with creation *ex nihilo* by God, himself), and it is progressing along a predetermined line toward an ending (the advent of the Messianic Age). Everything is unfolding according to the determinate counsel and foreknowledge of God (Acts 2:23). His plan for the ages is set and immutable (Romans 8:29, 30) and is based on his covenants, not man's actions.

In deference to man's free will God has chosen to limit his sovereignty so that each individual may choose his own destiny (Joshua 24:15). Men, therefore, either hear the voice of God and restore his will and ways in the earth, or they follow their own devices, repeating the same mistakes that destroyed their ancestors. Human infidelity has never altered nor can it ever negate God's fidelity and his immutability. God's will continues to progress rectilinearly despite his people's tendency to reverse course or proceed tangentially. Because of his faithfulness, God always finds people who will yield to his reforming hand and return to the precharted course of his will. Reformation and restoration, therefore, are repeating dynamics in salvation history.

History repeats itself not only in the secular realm but also in the spiritual world. This fundamental principle prompted Bildad to rationalize: "For inquire, please, of the former age, and consider the things discovered by their fathers; for we are but of yesterday, and know nothing, because our days on earth are a shadow. Will they not teach you and tell you, and utter words from their heart?" (Job 8:8-10).

The best way for us to learn something about God's will today is to inquire of ages past. We can be sure that an unchanging God will operate by the same principles by which he brought forth his will in the past. God simply does not have one will for one time and a different will for another, nor does he have one will for one people and a different will for another. He is ever consistent in his demands upon mankind and has even implanted the fundamental principles of that will in the genetic code, the very DNA of man: "For when Gentiles, who do not have the law, by nature do the things contained in the law, these, although not having the law, are a law to themselves, who show the work of the law written in their hearts, their conscience also bearing witness, and between themselves their thoughts accusing or else excusing . . ." (Romans 2:14, 15).

IT'S IN THE NUMBERS

Numbers are code words that a Bible student can use to understand the working of God. The immutability of God requires that they be repeated consistently. The circumstances and applications vary; however, the principles remain immutable.

Three is the fundamental building block of many important aspects of heaven and earth. There are three personalities manifest in the one Being of substance called God. There are exactly three components of the universe: time, space, and energy (which includes matter). There are three and only three colors of light from which every other color is made (yellow, cyan, and magenta).

We find the number *twelve* (or its multiple) whenever judgment is set (Numbers 1:44; Matthew 19:28; Revelation 4:4) or when foundations are laid (Revelation 21:19, 20; Mark 3:13, 14). Seven is used when power is manifested (Joshua 6:4; Judges 16:19; Revelation 1:4; 15:6) and when light comes forth (Exodus 25:31-40; Zechariah 4:2-6; Revelation 1:12; 4:5). Other numbers, including ten, forty, and fifty, are repeated continually as God deals with his people in succeeding generations.

TYPES, SHADOWS, METAPHORS, ALLEGORIES, AND PROPHECY

One of the tools that God has given us to understand his revelation in the Messiah and in the church which he built is based entirely upon the principle of immutability. When we understand the immutability of God, we can comprehend how events in the life of Jesus and the earliest church duplicated many of the events and circumstances in the lives of Adam, Isaac, Moses, and numerous other characters in the Hebrew Scriptures. If God never changes, we might readily expect to see the same principles manifest in his chosen people and their leaders in succeeding generations.

Jesus, himself, tells us that "all the law and the prophets prophesied until John" (Matthew 11:13). Now we can readily understand how the prophets prophesied, but how is it possible that the law prophesied? The truth is that the law was only "a shadow of the good things to come, and not the very image of the things" (Hebrews 10:1). People and events in their lives under the first covenant were typical of people and events that occurred under the new covenant. God laid down types in his dealings with the people of the Hebrew Scriptures that were fulfilled in the antitypes of those in the Apostolic Writings. All of the Word of God in the first covenant was prophetic of Messiah and the new covenant. It contained similes, metaphors, and allegories (Galatians 4:23, 24) that were manifest in Jesus and the church. These were the shadows of things to come, but the reality was Christ (Colossians 2:17).

We can better understand this manifestation of divine immutability if we call the events of the first covenant pictures of the reality that was to come in the new covenant. They were blueprints of the actual structures that were to be manifest. Moses' life was a picture of the life of Jesus, the Messiah. Israel in the desert was propaedeutic of the church. This helps us to understand how types and shadows, allegories, and prophecy are part of the Judaic hermeneutic.

Even prophecy itself is subject to repeated fulfillments in different parallel eras so that it often can be seen to have a preteritist fulfillment, a spiritual fulfillment, and an eschatological fulfillment. Such is the case with Amos 9:11, 12: "On that day I will raise up the tabernacle of David, which has fallen down . . . that they may possess the remnant of Edom, and all the Gentiles who are called by my name." This prophecy was fulfilled historically in the rebuilding of Jerusalem and the temple in the days of

Zerubbabel, Joshua, Ezra, and Nehemiah; however, according to James, it was fulfilled again when Jesus reformed the congregation of God and Gentiles were added (Acts 15:16, 17). This same prophecy is again presently being fulfilled in the restoration of the nation of Israel into their land "no longer to be pulled up from the land" (Amos 9:15). It could also be said to be in the process of fulfillment with the present restoration of the church, which, like the temple of old, had suffered at the hands of a Babylonian system (Greco-Romanism). And, the words of Amos might be expected to be fulfilled ultimately in the Messianic kingdom that is yet to come.

UNDERSTANDING GOD'S RELIGION

The unchangeableness of God, then, is the underlying principle of types, shadows, allegories, analogies, and other principles which enable us to understand the working of God in a given time by observing what he did in previous eras. It has been rightly said that one cannot possibly understand the New Testament without knowing the Old Testament, for the symbolism of the New Testament is revealed in the Old.

When we fully comprehend the immutability of God, we can receive the full impact of Jesus' statement in Matthew 5:17: "Do not think that I came to destroy the Law or the Prophets. I did not come to destroy but to fulfill." Jesus could not destroy God's law or religion of fifteen hundred years to establish another. Knowing the full import of the unchangeableness of God, we can logically assert that if biblical Judaism were ever God's appointed religious system, in some form it must remain his system.

Since God is not subject to change, he can only reform and remake until the perfect product is achieved. This principle of reformation is revealed in Jeremiah 18:4, 6, where we are told that when the clay became marred in God's hand, he *made it again* into another vessel. God did not discard the clay (Israel). He reformed it again (and perhaps again and again) until it became the vessel of honor that he had desired in the beginning. God is simply not hampered by human frailty or failure. He never gives up on his people, for his gifts and callings are irrevocable (Romans 11:29).

What Jesus achieved was a reformation of Judaism, a reshaping of the substance of God's ancient religion, not a destruction of that system. Hebrews 9:10 clearly informs us that Jesus was a reformer who perfected forever God's religion through the introduction of the New Covenant in his blood. He is the author *and* the perfecter of our faith (Hebrews 12:2).

How can we know what God wants today? With all confidence, we can "inquire of the former age." To know his will today, we must hold to God's unchanging hand.

Chapter 3

Is God
Really All
That Fickle?

Chapter 3
IS GOD REALLY
ALL THAT FICKLE?

"Well, let's see . . . what can we do today? I think I'll try . . . No, I tried that before and it didn't work. Besides . . . I'm not sure that I like that idea after all . . . But, I'm tired of this same old routine. I just have do something new and exciting!"

If the thinking of many Christians today were correct, this might well have been a conversation between God and himself before he *finally decided* that he would send Jesus into the world to redeem fallen man. An amazing number of Christians think that God has been working on a hit-and-miss, stab-in-the-dark basis, flying blind, trying his best to salvage mankind, but always finding himself foiled by Satan and having to try something new.

First, God created man and gave him dominion over the earth, requiring only that he not partake of the tree of the knowledge of good and evil. But, that didn't work, and man failed. Then God tried to let man regain his favor in a dispensation of conscience. When that didn't work, God tried again—this time giving the law to Moses and Israel. After fifteen-hundred years, God finally realized this scheme would not work, so he decided to give up on the law and try something else. He would send his only begotten Son to bring a new religion called Christianity that would replace the flawed and unsuccessful religion called Judaism. Since we are Christians, we are sure that this time God has the right plan that will work.

But, does this make sense? Is God really all that fickle? Is he so limited in his foreknowledge that he was unaware that man would fail, that the law would not keep him from sin, and that he could not establish his righteousness through good works? Is God so inconsistent that he constantly wavers, changing his mind according to whim, giving up on one thing, throwing it out, and starting all over, trying something entirely different that he is not even sure will work?

The very idea is preposterous! God is both omniscient and omnipotent. He knows what has happened, what is happening, and what will happen. He is capable of doing anything he intends, and his power cannot be contravened. If God has such knowledge and power, why do many Christians consider him to be so fickle? Yet, the myth continues, and most Christians today envision God sitting in heaven waiting, not sure when, why, or how he will complete this era, just waiting for the notion to strike him to send Jesus back to earth. Rather than subscribe to this absurdity, surely we must believe that the God who by his own word caused Jesus to become incarnate "when the fullness of time was come" (Galatians 4:4) will prompt his return when "the fullness of time" is come again.

One's belief about the Bible and man's relationship toward God reflects his understanding of the fundamental nature of God. Unfortunately, most Christians' attitudes toward the working of God among men reflect a lack of confidence in his mental and emotional stability. The Holy Scriptures, however, paint an entirely different picture of the Almighty! Listen to these accounts:

"I am the Lord, I do not change" (Malachi 3:6); "I know that whatever God does, it shall be forever. Nothing can be added to it, and nothing taken from it. God does it, that men should fear before him. That which is has already been, and what is to be has already been; and God requires an account of what is past" (Ecclesiastes 3:14, 15); "The father of lights, with whom there is no variation or shadow of turning" (James 1:17); "Jesus Christ the same yesterday, today, and forever" (Hebrews 13:8); "Thus God, determining to show more abundantly to the heirs of promise the immutability of his counsel, confirmed it by an oath" (Hebrews 6:17).

COULD GOD START A NEW RELIGION?

Is it conceivable that a God to whom is ascribed such immutability throughout the Scriptures could be so fickle as to try anything until perchance he finds something that works? Hardly so! Could such a God give up on Judaism, a fifteen-hundred-year-old religion which he, himself, had authored, and start a completely new religion called Christianity?

Could God allow himself to be perceived as being schizophrenic by revealing himself as a God of anger, wrath, judgment, and legalism in Judaism and as a God of grace, mercy, love, compassion, and freedom in Christianity? Could God be God and admit that the religion which he authored at Sinai was a failure and that he would scrap it and begin anew with Christianity? If he could, would anyone want to serve a God so fickle?

AN UNCHANGING PLAN OF SALVATION

No, the unchangeable God has not been flying blind, so to speak. From the foundation of the world, his divine plan of salvation has been constantly unfolding in each succeeding generation and will yet continue to unfold until the end of the Sabbatical Millennium. Throughout the Old

Testament ages, God's plan was constantly added to and modified to bring it closer to the perfect day. When Christ completed the work of his humanity, the elements necessary for perfecting the plan of salvation were provided. Since that time, God has been calling out chosen vessels to make up the body of Christ to set the stage for the last remaining part of the plan, the reign of Christ upon the earth and the subsequent destruction of evil and death.

And, God certainly did not give the axe to Judaism and raise up a new religion called Christianity. He merely brought the Reformer into the world to bring perfection to the Jewish faith and to extend that faith to all mankind. The faith of the first century church was Judaism, perfected by a new covenant, a Judaeo-Christianity as it were. The earliest church was altogether a part of the Jewish community and made no attempt to break away from Judaism until after the passing of its first generation of leaders, the leaders established by Jesus, himself.

What is called Christianity today is the product of two millennia of tradition and attempts to syncretize the faith of the Bible with the religions and philosophies of the Gentiles. History offers abundant confirmation of this fact. Christianity was gradually divorced from biblical Judaism, and in the process both Jewish and Gentile believers were denied their heritage in Judaism.

In truth, if God's counsel is immutable (and we have his Word that it is), then we must conclude that the division between Judaism and Christianity today is man-made. Two religions that spring from the same source must be the same if there is no outside interference. It was not, and is not, God's intention for Judaism and Christianity to be different from one another or to define themselves *vis-à-vis* one another rather than in the context of one another. Human tradition and hardened hearts have parted the way between these two great faiths, for God is not the author of confusion (1 Corinthians 14:33). And, there is at least as much, if not more, responsibility for this debacle upon the church than there is on Israel and Judaism.

No, God is not fickle. His determinate counsel and foreknowledge have ordered and sealed forever his plan for the ages. And, his immutability will bring that plan to completion in the end of the age through the establishment of a Messianic Kingdom patterned after biblical Judaism.

Chapter 4

There's
Only One
Way!

Chapter 4
THERE'S ONLY ONE WAY!

According to Paul, there is only "one Lord, one faith, one baptism" (Ephesians 4:5). The apostle's entirely logical premise is that if there is only one God, there can be only one faith or religion ordained by him. While many propose the idea that the countless religions of the world, including the various fractured segments of Christianity, are but many ways to the one God, we must accept the authority of the Word of God that there is only one religious system that finds perfect acceptance before God and that that system is the religion which he, himself, authored and perfected.

If God never changes–and he swore an oath that he does not (Hebrews 6:17)–then we must assume that whatever religious system pleased him in the past must in some form still please him. This is not to say that the one religion for humanity is a syncretism of all of the various religions that man has employed, for what divine order could possibly be extracted from the maze of confusion that a world of religions offers today? It is a declaration that if God is one, then his religion is also one. If the first and greatest commandment is "Hear, O Israel, the Lord our God, the Lord is one," then we must assert that his faith (religion) is one.

WHERE DID THEY ALL COME FROM?

Before the creation of the world, there was only one religious system in heaven by which the angelic host worshipped the Eternal God. When man was brought forth upon the earth, his function was to bring the praise and honor of the Creator to this planet; therefore, God began to reveal to man some of the order of worship which pleased him. The pure lineage of Adam through Seth was maintained as a patriarchal priesthood to offer up sacrifices and worship to God.

On the other hand, the descendants of Adam through Cain followed after deception, polluting the pure worship of God to offer service to idols and material gods, even honoring the devil himself. The lineage of Seth became more and more contaminated with the seed of Cain and its accompanying religious perversion. Finally, the situation became so bad that God determined to destroy the earth.

At that time, Noah alone had maintained a perfect pedigree, keeping himself and his children separate from the daughters of men; therefore, he alone had the right to the priesthood to offer acceptable sacrifices unto God. For this reason, Noah found grace in the eyes of the Lord and was given a plan for the salvation of his household.

Following the great flood, Noah's son, Ham, was influenced to perpetuate evil in the world and the stage was set for subsequent generations to create the various pagan religions that worshipped the heavenly creation and engaged in wanton practices, glorifying the works of the flesh and exalting men themselves above the knowledge of God.

All religions of the earth, except the one true religion of the Eternal God, are but polluted copies of the original. They are all counterfeits, introducing their own gods, but maintaining the principles of the religion of Yahweh. All have an altar, all have sacrifices, all offer prayers, all believe in life after death, all have a priesthood. But, all are counterfeits of the true God, the true altar, the true sacrifice, the true resurrection, the true priesthood.

In the midst of this confusion of Babylon, however, God called a direct descendant of Adam through Seth and of Noah through Shem and directed him to leave his Syrian household in search of the land where the altar of God would be found, the city that had foundations whose builder and maker was God (Hebrews 11:10). This man was Abraham, the father of the faithful, the first human being who was chosen of God to enter into a covenant with his Maker (Genesis 12:1-4). God chose him because he had the faith to believe God's promise, because he was faithful to keep all of God's commandments (Genesis 26:5), and because God knew he would teach his children and grandchildren to be obedient to God (Genesis 18:18, 19).

GOD'S RELIGION FOR GOD'S NATION

Through Abraham's lineage, God perpetuated his chosen religious system until the time when over four hundred years after Abraham's call, he brought those descendants of the man of faith before his mountain, Sinai. It was there that God revealed to Moses and the children of Israel his divine system for praise, worship, and service. Moses was permitted by Yahweh to look into the heavens to behold the order employed by the angelic host in the worship of the Eternal. Finally, the man of God was instructed to establish that same order among Israel by making all things "according to their pattern" (Exodus 25:40; Hebrews 8:5).

The one religion which the Eternal God, himself, revealed to mankind was biblical Judaism. Since that time, many copies have been made. Some, like Islam, have taken the one God, given him a different name and another prophet and modified the system of service to please a different culture of men. Others, including Christians and Jews, have altered God's system by introducing traditions that have voided God's Word (Mark 7:9, 13). Many have used God's religion as a pretext for spreading their own ideas and concepts. In effect, they have created God in their own image and have created their own faith to worship the God they have made.

JUDAISM APPROVED OF GOD

Still, in it all, there is only one way–the old path wherein is the good way! The one religion which God authored and put his stamp of approval upon was biblical Judaism. The Holy Scriptures document the miraculous displays of divine glory that accompanied the proper observance of Judaism when the very *Shekhinah* of God was localized in a material manifestation of fire on the mercy seat of the ark of the covenant in the most holy place in the tabernacle and when overpowering smoke of his presence interrupted the priests' service in the temple that Solomon built and dedicated. The system that was employed in both of these settings was Judaism, the term that was used to describe the religion of the first covenant in Galatians 1:13, where Paul called his lifelong religion Ἰουδαισμός, (*Ioudaismos*). While many have suggested that this Pauline statement indicated the apostle's abandonment of his "old" religion in favor of the "new" Christianity, this view is glaringly inconsistent with Paul's unequivocal statements that his faith in Jesus was fulfilled by his "believing all things which are written in the law and in the prophets," which was the very essence of biblical Judaism (Acts 24:14). This *Ioudaismos* was the Judaism that Jesus himself defended and espoused throughout the time of his incarnation (Matthew 5:17; John 4:22, 23).

JUDAISM REFORMED AND PERFECTED

Since Jesus was the Son of God, we could rightly expect that he would perpetuate the system that God had developed through the centuries. And, so he did! In reality, Jesus was the divine *Memra* (the Hebrew/Aramaic word translated "*Logos*" in Greek and "Word" in English) who created everything "in the beginning" (Genesis 1:1). He was the theophany who wrestled with Jacob and commissioned him as Israel. He was the lawgiver at Sinai who defined God's will to Moses and gave Israel a national constitution called the Torah (law). When he became incarnate in the womb of the virgin Mary, was born in Bethlehem, lived his life as a Jew among his Jewish brethren, died at the hand of the Romans, resurrected, and ascended into heaven, how could he have done otherwise than to perpetuate and perfect Judaism, the religion that he had authored (Hebrews 12:2)?

Jesus was the prophet like Moses (Acts 3:22). The law (Old Covenant Judaism) came by Moses; grace and truth (New Covenant Judaism) came by Jesus Christ (John 1: 17). Jesus brought a perfected order to Judaism through a new covenant, based on new and better sacrifices and offering a new method of observing the unchanging laws of God. Then, he extended that one faith to all mankind, including all the nations of the world in the covenant of God with Abraham (Galatians 3:8). He was the Son of Jacob through whom Israel's light was taken to the Gentile nations of the entire world (Isaiah 42:6). He was the Son of David who was given the heathen for an inheritance (Psalm 2:8).

EARNESTLY CONTENDING FOR GOD'S FAITH

The one faith of God has always been the object of Satan's ire. He first tried to pollute it by drawing worship to himself from a third of the angelic host in heaven. He would "be like the Most High" (Isaiah 14:14; Ezekiel 28:12-15), he said. After he was cast out of heaven by Michael the archangel (Revelation 12:3-9), Satan sought to pollute every incidence of God's giving pure religion to mankind. Since that time, his quest has been unrelenting even to this day. Satan has never had anything original: he has only copied and perverted the pure faith of God.

This is why Paul warned the church that after his departure, "grievous wolves" would enter in among them, "not sparing the flock" (Acts 20:29). For this reason Paul was jealous over the church that he had established in Corinth, fearing that "as the serpent deceived Eve by his craftiness, so [their] minds may be corrupted from the simplicity that is in Christ" (2 Corinthians 11:2, 3). This knowledge also prompted Jude to plead with the church to "contend earnestly for the faith which was once for all delivered to the saints" (Jude 3), noting that certain men had crept in who were using the grace of God as a pretext for lasciviousness.

Both evil men and men of good, but misguided intentions have prevailed upon the New Covenant Judaism which Jesus and the apostles practiced and have changed it into something almost unrecognizable. Pagan and Greco-Roman traditions have so altered the face of Christianity that today it is barely recognizable as a "Jewish" faith.

Believers who have accepted Messiah Jesus into their lives as Lord and Savior have entered into the Judaism of the New Testament. They have undertaken the journey to acceptance before God that is found in the ancient path. Having begun this journey, they must "contend for the faith once for all delivered to the saints," worshipping the Father in the same way in which Jesus and the apostles did. Those who continue to search God's Word to find his will for their lives will become more and more obedient to the one faith of the one God, Judaism through Jesus–God's One Way.

Jewish Jesus
or
Cosmic Christ?

JEWISH JESUS OR COSMIC CHRIST?

Very shortly after the death, resurrection, and ascension of our Lord Jesus Christ, theological and Christological controversies began to arise among those who professed themselves to be the church. Just who and what was Jesus? Was he God, or was he man, or was he both God and man, and if both, to what degrees? From these and similar questions came forth a host of teachings about the nature of Jesus. Some were truth, others, heresy, and they all in one way or another have continued to influence the church to this day.

HERESY INFILTRATES THE CHURCH

The influence of the theological and Christological heresies on the church was considerable. It is a miracle that the truth prevailed in the midst of the pervasiveness of heresy. And, even though truth triumphed officially, heresy continued to shape far too much of the practical application of the church's orthodox teaching.

Among the first heresies which challenged the very existence of the church were Gnosticism and docetism. Both presented a perverted view of the nature of Jesus, in which his absolute humanity as a Jew among his Jewish brethren was denied in favor of a view that made him solely the cosmic Christ, the good God who stood in opposition to the malevolent Yahweh of the Old Testament.

The Gnostics believed that man was saved by esoteric knowledge, not by faith. Marcion developed his own version of Gnosticism by declaring that Yahweh, the God of the Old Testament, was the Demiurge who created the evil material world in which the immortal souls of men were trapped. He believed that Jesus was the good God who came to end this contamination by destroying Yahweh and his religion, Judaism, and establishing a completely new, unforeseen religion–Christianity. Marcion purported that Jesus was not the Jewish Messiah, was not born of Mary, was never incarnate, and only appeared in spirit during the time of his ministry.

The docetists, including their most extreme sect, the monophysites, believed that there was only one nature of Jesus–the divine. He was not human, did not suffer on the cross, and did not need a resurrection. His physical appearance was only a phantom, a disguise of his spirit so that men might perceive and worship him. This heresy totally denied the incarnation of Jesus as a Jew among his Jewish brethren.

Though both the Gnostics and the docetists were branded heretics by the church, their influence infiltrated the consciousness of the church so that it more and more tended to ignore the historical Jesus in favor of the cosmic Christ. As the church gradually denied its Judaic heritage in favor of the concepts of Greco-Roman philosophy and ideas from mystery religions, it became more and more simple to deny the Jewishness of Jesus and to look upon him as a mystical figure, the Christ (despite the fact that the word *Christ* is a Greek representation of the Hebrew word *Messiah*).

ORTHODOX THEOLOGY AND CHRISTOLOGY

Out of the raging inferno of several centuries of conflict and polemics, orthodox Christian theology and Christology emerged. The Nicene Council in 325 C.E. concluded that Jesus was very God, of one substance with the Father and with the Holy Spirit. There was one God in three persons, one Being of substance yet three personalities. It was the person of the Word of God who had become incarnate, lived, suffered, died, resurrected, and ascended. This was the teaching of the deity of Christ, the foundation of theology. Later, the Council of Chalcedon in 451 C.E. concluded that Jesus was both God and man, very God and very man, not part God and part man, but all God and all man at the same time. This was the teaching of the two natures of Christ, the foundation of orthodox Christology.

Both of these orthodox teachings recognized what is clear in the Apostolic Writings: Jesus is more than just a man; he is God (John 1:1-4, 14; Colossians 2:9; 1 Timothy 3:16). At the same time, in his incarnation, he was very much a man, less than God in the sense that he had limited his deity to his humanity (Philippians 2:6-8) and had become subject to death. He became man in order that he might complete the plan of salvation by overcoming sin in the flesh (Romans 8:3), providing an efficacious atonement for the sins of all mankind (Hebrews 9:26) through the offering of his perfected body on the cross (Hebrews 2:10, 14), and by resurrecting on the third day as proof of God's approval upon his sacrifice (Acts 2:23-36).

With these clear and irrefutable teachings in place in the church for over fourteen hundred years, how is it that a large part of the church today has virtually denied the historical Jesus in favor of the cosmic Christ? How is it that Jesus is hardly thought of as a Jew who lived his entire life in the midst of his fellow Israelis? How is it that we have so many different conceptions of Jesus, including the Nordic, Aryan Jesus with blonde hair and blue eyes, the African Jesus with black skin and hair like wool, the oriental Jesus with oriental features? And, these are only the Christian versions. What of the Jesus who is portrayed as a first-rate medium by the consciousness philosophers, who is one of the many incarnations of God in Eastern Monism, who is another of the prophets leading up to *the* prophet Mohammed in Islam, who is the healer of Christian Scientism, who is a rabbi among many Jews, who is the great moral example in nominal Christianity? Every religion and philosophy wants to claim Jesus for its own purposes and to create him in its own image. If we are to understand Jesus, however, we must accept the record of Holy Scripture that places him and his sayings in the historical and cultural milieu in which he was born, lived, died, resurrected, and ascended.

JESUS WAS A JEW!

The record of Scripture is clear: Jesus was born a Jew, he lived as a Jew; he died as a Jew, he resurrected a Jew, he ascended a Jew, he is seated at the Father's right hand in heaven a Jew, and he will return to earth a Jew.

When he became incarnate on earth, it was "evident that our Lord arose from Judah," the tribe whose name was contracted to form the word *Jew* (Hebrews 7:14). As "concerning the flesh" Christ came from the "Israelites" (Romans 9:4, 5). He was born in Bethlehem of Judea, the "son of David, the son of Abraham" (Matthew 1:1). He was (as was supposed) "the son of Joseph . . . the son of David . . . the son of Jacob . . . the son of Isaac . . . the son of Abraham . . . the son of Adam . . . the son of God" (Luke 3:23, 31, 34, 38). When the wise men from Babylon came to Jerusalem, they asked, "Where is he that is born King of the Jews?" (Matthew 2:2).

Jesus lived a normal life as a Jewish man among his Jewish brethren. There was no nimbus around his head, no fire coming from his fingers and toes, or any other distinguishing mark that would signal to others his divine origin. He was very man: he thirsted, he was hungry, he ate, he slept, he wept, and he died. As a child he was precocious in his knowledge of the Torah, the law of God, so much so that at the age of twelve he astounded the rabbis in the temple (Luke 2:42ff); however, there was nothing that would convince most of those around him that he was more than a rabbi (teacher) or perhaps even a prophet. In everything he was recognized as a proper, Torah-observant Jew. The woman at the well of Samaria recognized him as a Jew because of his manner of dress and demeanor (John 4:9). The woman with the issue of blood was healed when she touched the *tzitzit* (tassels) of his garment (Matthew 9:20), an important part of the dress of every Jewish man who observed God's commandments. It was not until late in his ministry that Peter understood by divine revelation that Jesus was the Messiah, the Son of God (Matthew 16:16).

When Jesus died, he was still a Jew. This is the superscription that appeared above his head as he hung on the cross: "This is Jesus the King of the Jews" (Matthew 27:37). Pilate legally recognized his Jewishness and his kingship in what was probably a bit of sarcasm directed toward the Jewish nation in comparing Jesus' fate with the status of Caesar.

When Jesus arose from the grave in the resurrection, he was still a Jew. This is the essence of Peter's sermon on the day of Pentecost in Acts 2:22-36. The resurrection of Jesus so that his flesh did not see "corruption" was required in order that God's oath to David could be fulfilled: "That of the fruit of his body, according to the flesh, he would raise up the Christ to sit on his throne, he, foreseeing this, spoke concerning the resurrection of the Christ. . . ." Jesus did not die a Jew and resurrect the cosmic Christ. He was the cosmic Christ from eternity past, but he became incarnate as a Jew, died as a Jew, and resurrected as a Jew so that God's oath to David could be fulfilled "according to the flesh."

Jesus ascended to heaven as a Jew. Hebrews 7:14, 15 tells us that in order for Jesus to become our High Priest at the right hand of the Father, the law of the priesthood had to be changed by reverting to the priesthood of the firstborn, the patriarchal priesthood of Melchizedek. The reason for this change was the fact that "For it is evident that our Lord arose from Judah, of which tribe Moses spoke nothing concerning priesthood." Jesus, then, is still of the tribe of Judah, a Jew–in glorified flesh, to be sure, but in Jewish flesh, nevertheless.

When Jesus returns, he will still be a Jew. The angels who witnessed the ascension of our Lord assured the disciples who were present: ". . . this same Jesus, who was taken up from you into heaven, will so come in like manner as you saw him go into heaven" (Acts 1:11). The same Jewish Jesus who resurrected in the flesh will return to the earth to sit on the throne of David in that same Jewish flesh, thereby fulfilling God's oath to David. Interestingly enough, this same Jesus will return to the same place from which he departed–the Mount of Olives (Acts 1:12; Zechariah 14:4)–and in the same manner in which he ascended–with clouds (Acts 1:9; Revelation 1:7).

While he was, is, and ever will be the cosmic Christ, in his incarnation, Jesus was, is, and will be a Jew according to the flesh until that time when he will deliver everything up to the Father so that God may be supreme (1 Corinthians 15:27, 28).

Jewish Jesus or Cosmic Christ? He was and is both–God and man, Creator and Redeemer, Author and Finisher of our faith.

Chapter 6

A Perfect Sacrifice–
The Foundation of
Christian Faith

A PERFECT SACRIFICE:
THE FOUNDATION OF CHRISTIAN FAITH

The inherent sinfulness of mankind and the consequent need for atonement form a concept that is uniquely Judaeo-Christian. From the animal that was slaughtered in order to provide a covering for Adam and Eve, to the sin offering that was available to Cain following his insufficient firstfruits offering, to the system of animal sacrifices under the law of Moses, to the eternally efficacious sin offering made once for all on the cross of Calvary through the body of Jesus Christ, the concept of the shedding of blood for the remission of sins has always been an identifying characteristic of Yahweh's religion.

The sinful nature of humanity is summed up in David's statement: "I was brought forth in iniquity, and in sin my mother conceived me" (Psalm 51:5). From David's words we understand that sin is inherent in human beings. Paul declared that no one has escaped this condition: "The scripture has confined all under sin" (Galatians 3:22); "For all have sinned, and fall short of the glory of God" (Romans 3:23). Even in rabbinical Judaism, the human situation and proclivity toward sin is described as the *yetzer hara,* the evil inclination that is believed to take residence in a person at the moment of birth. Though many have argued the difference between the Augustinian concept of original sin inherited at conception from one's parents and the rabbinic idea of *yetzer hara* acquired at birth, there are many similarities, and both confirm the nature of sin that wars within every human being from the time of his birth.

SEPARATION AND DEATH

The root of sin is rebellion against God and his will (1 John 3:4), and the penalty for sin is separation and alienation from God and his blessings (Genesis 2:17; 1 Corinthians 6:9; 15:56; Romans 6:23). Ultimately, the wages of sin is death (Romans 6:23). Since all men are concluded in sin, the need for a means of reconciliation is readily apparent. God's plan for bringing about such a reconciliation was set in motion in the Garden of Eden with the sacrifice of an animal to cover the nakedness of Adam and Eve Genesis 3:21.

God's plan was given further substance at Sinai, where for the first time he made an agreement with a nation that he would be their God, a covenant that was established in the law that provided a means of atonement. God's constitution for the nation of Israel (the Torah) provided initial covenantal relationship with God and a means of maintaining their relationship with him by making the prescribed sacrifices for sin.

BLOOD SACRIFICE FOR SIN–A JUDAIC CONCEPT

In order for a people to become God's chosen, it was necessary that their sins be remitted so that they could have access to God. This could be accomplished in only one way: "It is the blood that makes atonement for the soul" (Leviticus 17:11); ". . . without shedding of blood there is no remission" (Hebrews 9:22). This is why, when Moses first introduced God's covenant with Israel, both the people and the law were sprinkled with blood: "For when Moses had spoken every precept to all the people according to the law, he took the blood . . . and sprinkled both the book itself and all the people, saying 'This is the blood of the covenant which God has commanded you' " (Hebrews 9:19-20).

When God established the first covenant with his chosen people at Mount Sinai, then, he very carefully delineated the various blood sacrifices which were to be offered continually for the sins of the Jewish people. These animal sacrifices were necessary for a continuing atonement for sin and for the purification of the flesh and spirit. This was in keeping with Judaic holism that saw man as a whole, not as bifurcated parts, spirit and body, good and evil, as philosophies in the world around them asserted. The blood sacrifice was an absolute necessity: it was a requirement without which no individual could be justified before God. The covenant was the foundation of Judaism; however, the blood sacrificial system was its maintenance. The Jewish people were joined to God by the covenant; however, in order to maintain their relationship with God, they were required to offer sacrifices when they violated God's commandments. This was God's provision for covenant maintenance.

The concept of offering blood to atone for sin was unique to Judaism. While various Gentile religions involved sacrifices to appease their gods and court their favor (even the killing of human beings), Judaism stands out alone as a system of offering blood for the remission of sins and justification before God. The true and living God required something that was peculiarly his, something which came directly from him which could not be maintained without him: the life that is in the blood (Genesis 9:4). The shedding of blood was the taking or offering up of a life and was in keeping with the concept of a life for a life (Deuteronomy 19:21). Since the penalty of sin was death (Genesis 3:3; Romans 6:23), a life had to be taken to forestall immediate death and achieve reconciliation or atonement with God.

OLD TESTAMENT SACRIFICES INCOMPLETE

The blood sacrifices of the Old Testament were incomplete. They served only as a temporary means of atonement and prefigured the coming Atonement which would be complete and perfect. The sacrificial law's weakness was the fact that its atonement was not perpetual: "For the law, having a shadow of the good things to come, and not the very image of the things, can never with these same sacrifices, which they offer continually year by year, make those who approach perfect. For then would they not have ceased to be offered? For the worshipers, once purified, would have had no more consciousness of sins" (Hebrews 10:1, 2).

This inefficiency in the sacrificial system of the Old Covenant was the reason for the prophet's prediction of the coming New Covenant (Jeremiah 31:31). The sacrifices of the Old Covenant were, in fact, only shadowy symbols that prefigured the reality that was to come. The New Covenant was to bring a purification from sin by a better sacrifice than that of the Old Covenant (Hebrews 9:23).

The nature of the sacrificial change which brought about the New Covenant was this: "Sacrifice and offering you do not desire, but a body you have prepared me" (Hebrews 10:5). A human body was prepared as a vicarious sacrifice for the sins of mankind in fulfillment of the type established when Abraham prepared Isaac to be sacrificed. Just as a ram was substituted in Isaac's place, so the Lamb of God was substituted in the place of the human race, all of which deserved death because of sin. The Jewish concept of vicarious atonement originated in Isaac and was completed in Jesus, with both sacrifices offered on Mount Moriah.

MESSIAH, THE PERFECTED ATONEMENT

Various Jewish prophets foretold the day when a man would shed his blood for the remission of sins. Most notable among these was Isaiah who predicted, "He was wounded for our transgressions, he was bruised for our iniquities; the chastisement for our peace was upon him, and by his stripes we are healed. All we like sheep have gone astray; we have turned, every one, to his own way; and the Lord has laid on him the iniquity of us all . . . he was cut off from the land of the living: for the transgressions of my people he was stricken . . . Yet it pleased the Lord to bruise him; he has put him to grief. When you make his soul an offering for sin, he shall see his seed, he shall prolong his days . . . and he bore the sin of many, and made intercession for the transgressors" (Isaiah 53).

King David was swept up in the spirit of this man's suffering and described the experience: "They pierced my hands and my feet . . . They divide my garments among them, and for my clothing they cast lots." (Psalm 22:16, 18). Zechariah predicted that "they will look on me whom they pierced. Yes, they will mourn for him as one mourns for his only son" (Zechariah 12:10). Daniel foretold the coming sacrifice and its timing: "After the sixty-two weeks Messiah shall be cut off, but not for himself . . . in the middle of the week he shall bring an end to sacrifice and offering" (Daniel 9:26, 27).

But, how could the death of a mere human being have any more effect in atoning for sin than the death of an animal when we understand that "all have sinned and fall short of the glory of God" (Romans 3:23)? The prophets also provided the answer to this dilemma: "Behold, the virgin shall conceive and bear a son, and shall call his name Immanuel"(Isaiah 7:14). The perfect means for a perfect sacrifice and perpetual atonement was achieved, then, when the Virgin Mary conceived of the Holy Spirit and brought forth Yeshua (Jesus of Nazareth), the first man since Adam who was not conceived in sin. Of Jesus and of him alone could it be said that he "committed no sin, nor was deceit found in his mouth" (1 Peter 2:22). The very nature of sin is transmitted from generation to generation by the seed of the man, not the woman, for Adam sinned willfully while Eve was deceived (1 Timothy 2:14). Though Mary was sinful (as is every human being), her son was not conceived in sin because he was not produced through the natural process of human reproduction. He was conceived of the Holy Spirit; therefore, that "holy thing" was the Son of God (Luke 1:35). He was literally "made of woman . . . under the law" (Galatians 4:4), for he had no earthly father. This is not to say that a man was exalted to become God but that God, himself, became fully human in the person of his Son.

In order for Jesus to be offered as a perfect sacrifice, however, it was necessary that his humanity be perfected by being tempted in all points, that he suffer affliction, and that he endure the trial of Satan. "For it was fitting for him . . . to make the author of their salvation perfect through sufferings" (Hebrews 2:10). When the appointed time of his offering came, he could say in all truth, "The ruler of this world is coming, and he has nothing in me" (John 14:30). A sinless body that had been perfected through sufferings was a sacrifice that was sufficient to meet the forensic demands of divine justice for the sins of mankind.

As Jesus hung on the cross outside Jerusalem, he fulfilled every type and shadow of the sacrificial law of the Old Testament. In particular, he was the Passover Lamb, slain from the foundation of the world, whose blood could be applied to the hearts of believers by the millions, causing eternal death to pass over them. He was the vicarious sacrifice and atonement prefigured for Judaism in Isaac. He was both the Yahweh goat and the scapegoat that atoned for and carried the sin of all mankind outside the camp (Leviticus 16:7-26; Hebrews 13:13).

Jesus' sinless state resulted from his meticulous observance of the law. Because he was born under the law, he was responsible to keep it. Had he violated any of the commandments (*mitzvot*), he would have been a sinner, for "sin is the transgression of the law" (1 John 3:4). Since he overcame every temptation, however, Jesus established his own righteousness by the righteousness of the law and provided for the substitutionary imputation of his righteousness to every believer for his faith.

THE CROSS–THE FOUNDATION OF THE NEW COVENANT

The atonement of the cross was the foundation of the New Covenant which Jesus brought to Judaism, Yahweh's religion. In the Old Covenant, the gifts and sacrifices "concerned only with foods and drinks, various washings, and fleshly ordinances," and they were imposed upon Israel only "until the time of reformation" (Hebrews 9:10). This was the work of the suffering Messiah: "But Christ came as High Priest of the good things to come . . . Not with the blood of goats and calves, but with his own blood he entered the Most Holy Place once for all, having obtained eternal redemption . . . how much more shall the blood of Christ, who through the eternal Spirit offered himself without spot to God, purge your conscience from dead works to serve the living God? And for this reason he is the Mediator of the new covenant" (Hebrews 9:11-15).

The one Passover sacrifice of Jesus provided perpetual and eternal atonement: "Not that he should offer himself often, as the high priest enters the Most Holy Place every year with blood of another. He then would have had to suffer often since the foundation of the world; but now, once at the end of the ages, he has appeared to put away sin by the sacrifice of himself" (Hebrews 9:25, 26). When he appears the second time, it will be apart from sin unto salvation (Hebrews 9:28).

Is it any wonder then that there is now no continuing animal sacrifice? It is not mere coincidence that the blood sacrifice was suspended in Judaism with the destruction of the temple in Jerusalem. The one eternal sacrifice had been offered for all men and for all time in the blood of Jesus Christ (Hebrews 9:28). The temple sacrifices ceased in 70 C.E., forty years after Jesus died on the cross. These forty years were a probationary period for the nation of Israel and its leadership, part of the prophetic type of Jonah which Jesus said was the only sign that he would give to Israel to validate his claim of Messiahship (Matthew 12:39-41). Jonah's forty days of witness to Nineveh were prophetic of God's withholding judgment on Jerusalem and its leaders for forty years, just as the fact that Jonah was in the belly of the whale for three days and nights was prophetic of the duration of Jesus' entombment. The historical and prophetic cessation of temple sacrifices in 70 C.E., forty years after the death of Jesus, confirmed the fact that Yahweh's ultimate sacrifice for sin had been made once and for all in the person of Jesus Christ. The resurrection of Jesus, which paralleled Jonah's release from the whale, validated both his Messiahship and the eternal efficacy of his sacrifice for sin.

A PERFECT SACRIFICE PERFECTS JUDAISM

This perfect sacrifice perfected Judaism and extended it to all men, providing eternal life to everyone who believes. This sacrifice became the foundation of a new order for Judaism that came to be called Christianity in subsequent generations. It was never God's intention to abolish Judaism, a fact witnessed by Jesus and the apostles themselves. It was, however, his intention to complete the faith that was outlined for Israel at Sinai and to extend it to the nations for the obedience of faith. This truth is also in keeping with some rabbinic understanding that predated the time of Christ which said that when the Messiah would come he would change the law (Torah) in order to complete it. The fulfillment of the sacrificial law in the life, death, and resurrection of Jesus offered a perfect system, one which the writer of Hebrews tells us is better than the original system. It was not that the first covenant was bad and the new covenant was good; it was that the first covenant was good and the new covenant was better. While everything in the old economy was good, it all paled in significance when compared with the birth, life, death, resurrection, and ascension of Jesus.

Once we have recognized God's one sacrifice for sin, Jesus Christ, and have received his righteousness by imputation for our faith, we enter into relationship with Yahweh, the God of the Jews, and are then ready to practice the faith "once for all delivered to the saints" (Jude 3), the faith which Jesus and the apostles observed throughout their lives: biblical Judaism. We are simply not called to a religion that is foreign from Judaism. We are called to worship the God of the Jews, to read the Hebrew Scriptures, to exalt the Jewish Messiah, and to share in the salvation that is from the Jews. The perfect sacrifice for sin that was offered once and for all at Calvary is for us the foundation of faith that produces a lifestyle of obedience to God, patterned after the Judaism of Jesus and his apostles.

Christ,
Our
Righteousness

CHRIST,
OUR RIGHTEOUSNESS

Second Temple Judaism, from which the reformation of Jesus Christ brought forth the perfected religion of the New Testament, was the scene of constant debate over what was required to establish righteousness. Nearly two thousand years later, the debate still continues, as people of widely differing backgrounds offer their advice on the standards that in their opinion one must maintain in order to be accepted before God.

Some today, like the Pharisees of old, are persuaded that righteousness is measured by outward appearance. Much of this is a legalism, a self righteousness that is based in cultural baggage rather than in the word of God. Others insist that works of righteousness are not required and that direct violations of the commandments of God are also overlooked by a God of grace and mercy. This approach results in what Dietrich Bonhoffer described as a "cheap grace," which is no grace at all, and what others have characterized as "sloppy *agape*," which is no love at all.

From the time of the fall of Adam until Christ, it could be accurately stated that there was none righteous, no not one (Romans 3:10). All men were conceived in sin and brought forth in iniquity (Psalm 51:5), and all had sinned and fallen short of the glory of God (Romans 3:23). Sin was inherited along with mortality so that all men were as incapable of refraining from sin as they were unable to escape death.

Even the great event of the giving of the law of God at Sinai was not intended as a panacea for sin. As Yahweh thundered out his commandments from the frightful mount, the children of Israel cried out, " 'Let me not hear the voice of the Lord my God, nor let me see this great fire anymore. . .' ", whereupon Yahweh said, "What they have spoken is good. I will raise up for them a Prophet like you from among their brethren, and will put my words in his mouth, and he shall speak them all that I command him. 'And it shall be that whoever will not hear my words, which he speaks in my name, I will require it of him.' "(Deuteronomy 18:16-19; cf. Acts 3:26). Traditional Judaism has suggested that this prophet was Joshua; however, there is no evidence that Joshua gave laws that were added to the Mosaic corpus, the violation of which would bring judgment upon Israel. This prophet was Jesus of Nazareth, Israel's Messiah and the world's Savior.

The law became a guardian (Galatians 3:24) to protect the Jewish people and to control the conduct of the Israelite nation until the time when this prophet would come to redeem them from sin and teach them the full understanding of God's will and ways. Jesus was that prophet who completed and perfected the law and provided the means by which it could be established and fulfilled (Romans 3:31). Until Jesus came, the Scriptures tell us that there was no flesh justified or righteous in the sight of God (Psalm 14:1; Romans 3:10).

It should be noted that the words *righteous* and *justified* both are used to translate the same Greek word *dikaios* and mean essentially the same thing. They indicate the status of acceptance before God. While the law protected Israel and set standards for personal deportment, it could not complete the faith of its adherents because of the sin that was continually manifest in their lives. This required the work of the prophet to whom Moses referred, the Messiah, himself.

BORN OF WOMAN, UNDER THE LAW

It was fitting and proper then, that in the fullness of time, God sent forth his son, made of woman (after the flesh), made under the law (responsible to observe the law). His personal righteousness was established by his keeping all the law (Romans 10:5). His eternal purpose in doing so was to redeem those who were under the law that they might receive the adoption of sons (Galatians 4:4, 5).

The first and essential element which made this possible was the miraculous virgin birth that brought the Son of God into the world without inherent sin (Luke 1:27-35). His mother was told: "The Holy Spirit will come upon you, and the power of the Highest will overshadow you; therefore, also, that Holy One who is to be born will be called the Son of God." Jesus was the first human since Adam who was not conceived in sin and formed in iniquity (Psalm 51:5).

The second essential element which made it possible for man to be redeemed from sin was the fact that Jesus Christ was the first man who kept the law of God in its entirety, not giving offense in a single point. He was in all points tempted just common to man, yet remained without sin (Hebrews 4:15). He knew no sin, neither was deceit found in his mouth (1 Peter 2:22). He who knew no sin became sin in one moment of time when he bore the sins of all mankind in his body on the tree (2 Corinthians 5:21; 1 Peter 2:24). He who had never warranted a curse from God because of his sinless life became a curse as he hung on the cross and assumed to himself the curses of the law that were pronounced upon those who violated its commandments (Galatians 3:13). It was appropriate for him to "fulfill all righteousness," including Judaism's ritual immersion (Matthew 3:15). In everything, Jesus was fully submitted to the Father's will.

All that Jesus did in obedience to the will of the Father brought about the perfection of his flesh (Hebrews 2:10) so that his body could be offered as a perfect, perpetual atonement for the sins of all mankind (Hebrews 9:14). Through his obedience and suffering of temptation without sin, Jesus in his humanity established his own personal righteousness. His voluntary suffering in the limitations of human flesh (Philippians 2:6-8) satisfied the demands of divine justice so that he now stands as the embodiment of the righteousness and justification of God for all mankind (1 Corinthians 1:30). Jesus established his own personal righteousness and died a death that was not demanded by divine justice; therefore, his death could balance the scales of justice and provide atonement for those who would believe, and his righteousness could be imputed to them for their faith. As Abraham believed and was consequently credited to him for righteousness by God, so the believer who accepts God's provision for sin in Christ receives the righteousness of Christ.

A VICARIOUS ATONEMENT

All that Christ did, he did for us and in our stead. This was in keeping with the Judaic principle of vicarious atonement that was first manifest in Abraham's sacrifice of Isaac. What we were (and are) not able to do through the weakness of the flesh, God, sending his Son in the likeness of sinful flesh, condemned sin in the flesh and accomplished redemption in our stead (Romans 8:3). Believers are vicarious participants in the obedience of Christ: they kept the law through him; they died in Christ; they were crucified with him (Romans 6:3, 6); they were delivered from the curse that the law pronounced upon its violator through his being made a curse for them by hanging on a tree (Galatians 3:10, 13). They were freed from the contract with the law by the body of Christ (Romans 7:4); therefore, he is the end, or the teleological goal, of the law for righteousness or justification to those who believe (Romans 10:4). As through the disobedience of one, all die, so through the obedience of one, many are made righteous (Romans 5:19). He who knew no sin was made sin for us that we might be made the righteousness of God in him (2 Corinthians 5:21).

Paul explains the righteousness of God in Romans 3:9ff: "For we have previously charged both Jews and Greeks that they are all under sin. As it is written: 'There is none righteous, no, not one . . . Therefore by the deeds of the law no flesh will be justified in his sight . . . But now the righteousness of God apart from the law is revealed, being witnessed by the Law and the Prophets, even the righteousness of God, which is through faith in Jesus Christ, to all and on all who believe. . . . being justified freely by his grace through the redemption that is in Christ Jesus, whom God set forth to be a propitiation by his blood, through faith, to demonstrate his righteousness, because in his forbearance God had passed over the sins that were previously committed . . . that he might be just and the justifier of the one who has faith in Jesus. . . . therefore we conclude that a man is justified by faith apart from the deeds of the law. . . . Do we then make void the law through faith? Certainly not! On the contrary, we establish the law." Faith righteousness establishes and fulfills God's law in the lives of believers.

A FAITH RIGHTEOUSNESS

The concept of faith righteousness had been foundational to Yahweh's religion from the time of Abraham. All those who were justified before God in the Old Testament were righteous through faith. Hebrews 11 is a roll call of faith from the Old Testament, detailing men and women who believed God and did what he had commanded them. They were participants in faith righteousness.

When Jesus came, this concept of faith righteousness came to completeness or perfection, resting on a perfect sacrifice and forming a better covenant. The righteousness of Christ is a faith righteousness, and it can be imputed unto us only through our faith in the Son of God, "For with the heart one believes to righteousness, and with the mouth confession is made to salvation" (Romans 10:10). Does this faith, then, make void the law of God? Certainly not; for, in effect, it serves to establish the law in that it accomplishes the objective of the law by making the comer thereunto obedient to God. When we accept the substitutionary righteousness of Christ through faith in his atoning death and his glorious resurrection, we become completely justified before God, and we need not offer further sacrifice or do additional works to complete or maintain our status of righteousness before God (Romans 5:1; 3:21, 22).

Through this imputed righteousness, we are enabled and empowered to keep the law of God through faith. Should we, then, continue in sin that grace may abound? Let it never be! (Romans 6:1). Should we violate the commandments and the law of God so that we may prove that we are of the faith of Jesus? No, let it never be! Rather, because Christ is righteous and we through faith have partaken of his righteousness, we should live righteously and godly in this present world (Titus 2:12).

When we as believers accept the new covenant through the blood of Jesus, we partake of this agreement: "I will put my laws into their hearts, in their minds I will write them." Therefore, "by a new and living way" we have access to the holiest of all by the blood of Jesus (Hebrews 10:16-20). Having been imputed total righteousness through Christ, we are then empowered to "work the works of righteousness," to be completely equipped by the Hebrew Scriptures unto all the good works that God seeks (2 Timothy 3:16, 17).

HOLINESS A MANIFESTATION OF RIGHTEOUSNESS

While our righteousness and justification are obtained through Christ apart from the law of God, we are not at liberty to conduct ourselves as we please with total disregard for the will of God. While Christ was the end of the law for righteousness or justification, he was not the destroyer of the law. Indeed, he was the fulfiller of the law (Matthew 5:17-19).

This is the thrust of James' general epistle: "Show me your faith apart from your works, and I by my works will show you my faith" (James 2:18). If we have the righteousness or justification of God within us through faith, then that righteousness will manifest itself in our works. Jesus said, "Ye shall know them by their fruits " (Matthew 7:16). According to James, the faith of Abraham, which was credited to him for righteousness, was not completed until he acted and offered Isaac in obedience to the commandment of God. Likewise, our faith is not complete until we witness it by obeying the commandments of God and living a set-apart or sanctified life. This is the essence of Judaism and Christianity—a call to holiness.

Righteousness or justification is imputed, not earned, through faith (Romans 4:6); however, we must be obedient to God's will and be a separate or holy people. God requires that we be set forth in contradistinction to the elements of the world. This is the condition of being holy or set apart. Holiness is not an addition to righteousness or justification; however, it is a manifestation of righteousness. If we are righteous and remain so, we will be a holy, set apart, sanctified people, qualified for the Master's use (Titus 2:12; 2 Timothy 2:21). James was correct, then, when he declared that "by works a man is justified, and not by faith only" (James 2:24).

"Therefore, having been justified by faith, we have peace with God through our Lord Jesus Christ, through whom also we have access by faith into this grace in which we stand, and rejoice in hope of the glory of God" (Romans 5:1, 2). We lift up our hands and hearts in thanksgiving to God for his amazing grace, for his gratuitous pardon, for his free justification, for his imputation of the righteousness of the Messiah, and for his empowering us to live a life of sanctification in holiness.

Raised Again
For Our
Justification

RAISED AGAIN
FOR OUR JUSTIFICATION

"[Jesus] was delivered up because of our offenses, and was raised because of our justification" (Romans 4:25).

As Christians, we hear much discussion concerning the crucifixion of our Lord Jesus Christ, and, indeed, "worthy is the Lamb who was slain to receive power and riches and wisdom and strength and honor and glory and blessing!" (Revelation 5:12). Often, however, we become so involved in paying tribute to the sacrificed Lamb for his act of unfathomable love in offering himself without sin to atone for the sins of all mankind, that we lose sight of a greater act performed in the life of Jesus which speaks of greater, more far-reaching consequences than the Calvary experience.

The single most important event in all of human history was the resurrection from the dead of the only begotten Son of God. The Heavenly Father attached profound significance to the resurrection of the Son by declaring: "You are my Son, today I have begotten you" (Acts 13:33). Peter declared in Acts 2:30, 31 that the resurrection, not the birth, of Jesus was the fulfillment of God's oath to David in Psalm 132:11. While the birth of Jesus in Bethlehem provided a body of flesh in which God could become incarnate, the manifestation of divine power which brought his uncorrupted body forth from the tomb was that act which confirmed and established forever his Messiahship and his divinity. While the death of Jesus on the cross of Calvary provided perpetual and eternal atonement for sin for all who would believe in the redemptive power of his blood, his resurrection from the dead justifies believers in a way in which no sacrifice for sin could accomplish.

Romans 5:10 clarifies this premise: "For if when we were enemies we were reconciled to God through the death of his Son, much more, having been reconciled, we shall be saved *by his life*." While the shed blood of Jesus reconciled fallen man to God through the forgiveness of sins, the resurrection and life of Christ justified man from the inherent sin of Adam and reinstated the promise of eternal life. Jesus, himself, through his divinity, brought forth his body from the grave, as he had promised: I have power to lay [my life] down, and I have power to take it again" (John 10:18). "Destroy this temple, and in three days I will raise it up " (John 2:19). While the crucifixion of Jesus proved that he was man (Hebrews 2:9), his resurrection proved that he was God (Acts 2:36) and therefore endowed with the power of life. Had he not resurrected, what evidence would there be that his death was more than the death of any other man or that his sacrifice for sin was efficacious?

POWER OVER DEATH DEMONSTRATED

Through his resurrection, Jesus demonstrated that it is possible for humanity to inherit life through faith. No one had ever before achieved this of himself though it was prefigured in Enoch and Elijah and perhaps even in Moses. What the law could not do, the resurrection of Jesus did (Acts 13:39). If his righteousness was sufficient for him to acquire the promise of eternal life first given to Adam, then we have the distinct probability that through faith in him and his resurrection, we can partake of his righteousness and be resurrected ourselves. The resurrection of Jesus, therefore, takes on greater dimensions than the mere forgiveness of sins of mankind and provides the means for reinstating the opportunity for mankind to obtain eternal life.

According to Revelation 1:5 and 2 Corinthians 15:23, Jesus is the first begotten from the dead or the firstfruits of the resurrection. In this capacity, he stands forth as an object of faith for the believer, for as in the sin of Adam all die (and we are assured of this fact beyond doubt), so in Christ shall all be made alive (Romans 5:17). If Christ is the firstfruits of the resurrection, he is proof that a great harvest of resurrection is to come when at the end of the age God sends his angels to gather together all of his chosen, both in heaven and earth (Matthew 24:31; Ephesians 1:10).

In 1 Corinthians 15:3, 4, 12-14, 16, 17, 20-22, Paul further elaborates on this theme: "For I delivered to you first of all that which I also received: that Christ died for our sins according to the Scriptures, and that he was buried, and that he rose again the third day according to the Scriptures. . . now if Christ is preached that he has been raised from the dead, how do some among you say that there is no resurrection of the dead? But if there is no resurrection of the dead, then Christ is not risen. And if Christ is not risen, then our preaching is vain and your faith is also vain. . . and if Christ is not risen, your faith is futile; you are still in your sins! . . . but now Christ is risen from the dead, and has become the firstfruits of those who have fallen asleep. For since by man came death, by Man also came the resurrection of the dead. For as in Adam all die, even so in Christ all shall be made alive." Paul declares that if there is no resurrection of the dead, then Christ is not raised. The converse of this is also true: If Christ is raised from the dead, then there will be a resurrection of the dead, the order and nature of which the apostle proceeds to explain in the remainder of 1 Corinthians 15. The acquisition of a new body "like his glorious body" (Philippians 3:21) is explained in 2 Corinthians 5:1: "For we know that if our earthly house, this tent, is destroyed, we have a building from God, a house not made with hands, eternal in the heavens."

The assurance of our hope of resurrection and life after death, then, is totally contingent upon our confidence in the resurrection of the Lord Jesus Christ. This is the reason for the apostle's assertion in Romans 10:9, 10 that the method and order which brings about the crisis experience of the rebirth is this: "that if you confess with your mouth the Lord Jesus and believe in your heart that God has raised him from the dead, you will be saved. For with the heart one believes to righteousness, and with the mouth confession is made unto salvation."

Man's justification through faith in the resurrection of Jesus, then, is in itself his investiture of the attribute of righteousness. According to Paul, believing with the heart and confessing with the mouth that God raised Jesus from the dead produces the imputation of substitutionary righteousness and salvation (Romans 10:9, 10). The imputed righteousness is, however, totally unmerited by man and is the direct result of divine grace.

HISTORICAL AND PROPHETIC FACT

It is important to note that more is required than belief in the death of Jesus, for salvation in the ultimate sense is unattainable without the resurrection of Jesus Christ. In order to be born from above both in spirit and in the body, we must believe in the resurrection. The Christian promise is not just a rebirth in spirit or absorption into the divine that occurs with the shedding of the material body (as with neo-Platonism and Eastern Monism). It is the fruition of the promise of God's Word espoused by the Pharisees of Jesus' time–the resurrection of the body to rule with Messiah on earth during the Messianic Age.

Belief in the resurrection is not, however, blind faith, for there is ample testimony to corroborate the fact that Jesus did, in fact, rise from the dead. From the standpoint of history alone, all the requirements for the documentation of a simple historical event are met. The infallible word of prophecy predicted it, and the eyewitnesses of the New Testament confirmed it.

The same prophecies which foretold the suffering and death of the Son of God also predicted his resurrection. "For you will not leave my soul in Sheol, nor will you allow your Holy One to see corruption." (Psalm 16:10). "Yet it pleased the Lord to bruise Him; he has put him to grief. When you make his soul an offering for sin, he shall see his seed, *he shall prolong his days* . . . By his knowledge my righteous Servant shall justify many. . ."

(Isaiah 53:10, 11).

Those who wereeyewitnesses of the resurrection and ascension of Jesus testified: ". . . to the apostles whom he had chosen, to whom he also presented himself alive after his suffering by many infallible proofs, being seen by them during forty days and speaking of the things pertaining to the kingdom of God"(Acts 1:2, 3). "Therefore, of these men . . . one . . . must become a witness with us of his resurrection. . . ." (Acts 1:21, 22). "This Jesus God has raised up, of which we are all witnesses" (Acts 2:32). If the resurrection were a hoax or a phantasmagoria, would all of the disciples–without exception–give up their lives rather than recant their testimony?

THE BLESSED HOPE

Without the resurrection of Jesus Christ and our hope of a similar experience through faith in him, we are of all men most miserable (1 Corinthians 15:19). Even Epicureans and hedonists live by the premise, "Eat, drink, and be merry; for tomorrow we may die." Through faith in Jesus and his resurrection, we are able to lay hold on that "blessed hope," the "glorious appearing of our great God and Savior Jesus Christ" (Titus 2:13) when "in a moment, in the twinkling of an eye, at the last trumpet . . . the dead will be raised incorruptible, and we shall be changed" (1 Corinthians 15:52). We can shout with Paul: "Thanks be to God, who gives us the victory through our Lord Jesus Christ" (1 Corinthians 15:57), and with John we can exclaim: "Even so, come, Lord Jesus" (Revelation 22:20).

Nailed
To
The Cross!

NAILED TO THE CROSS!

For nearly two thousand years theologians and Bible teachers of various persuasions have had their hammers out, nailing a wide variety of things to the cross of Christ. Some have nailed the ceremonial law to the cross. Others have impaled all the law of Moses there. Still others have hung the entire Hebrew Scriptures on the cross. A fair question for a believer to ask is, just what was nailed to the cross?

First we must understand that all that was literally nailed to the cross of Calvary was the fleshly body of Jesus of Nazareth and the inscription of Pilate that Jesus was the King of the Jews. The question of controversy arises over Colossians 2:14. And, the answer to the question of the symbolic language of this passage is found in the literal event which occurred on Golgotha. We shall find that the principle of the grammatico-historical hermeneutic that "context interprets text" will provide a reliable exegesis of this passage as it does with all Scripture.

"In him also ye are circumcised with the circumcision made without hands, in putting off the body of the sins of the flesh, by the circumcision of Christ... And you, being dead in your trespasses and the uncircumcision of your flesh, he has made alive together with him, having forgiven you all trespasses, having wiped out the handwriting of requirements that was against us, which was contrary to us. And he has taken it out of the way, having nailed it to the cross ...Therefore, if you died with Christ from the basic principles of the world, why, as though living in the world, do you subject yourselves to regulations ..." (Colossians 2:11, 13, 14, 20).

What is the meaning of the term *handwriting of ordinances*? How and why were they "against us"? How did Christ's death free us from them? What impact did Christ's "blotting [*them*] out" have on the Judaism of his day? Were the ordinances God's commandments, or was the issue not so much of laws but of sin?

A BURDENSOME EXERCISE

By the time of Christ, much of Judaism had become a burdensome exercise that was contrary to the nature of man (Acts 15:10). Some had come to demand that each individual establish his own righteousness or justification before God through works. Despite the fact that all of biblical Judaism has recognized that man's justification and relationship with God was effected solely by faith and the *chesed* (loving kindness) of God, many had come to believe that their righteousness was achieved by their response to God's commandments rather than by a sovereign act of divine grace through faith. The religion of Sinai that had been birthed in the faith of Abraham was gradually developed into an endless maze of *mitzvot* (commandments) and *halachot* (interpretations of commandments) that were designed to govern all areas of human conduct.

The Pharisaic community sought to "build a fence around the law" so one would not come close to breaking one of the actual commandments. Rather than continue to be justified by faith as Abraham was, many of Israel's leaders sought security in a complex system of traditions that added to God's requirements in the written Torah (law) what came to be known as the "Oral Torah." These restrictions were designed to place a fence of warning that would signal one's proximity to the breaking of a biblical commandment. Instead, they often caused men to seek to be more righteous than God (Ecclesiastes 7:16), promoted self-righteousness, and even voided God's commandments (Matthew 15:6). The intentions of the ancient sages and subsequent rabbis were good; however, they were misguided and produced in Judaism a reliance on works rather than on faith as a means of establishing and/or maintaining one's status with God. They did not trust the Spirit to direct people in observing the commandments; therefore, they resorted to restrictions that God, himself, had not required of his people.

The extreme care that this multiplicity of commandments of the Oral Law required made it impossible for anyone to be faultless in every respect. Even in fulfilling the written law when one observed one commandment he would often break another commandment (e.g. what would one do when the commandment to circumcise on the eighth day must be fulfilled on the Sabbath?). This was, no doubt, the reason Peter called the rabbinic model of Judaism "a yoke . . . which neither our ancestors nor we were able to bear?" (Acts 15:10). It also helps us understand Paul's observation that all have sinned and come short of the glory of God, even those who were punctilious in their detailed observance of the commandments both of the written Torah and the oral Torah (Romans 3:23).

It was impossible that men, who were sinners by nature, could establish perfect and lasting righteousness before God by fleshly works. While the law was "holy" and the commandment "holy, and just, and good" (Romans 7:12) and was "perfect, converting the soul" (Psalm 19:7), the flesh of man was the only weakness of that system, making its perfect fulfillment impossible. The only possible means of justification for man is through the judicial proclamation of God that he is righteous, and this can be accomplished only through a divine act of grace that generates faith in men. It can be applied only because Jesus paid the price to ransom the souls of men. It is not, therefore, of man's works–never has been, and never will be!

A BODY OF FLESH MAKES FLESHLY WORKS UNNECESSARY

When a sinless body of flesh that had been perfected through sufferings and temptations was nailed to the cross, the need for fleshly works of righteousness ended. Consequently, the laws and ordinances which prescribed ritual for establishing such, including the sacrificial law, became obsolete and outmoded. So, metaphorically speaking, these ordinances were nailed to the cross in the body of Jesus. This is why the apostle tells us that we are not to be judged by what we eat, or by what we drink, or by what days we observe (Colossians 2:16). In short, we are not subject to carnal ordinances or rules governing fleshly purification and righteousness (Hebrews 9:10).

The problem was sin, not God's law. It was sin that was against mankind, not God's law. The Messiah came to remove sin. In a very real sense, all the sin of the human race was nailed to the cross of Christ when it was laid upon him to such a degree that "he became sin for us." In order to redeem those who would believe, the price that was adequate to atone for the sins of all mankind was paid.

It was not the intention of the New Testament writers, however, to imply that the law had been abolished or that there was no continuing value in Judaism. The principles of the Judaic faith remained the same; however, their function and manifestation were altered. God, who requested that his people remember his festival times forever, did not suddenly change his mind and abolish them. He merely restored them as media of praise and worship rather than as means of establishing justification. This is why we find the apostle who said that no one's salvation should be judged by the days he observed (Colossians 2:16, 17) nonetheless urging Gentiles in Corinth to keep the Feast of Passover (1 Corinthians 5:8). We also find Paul shaving his head and going through the rites of purification in the temple so he could prove that he walked orderly and kept the law (Acts 21:20-24) and making all haste so that he could be at Jerusalem for the observance of the Feast of Pentecost (Acts 20:16).

When Jesus said, "Do not think that I have come to abolish the law" (Matthew 5:17), he meant exactly what he said. The eternal laws and principles of God were never abolished; however, the requirement for fleshly works was rendered unnecessary through the personal righteousness of Christ. The body of Christ, nailed to the cross of Calvary, freed the believer for all time from the bondage and yoke of fleshly works so that he might freely serve the living God in the Spirit.

HANDWRITING AGAINST US?

What was meant by the apostle's statement that the "handwriting of ordinances" that was "against us" was "nailed to his cross"? Much of the church has insisted that the handwriting was the "Law of Moses" which was added to the "Law of God." Some have suggested that it was the Oral Torah which was added by the sages and rabbis of Israel. A third and possibly more feasible explanation of this statement is that the "handwriting" is the record of men's sins that have been recorded in heaven in the Book of Works since the beginning of time. This record enumerates each individual's violations of God's commandments. When all the sins of humanity were placed upon Jesus as he hung upon the cross (Isaiah 53:6), the provision for blotting out that sin record (the "handwriting" from the ordinances against men) was made in his efficacious sacrifice. That sin record ("handwriting") was, therefore, nailed to the cross in the body of Jesus.

What was nailed to the cross? Flesh and carnal works, that the Spirit and faith might be exalted! Sin, so that all men might be freed from its enslaving power. The carnal ordinances, so that God's religion might be restored to its original ideal–faith!

The Faith of Abraham and God's Covenant People

Chapter 10
THE FAITH OF ABRAHAM AND GOD'S COVENANT PEOPLE

The biblical concept of election is founded in the sovereignty of God. It is God who has sought a man and a people with whom he could have relationship. As Abraham Joshua Heschel has said, history is not a record of man's search for God but of God's search for man. Jesus, himself, confirmed this truth in John 4:23: "But the hour cometh, and now is, when the true worshipers will worship the Father in spirit and truth: for the Father is *seeking such* to worship him."

This fundamental truth helps us to understand that history is linear and covenantal. Salvation history started somewhere (with creation) and ends somewhere (with the Messianic Age), and it is based on God's sovereign covenantal election of a people to be uniquely his. This kind of special relationship implies an agreement, for which the scriptural term is covenant. So we may state from the outset that God's chosen people have been and remain those with whom he has established his covenant.

GOD'S FIRST COVENANT WITH HUMANITY

Immediately after the fall of Adam and Eve in the Garden of Eden, God made this promise in his declaration to the serpent: "And I will put enmity between you and the woman, and between your seed and her Seed; *he shall bruise your head*, and you shall bruise his heel" (Genesis 3:15). Later in Noah's time, immediately following the flood, God established a covenant with all the earth declaring that he would never destroy the earth again with water (Genesis 9:8-17). Neither of these events, however, represented a covenant with an individual, electing him above all others.

In Bible history, the first time that Yahweh, the Eternal God, entered into a covenant with anyone is found in Genesis 15, where Abraham was chosen because of his implicit faith in God's Word. Abraham had left his father's house in Haran of Syria to look for the land to which God had sent him, and when he finally came into the land, he implored the Lord in this manner: "Lord God, how shall I know that I will inherit [*this* land]?" (Genesis 15:8). God required Abraham to make a sacrificial offering, after which he spoke to him in this manner: "To your descendants have I given this land, from the river of Egypt unto the great river, the River Euphrates . . ." (Genesis 15:18). The record continues, declaring that "On the same day the Lord made a covenant with Abram."

Abraham, therefore, was the first man with whom God entered into a covenant, promising a special relationship with him and with his children forever. "The Lord appeared to Abram and said to him . . . And I will establish my covenant between me and you and your descendants after you in their generations, for an everlasting covenant, to be God to you and your descendants after you. Also I give to you and your descendants after you the land in which you are a stranger, all the land of Canaan, as an everlasting possession; and I will be their God" (Genesis 17:1, 7, 8). The seal of God's covenant was to be the rite of circumcision.

This agreement between God and Abraham brought about a startling transformation. Abraham, who was a Babylonian by birth and a Syrian by nationality (Genesis 11:31), became the father of another nation, the nation of faith in the Eternal God. As far as God was concerned, Abraham was transformed from a Gentile into a chosen vessel to father a holy nation that would bear his name among the Gentiles.

From the time that Abraham had crossed over the river Euphrates, he had been called a Hebrew from the word *eber*, meaning to cross over. His leaving the land of Ur of the Chaldees and later departing from his father's house in Haran of Syria were the acts of faith which prompted God to extend his promise and covenant to Abraham. So, after the making of the covenant, Abraham became more than a Hebrew–he became the father of the faithful.

Just as God had promised Abraham, it was some four hundred years before the benefits of his covenant became reality (Genesis 15:13). Through those ensuing years, Abraham's progeny through his promised son Isaac were God's chosen people because of the Abrahamic covenant. The children of Abraham continued to be known as Syrians until after the time of Jacob as Deuteronomy 26:5 declares: "My father was a Syrian, about to perish, and he went down to Egypt and sojourned there, few in number; and there he became a nation, great, mighty, and populous." Still, the children of Israel were a chosen people within the nation of Syria. While seventy souls entered into the land of Egypt during the time of the famine, at the end of four hundred years, six hundred thousand men, together with women and children, were ready to be delivered from the slavery into which they had been forced.

ISRAEL, A COVENANT NATION

A profound deliverance was effected by God's intervention through the hand of his servant Moses. The children of Abraham through Isaac and

Jacob passed through the Red Sea and gathered before the great mountain of the Lord called Sinai to make a covenant with God that would transfer them into his holy nation, chosen above all the people of the earth (Deuteronomy 10:15). When this covenant was made, however, it merely amended the covenant that Yahweh and Abraham had made four hundred years before, for it could never replace or abrogate that covenant: "The law, which was four hundred and thirty years later, cannot annul the [Abrahamic] covenant that was confirmed before by God in Christ, that it should make the promise of no effect"(Galatians 3:17).

Speaking expressly and shockingly to them, God delivered the Ten Commandments to the Israelites as they stood in fear and awe before Sinai. Both Israel and the entire world heard the proclamation of God's commandments that day (Exodus 19:18, 19; Psalm 68:8; Hebrews 12:26). Israel, however, responded affirmatively to God's command, saying, "All that you have said we will do and we will hear." Israel had such faith in God's Word that they agreed to do his commandments before they understood (heard) them! So, God chose all of Israel as his nation and established his covenant with them; however, the Word of God tells us that at that same time he made further selection and separated a part of Israel to be a special people unto him. "When Israel went out of Egypt, the house of Jacob from a people of strange language, Judah became his sanctuary, and Israel his dominion"(Psalm 114:1, 2); "Moreover he rejected the tent of Joseph, and did not choose the tribe of Ephraim: but chose the tribe of Judah, mount Zion which he loved" (Psalm 78:67, 68). The tribe of Judah, then, became a peculiarly chosen people unto God–a nation within a nation, as it were. It was Judah to whom God entrusted his sayings. And, it was Judah, more than all of the other tribes of Israel, that was zealous for the law and the Word of God.

THE ORIGIN OF THE TERM *JEW*

As time progressed, particularly following the reigns of David and Solomon, the tribe of Judah, with Benjamin and much of Levi, became even more separated from the rest of Israel in the divided kingdom. The northern tribes followed Jeroboam while Judah, Benjamin, and Levi followed Rehoboam, Solomon's son. God's wisdom in choosing Judah above the others is validated in the fact that Judah continued to maintain God's religious system while the ten tribes entered into idolatry and experienced the first Diaspora when God brought the Assyrian armies against them.

It was during this time that the members of the tribe of Judah came to be known as Jews, a contraction of the word *Judah* (*Yehudah*). The first scriptural record of this term is found in 2 Kings 16:6. Initially "Jew" was a term of derision applied by others and not by the bearers of the name (as is also the case with the term *Christian*, an aspersion against the early believers in Jesus). Through succeeding generations, this term came to be synonymous with God's chosen people, so much so that members of other tribes came to be called Jews also (Acts 19:14, 34; 21:39).

From that time, the term *Jew* came to connote the chosen people of God. Jews as a nationality included the Hebrews who had made a covenant to become God's chosen people. The term *nationality* is a particularly apropos description of the Jews. While the more common usage of the term *race* is sometimes applied to them, in the strictest sense of the meaning of this word, Jews are not a race within themselves.

HOW DID ONE BECOME A JEW?

In the pre-Christian era, there were two ways in which one could become a Jew. First, one's being born of Israelite parents automatically made him a Jew through the covenant to Abraham and his descendants. Secondly, provision was made for those who wished to accept the law of God through faith to become fellow citizens with those Jews of fleshly lineage. From the very outset of the exodus, the Lord said, "And when a stranger . . . wants to keep the Passover to the Lord, let all his males be circumcised, and then let him come near and keep it; and he shall be as a native of the land" (Exodus 12:48). Leviticus 19:34 reconfirms this position: "The stranger who dwells among you shall be to you as one born among you, and you shall love him as yourself . . ." For those Gentiles who would be included in Israel there were certain initiation requirements, including circumcision, ritual immersion, sacrifice, and learning the Torah.

Is it possible that those Gentiles in the flesh actually became Jews? As far as God was concerned their acceptance of the terms of the covenant between himself and the children of Israel transformed them into Jews just as it had transformed Abraham, the Babylonian/Syrian, into a Jew. Though at first they were called proselytes and were considered second-class citizens by many elitist Jews, those who accepted the covenant of God eventually became recognized as Jews. The exclusivity of the Jews did not obviate the impartiality of God. According to Isaiah 56:3-7 the Gentiles who accepted God's covenant were to have a place in his house *better than* that of sons and daughters.

Since God has no respect of persons, the thing which made Abraham the chosen of God (in a sense, the first Jew) can make any man a Jew. As Abraham's selection was totally predicated upon his faith in God, so in both Old and New Testament eras, becoming chosen of God was by faith in God to accept his will and system for that particular era. This faith transformed a Syrian into a Hebrew, and it has transformed many strangers of various nationalities into Jews.

Such was the case in the days of Esther. We are told that when the Jews were given permission to defend themselves on the day on which Haman planned their genocide, "many of the people of the land *became Jews*, because fear of the Jews fell upon them" (Esther 8:17). Apparently, many of the people of the Persian empire so believed in the protection of the Jews by their God that they were willing to become Jews. Whether their instinct was faith or self-preservation, the simple fact is that the Scripture tells us they "*became Jews.*"

Throughout the Hebrew Scriptures, the Eternal God continued to recognize those who accepted his covenants as being his chosen people or Jews, as they came to be known. It was in his divine plan, however, to make the way easier so that all men might become his chosen. In the fullness of time, it was the covenant that he had made with Abraham that prompted the Father to send his Son, made of woman under the law to redeem them that were under the law (Galatians 4:4, 5). Zacharias, the father of John, prophesied: "Blessed is the Lord God of Israel; for he has visited and redeemed his people, and has raised up a horn of salvation for us in the house of his servant David . . . to perform the mercy promised to our fathers and *to remember his holy covenant*, the oath which he swore to our ancestor Abraham . . ." (Luke 1:68, 69, 72, 73). Jesus was the fulfillment of God's promise, "In Isaac your *seed* shall be called" (Hebrews 11:18).

THE COVENANT FOR JEWS ONLY

From the very beginning of his ministry, Jesus practiced the covenantal religious system under which he had been born. He staunchly maintained that the Jews alone (including those Gentiles who had fully embraced the covenant of Judaism) were God's chosen people. He declared that he was sent only to the lost sheep of the house of Israel (Matthew 15:24) and admonished his apostles not to go in the way of the Gentiles (Matthew 10:5, 6). Jesus well knew that the law of God (Torah) was to go forth from Zion and the word of the Lord from Jerusalem (Isaiah 2:3). He knew that to the Israelites alone belong "the adoption, the glory, the covenants, the giving of the law, the service of God, and the promises" (Romans 9:4). It was of the Israelites "from whom, according to the flesh, Christ came" (Romans 9:5). Even when addressing one of these lost sheep of Israel (a Samaritan), the Savior declared: "We know what we worship: for salvation is [*from*] the Jews" (John 4:22).

In his conversation with the Samaritan woman at the well of Jacob, however, Jesus predicted that a time would soon come when a change would take place in the practice of God's chosen religion, which also implied a change in the manner of God's choosing his people. He declared that the true worshipers of the Eternal God must begin to worship him in Spirit as well as in truth. Until that time, the people had worshiped Yahweh in a system that had been given by God and was a revelation of divine truth; however, the worshipers had carried out their ritual by an obedience to the commandments that was often lifeless. The time was coming that those who would offer acceptable worship to God would have to do so willingly and with the motivation of the Holy Spirit. The Messiah declared that since God is Spirit, they who worship him must do so in Spirit as well as in the truth which he has given (John 4:24). This is why Paul, himself a Pharisee, declared, ". . .the letter [*of the law*] kills, but the Spirit gives life" (2 Corinthians 3:6). Mere ritualistic obedience would no longer suffice: the worshipers must worship in Spirit as well as in truth. Indeed, the *hendiadys* of John 5:24 can be interpreted to mean that the true worshipers must worship the Father in the Spirit, *which is the truth*. It can also be interpreted that they will worship in *spiritual truth*.

EXTENDING THE ONE COVENANT FOR ALL PEOPLE

Since the covenants of God until that time had pertained only to the natural children, Jesus could not direct his earthly ministry outside that sphere; however, when the time came for the new covenant to be established to renew and expand the Abrahamic covenant and its Sinai emendation, the Word of God predicted that others besides the fleshly Jews would have access to that covenant. Isaiah had foretold this great event: "I, the Lord, have called you in righteousness . . . I will keep you and *give you as a covenant to the people*, as *a light to the Gentiles*" (Isaiah 42:6). Simeon, the priest who dedicated the Son of God, reiterated it in Luke 2:32. Jesus claimed it in Luke 4:18.

In John 10:11-16, Jesus set the stage for expanding the covenant to the Gentiles on the basis of spiritual rather than physical fulfillments of God's Word. He declared, "Other sheep I have which are not of this fold; them also I must bring . . . *and there will be one flock and one shepherd.*" The Son of God predicted that there would be a time when there would be one religion for all men, one fold in which all God's sheep would be gathered together. What had been required of Israel physically would now be required of the Gentiles spiritually (e.g., circumcision).

Prior to the time when the new testament in the blood of Jesus was sealed through the testator's death (Hebrews 9:15-17), the message of the Messiah had been directed only to the children of the fleshly covenant. After the death and resurrection of the Son of God, however, his commission to his disciples was this: "Go into all the world and preach the gospel to every creature" (Mark 16:15); "You shall be witnesses to me in Jerusalem, and in all Judea and Samaria, and to the end of the earth" (Acts 1:8).

As the door of salvation was opened to the Gentiles, the immutable principle of accepting God's covenant remained constant. Psalms 50:5 tells us that only those who have made a covenant with God are qualified to inherit with Christ. The new covenant that Yahweh made with Israel and the rest of the world through the death of his Son was this: "I will put my laws in their mind and write them on their heart; and I will be their God, and they shall be my people" (Hebrews 8:10).

The renewal and expansion of God's covenant was made available to the entire world, including the Gentiles, and was to be predicated upon only one thing–faith. This was the covenant which God made with the world: "That whoever believes in him should have . . . everlasting life" (John 3:16). Inclusion among God's chosen people was contingent upon accepting by faith that Messiah Jesus is the everlasting atonement for sin. Just as Abraham was justified by faith, so all the just "shall live by faith" (Romans 5:1; Galatians 3:11).

Confession of faith in the atoning death and glorious resurrection of the Jewish Messiah effected the rebirth and the spiritual circumcision of the heart that Moses (Deuteronomy 10:16) and Jeremiah had predicted (4:4). The believer's subsequent baptism in water was an outward demonstration of his death to sin, his burial, and his resurrection to newness of life. It was a fulfillment of Judaism's requirement that converts to Yahweh's religion immerse themselves in the *mikveh.* Those who were baptized became catecumenates and were taught the Word of God in like manner as proselytes to Judaism were taught the same Torah. They also participated in the one sacrifice for sin under the new covenant–Jesus, himself–and they shared in the new sacrificial system of praise, prayer, and worship of God in the Spirit (Hebrews 13:15, 16; Revelation 5:8; 8:3; Philippians 4:18).

While previously God's covenants had applied to the *fleshly* lineage and had been sealed with the *fleshly* sign of circumcision, the Messiah established a *spiritual* covenant which by a *spiritual* birth translated the believer into the *spiritual* Israel, the spiritual Kingdom of God, which then functioned alongside natural Israel in God's election. The principle of becoming chosen of God by making a covenant with him remained constant.

THE ABRAHAMIC COVENANT OF FAITH

The great similarity between the covenant of Abraham and that of Christ is immediately noticed. Both were given because of faith, and both promised an inheritance. Paul notes this similarity in Galatians 3:6-8, 13, 14, 26, 29: "Just as Abraham believed God, and it was accounted to him for righteousness. Therefore know that only those who are of faith are sons of Abraham. And the Scripture, foreseeing that God would justify the nations by faith, preached the gospel to Abraham beforehand, saying, In you all the nations shall be blessed . . . Christ has redeemed us from the curse of the law . . . that the blessing of Abraham might come upon the Gentiles in Jesus Christ; that we might receive the promise of the Spirit through faith . . . For you are all sons of God by faith in Christ Jesus. . . . And if you are Christ's, then are you Abraham's seed, and heirs according to the promise."

The Abrahamic covenant, then, was not abolished in Christ, but rather was extended by him to all men, both Jew and Gentile. All believers in Jesus, Jew and Gentile, become the spiritual children of Abraham by virtue of their faith. This is further explained in Romans 9:6-8, 23-26: "For they are not all Israel who are of Israel, nor are they all children because they are the seed of Abraham; but, in Isaac shall your seed be called. That is, those who are the children of the flesh, these are not the children of God; but the children of the promise are counted as the seed."

THE RENEWED COVENANT OF THE TORAH

The covenant of the Torah given at Sinai was a system of praise, worship, and service that came to be called Judaism by the time of the first century C.E. This Judaism was never obviated or superseded by the ministry of Jesus. Since Jesus, himself, confessed that he had not come to destroy the Torah (law) but to complete it (Matthew 5:17), the new covenant was not a totally unexpected religion but a renewal of the first covenant on the basis of a better sacrifice. It was another step in God's unfolding plan for the ages and the religion that he had given and would perfect.

It was not that the first covenant was bad and the second good. The first covenant was good (Romans 7:12), and the second was better (Hebrews 7:19-22). The new covenant expanded the Sinai covenant in the same way in which the Sinai Covenant had expanded the Abrahamic covenant. The Abrahamic covenant was of grace and faith as Hebrews 11 demonstrates. The new covenant brought an expansion of the grace and truth which the

Sinai covenant manifested restrictively. The Sinai covenant needed only perfection (completion) and renewal, not abrogation and supersession.

GENTILES BECOME SPIRITUAL JEWS IN THE NEW TESTAMENT

Ephesians 2:11-13 expands upon the thought of Gentile inclusion: "Therefore remember that you, once Gentiles in the flesh . . . were without Christ, being aliens from the commonwealth of Israel and strangers from the *covenants of promise,* having no hope and without God in the world. But now in Christ Jesus you who once were far off have been made near by the blood of Christ." Those who were formerly nothing more than "Gentiles in the flesh" and aliens from Israel and its covenants, were now translated into the kingdom of God (Colossians 1:13), becoming his chosen people (in effect, becoming Jewish or naturalized citizens of Israel.)

Paul declared that to the apostles alone was revealed this mystery that the Gentiles should be accepted before God on equal terms with the Jews: ". . .[this] mystery . . . in other ages was not made known to the sons of men, as it has now been revealed by the Spirit to his holy apostles and prophets: that the Gentiles should be fellow heirs, of the same body, and partakers of his promise in Christ through the Gospel" (Ephesians 3:5, 6).

The Abrahamic covenant and its more far-reaching implications then were applicable not only to the children of the flesh but also to the children of faith. Circumcision, the fleshly sign in which the Jews according to the flesh had come to trust, was totally secondary to the spiritual faith which Abraham had had when he was chosen of God. "For the promise that he would be the heir of the world was not to Abraham or to his seed through the law, but through the righteousness of faith. For if those who are of the law are heirs, faith is made void . . . therefore, it is of faith that it might be according to grace, so that the *promise might be sure to all the seed,* not only to those who are of the law, but also to those who are of the faith of Abraham, who is the father of us all" (Romans 4:13-16).

In Romans 2:25-29 the apostle Paul further explained the principle of faith and obedience to God through which the Gentiles could be accepted before God on equal terms with the Jews. "For circumcision is indeed profitable if you keep the law; but if you are a breaker of the law, your circumcision has become uncircumcision. Therefore, if an uncircumcised man keeps the righteous requirements of the law, will not his uncircumcision be counted as circumcision? . . . For he is not a Jew who is one outwardly, nor is that circumcision which is outward in the flesh; but he is a Jew who is one inwardly; and circumcision is that of the heart, in the Spirit, and not in the letter; whose praise is not from men but from God."

THE CHILDREN OF FAITH *COUNTED FOR* FLESHLY CHILDREN

A Gentile's having the righteousness of God, then, is *counted as* circumcision so that he, in effect, becomes Jewish. Since the righteousness of God is solely the person of Jesus Christ (Romans 10:4; 1 Corinthians 1:30), the Gentile as well as the Jew receives righteousness through faith in Jesus. This faith righteousness is then *counted as* circumcision of the flesh so that circumcision becomes a spiritual experience rather than a fleshly rite. The Greek word translated "counted for" is *logizomai*. It is the same word used in Romans 4:3: "Abraham believed God, and it was *accounted to* him for righteousness," and in Romans 9:8: "The children of the promise are *counted as* the seed." Just as Abraham's faith was *counted as* righteousness, so the substitutionary righteousness of Christ in the heart of the uncircumcised believer is *counted as* circumcision and the reborn child of the promise of God is *counted as* the fleshly seed.

This is the principle upon which a Gentile by circumcision of the heart (rebirth) can become a spiritual Jew. The spiritual Jew is the spiritual seed of Abraham through faith. What the apostle is saying here is that both fleshly Jews and fleshly Gentiles can become spiritual Jews through the circumcision of the heart. This does not replace the natural Jews in God's covenantal purposes, for the gifts and callings of God, both natural and spiritual, are irrevocable (Romans 11:29).

Some have suggested that the spiritual seed utterly replaced the natural Jews and that Christianity superseded Judaism. This position is based on an arrogant ignorance of hundreds of prophesies of the Old Testament and the writings of the apostles. Anyone who honestly studies the New Testament in the context of its first century culture, history, and grammar instantly recognizes the continuity of biblical faith.

Others have suggested that only fleshly Jews who believe upon Christ can become spiritual Jews. Those who propose this argument state that Gentiles who believe upon the Messiah are called spiritual Gentiles, an argument that falls short on two points:

(1) The term *spiritual* does not always denote spirituality or a higher plane of maturity in the Spirit of God. It is used to reveal something of the spirit, or the intangible, as opposed to something of the flesh, or the tangible. Such is the case in 1 Corinthians 15:44, where we are told that there is a natural body and a *spiritual* body; in Ephesians 5:19, where we are admonished to sing *spiritual* songs; in Ephesians 6:12, where the nature of our warfare is described as being against *spiritual* wickedness in high places;

and in Revelation 11:8, where Jerusalem is *spiritually* called Sodom and Egypt. While *spiritual* can be an adjective denoting spirituality, it is also used as a substitute for the prepositional phrase *in spirit.*

(2) By the time of the New Testament, the term *Jew* had become the word which was used to identify God's chosen people, whether they were of the tribe of Judah, Benjamin, Levi, or whatever. If the Gentiles were "fellowheirs, of the same body, and partakers of his promise" (Ephesians 3:6) and were no more strangers "from the covenants of promise" (Ephesians 2:12), then they most surely could be recognized as "Jewish" or chosen of God.

And, indeed, this was the case, for we find Peter, the apostle to the Jews, making this statement: "To the pilgrims of the dispersion . . . you also, as living stones, are being built up a spiritual house . . . you are a chosen generation, a royal priesthood, a holy nation, his own special people . . . who once were not a people but are now the people of God" (1 Peter 1:1; 2:5, 9, 10). This specific quotation of Hosea 1:6, 9 shows us that Gentiles who have experienced the rebirth considered spiritually and prophetically to be "Israelites."

A NATURAL INHERITANCE A PROVISION OF THE COVENANT

By accepting the Lord Jesus Christ and his righteousness, the Gentiles became a part of God's holy nation, his chosen people. They became spiritual Jews and children of Abraham. As such, they also became heirs of the world, as God had promised to Abraham (Romans 4:13).

This is the reason that the kingdom of God will be established in the nation of Israel rather than in some other nation of the world. The camp of the saints of the Most High God will be in the Holy City for the thousand years of the kingdom of God upon the earth (Revelation 20:9). The inheritance of the land from the Euphrates to the river of Egypt is promised to the children of Abraham, both the natural and spiritual Jews, who will reign with Jesus Christ for one thousand years over the entire earth from his headquarters in Jerusalem, Israel.

The identification of the spiritual Jews of today is simple. Those who believe upon Messiah Yeshua (Christ Jesus) are the children of the promise, the seed of Abraham through faith. They have come alongside natural Israel as spiritual partners in the promises and covenants of God.

GOD'S CHOSEN COVENANT RELIGION

If there is only one God, then there is only one religion for all mankind, both Jew and Gentile according to the flesh. Paul declares this to be true in

Ephesians 4:5: "One Lord, one faith . . . " There is not, as some would have it, a religion for the Jews, called Judaism, and a religion for the Gentiles, called Christianity. And, in the ranks of believers in Jesus, there is not one religion for the Jews, called Messianic Judaism, and another different religion for the Gentiles, called Christianity. Ultimately, there is only one faith or religious system for all men.

It is not necessary for us to persuade the believer that God is an unchanging God. Everyone knows that Jesus Christ is the same yesterday, today, and forever (Hebrews 13:8). Since the Lord is Yahweh who changes not (Malachi 3:6), then we must emphatically assert that if Judaism were ever his chosen system of praise, worship, and service, then in some form it must remain such.

But what effect did the ministry of Messiah Yeshua have on Judaism? The truth is revealed in the nature of the Eternal God as a Perfecter. God simply does not discard what he has done in one era in favor of a totally different thing in another. What he does do is to modify and restructure in order to bring about perfection in the linear development of his plan for the ages. Jeremiah 18:1-6 reveals the nature of the work that the Son of God did in Israel. He took the same marred lump of clay that God had been molding for centuries and from it re-formed a vessel of honor.

The role of Jesus as a reformer is very specifically applied to the religious system called Judaism in Hebrews 9:8,10: " . . . the way into the Holiest of All was not yet made manifest while the first tabernacle was still standing . . . concerned only with and food and drinks, various washings, and fleshly ordinances, imposed until *the time of reformation*." Jesus was a reformer, not an innovator. His purpose was to perfect what God had done through centuries of dealing with the Israelites by introducing the new covenant sealed in his own blood. He declared to the Jewish leaders who thought that he had come to introduce some new religion, "Think not that I have come to destroy the law, or the prophets: I have not come to destroy, but to *fulfill*" (Matthew 5:17).

Through the Messiah, the yoke of Judaism was made easy and the burden light (Matthew 11:28-30), for those parts of Judaism that were rendered superfluous through his becoming the perfect atonement once for all, were nailed to his cross, leaving only the eternal immutable principles of God intact, with a new order for their observance. Whereas the Judaism of the first covenant had become for many a burdensome, ritual-filled religion, the Judaism of the new covenant became a vibrant, exciting, Spirit-filled way of life. Whereas fleshly Jews had gravitated toward a largely ritualistic religion, old covenant Judaism, spiritual Jews (both Jews and

Gentiles who have believed upon Jesus) have inherited a spiritual religion, new covenant Judaism.

If those who believe on the Son of God are the true seed of Abraham, the spiritual Jews, then it is only fitting that their religious system be the reformed Judaism of the New Testament or new covenant. And so it was: New Testament Christianity was a Judaism among the many Judaisms of that day. And so it must be: today's over-Hellenized, over-Latinized Christianity must reconnect with its Jewish roots, rebuild its Hebrew foundations, and return to its Judaic heritage. In order to realize its fullness, Christianity must be restored to the religion which Jesus and the apostles practiced.

IRREVOCABLE COVENANTS AND NATURAL ISRAEL

God's plan to include the Gentiles did not require the exclusion of the Jews. Natural Israel, the Jews according to the flesh, continue in covenantal relationship with God. Romans 11:29 tells us that the gifts and calling of God are irrevocable. For this reason and for this reason alone, the natural, physical benefits of the covenant that God made with Abraham and his lineage according to the flesh still pertain to the fleshly Jews. Romans 9:29 declares that except the Lord of Sabaoth had left Israel a seed, they would have been as Sodom and Gomorrah; however, Yahweh's promise was that a remnant would be saved. Indeed, this is the proof of God's immutability: "For I am the Lord, I do not change; therefore, you are not consumed, O sons of Jacob" (Malachi 3:6). Because God can never change, his personal commitments to the children of Abraham continue to be fulfilled.

TORAH STILL A SCHOOLMASTER

In Galatians 3:24, Paul declared that the law (Torah) was a schoolmaster to bring Israel to Messiah. In the Hellenic world, of which Galatia was a part, a schoolmaster (*paidagogos*) was a family servant whose responsibility was to protect the children, to train them in proper etiquette and deportment, and to accompany them to their teachers. The law, then, was designed by God to be a means of protecting Israel and keeping them from the evils of the Gentile world until they could be brought to Messiah, their teacher.

The purpose of the Torah has never changed. Through the centuries and even to this day it has remained as a guardian of the Jewish people, ensuring the continuity of their faith in Yahweh, the only God. It has maintained the Jewish people as a distinct and recognizable entity in the world despite unrelenting attempts by the tyrants of history to effect their genocide. If it ever were a schoolmaster to bring Israel to Messiah, the Torah (law) remains so today and will remain so until the time that Messiah comes to teach Israel all his ways.

A PROPHETIC RESTORATION

God's plan for the Jewish people and the nation of Israel is a threefold restoration: the land of Israel is to be restored to the people of Israel; the people of Israel are to be restored to the land of Israel; and the people of Israel are to be restored to their God. The Zionist movement that has brought millions of Jewish people back to the land of Israel from the dispersion among the nations and has brought about the reestablishing of the nation of Israel in a part of the land which God promised to Abraham is a direct result of the faith of those Jews in God's promise to Abraham. Their faith in God's covenant has brought the fleshly benefits to them even though they have not come to faith in Jesus as Messiah. Through this means, the land has been restored to the people, and the people have been restored to the land.

The next stage of restoration is for the people of Israel to be restored to God. A large percentage of the Jewish world population is either non-observant, secular, agnostic, or atheistic. A move of God must take place to turn the hearts of the Jewish people and the nation of Israel back to God and to his Word. Then, and only then, can they come to understand that the one from among them who brought Israel's light to the Gentiles is, indeed, Messiah.

ALL OF GOD'S COVENANT HOLY ONES INHERIT

The great purpose of God in returning the land of Israel to the people, bringing the Jews again from the Diaspora, and turning their hearts again to God is to set the stage for Israel's national day of salvation (Zechariah 12:10; 13:1; Romans 9:27) and the subsequent coming of Messiah. When this great prophetic event occurs, those who are of the faith of Abraham, God's chosen people of every generation–both Jew and Gentile–will inherit the earth, just as Jesus promised (Matthew 5:5; 25:34). Yahweh God's four-thousand-year-old covenant with Abraham will have been made sure to all the seed, both the natural and the spiritual (Romans 4:16), and they will rule and reign with Messiah over all the earth for one thousand years in a kingdom that will continue to reflect the nature of its unchanging God by being patterned after biblical Judaism.

Chapter 11

Love: God's Eternal Plan Fulfilled

Chapter 11
LOVE: GOD'S ETERNAL PLAN FULFILLED

The first thing that the Holy Scriptures cause us to understand about the nature of man is that he is created in the image of God (Genesis 1:27). Because the desire to love and to be loved is at the heart of the personality of every man, we may, by casual reasoning, assert that love is central to the personality of God. We may assume, then, that a God of love would have created mankind for this express purpose–to love the Creator and to be loved by him. While we may assert that God is complete and has no need or lack, we also understand that mankind was created because God sought relationship with beings who would love him. In order to be genuine, however, love must be freely and voluntarily expressed. For this reason, God created man a free moral agent, with the power to choose between the good and the evil, between loving and serving God and hating and rebelling against him. The direct result of this innate characteristic in man was the introduction of sin and death into the world.

But, did the fall of man obviate God's plan in creating him? Did God then realize that he had made a mistake and set in motion another plan which he hoped would cause man to love him? Certainly not! God is not as most men, who experience and react. In his infinite wisdom, he plans and then acts. From the time that he created the world, the counsel of the Almighty has been predetermined. He was then aware that man would sin, and he had already devised the plan which would reconcile men to God. First man had to be barred from immortality (Genesis 3:22), else he would be an eternal sinner without hope of redemption as are the angels who left their first estate (Jude 6). Second, man had to be punished for his sin (Genesis 3:17-19). And, third, a means of reconciliation to God had to be established (Genesis 3:15). From the time of the fall, therefore, we see men offering sacrifices for their sins and seeking the presence of God.

After a time, God's plan for the ages called for the introduction of a codified law, which would stand forever as an outline of his basic likes and dislikes, his instruction (as the Hebrew word for law [Torah] is more accurately rendered). These instructions were not designed to cause man to extend voluntary love to the Creator; their purpose was to define sin in exact terms and thereby make it exceedingly sinful (Romans 7:13). The law was set forth to act as a guardian to keep the chosen people in check and to maintain a righteous seed through which the ultimate plan of re-demption would be expressed (Galatians 3:24). In later times, the law of God came to be known as Judaism (the term which Paul used in Galatians 1:13, 14 to describe his religious faith), God's chosen system of praise, worship, and service.

But, was the establishment of Judaism another admission of fault with God? Did he devise this system because what he had done before had failed? Of course not! God cannot fail, nor may his purpose know defeat! For fifteen hundred years Israel lived under the law of Judaism. Many chose the life that Judaism offered to those who would keep its precepts; others chose the death that its curse pronounced on those who would not obey the law (Deuteronomy 30:19). Those who chose life by obeying the command-ments were justified by their faith in God's Word, just as Abraham had been justified by his faith in God's Word. As Jesus said of that era, "If you would enter into life, *keep the commandments*" (Matthew 19:17).

Shortly before the time of Jesus, some of the sages of Israel began to emphasize the fact that more was required than mere ritualistic compliance with God's religious system. Perhaps in reaction to the prophets' denun-ciation of their observances of feasts, sabbaths, and fasts, they began to emphasize that service to God had to be based on love for the Creator, not on fear or on ritualism.

THE SUPREME EXAMPLE OF LOVE

Finally, in the fullness of time, God manifested what would be the piv-otal point of his plan for the ages when he sent forth his Son, his express image, made in the likeness of sinful flesh, subject to the law of Judaism (Hebrews 1:1, 2; Romans 8:3; Galatians 4:4). What greater example of voluntary love could the Creator establish than to permit his only begotten Son to become flesh so as to redeem mankind, which by all rights was totally and irrevocably lost and separated from his holy presence? God did not choose a man to be offered as a sacrifice for sins; he came himself in the person of his Son and offered himself as the sacrifice for us.

But, was God again giving up on another plan which had failed? Was he acknowledging defeat of his law revealed in Judaism and trying something else that he hoped would work? If he were doing so, what would give us any confidence that his new plan would work? Did Judaism represent a failure on God's part? Of course not! The coming of Jesus Christ to the earth was the most important event in human history; however, it was just another chapter in God's unfolding plan for the ages, a plan that had been conceived and set in motion before the foundation of the world (Revelation 13:8).

What the law of Judaism could not do because of the weakness of the flesh, Jesus Christ accomplished when he lived a sinless life, offered himself as a perfect sacrifice and an eternal atonement for the sins of mankind, and resurrected in an obvious demonstration that eternal life could be had through him. Jesus stands forever as the ultimate expression of the Creator's love.

A NEW MOTIVE: LOVE

Under the time of the law, many of God's people had only one motive for serving and obeying God: the fear of death. While there were those like David who "delighted in the law of God," much of Israel was obedient to the law through fear. For many, if love were obliquely involved, it was expressed from fear. If such is the case, this love is not the kind of love that the Creator, himself, expresses. God's ultimate plan, then, was to empower man to love as he loves, to choose the good and hate the evil because he loves his God.

It is only logical, then, that the perfected plan for man's redemption should be a religious system based on love. And so it was with the New Testament order of Judaism. Jesus encapsulated the entire legal code of the Old Testament in these two commandments: "You shall love the Lord thy God with all thy heart, with all your soul, and with all your mind," and "You shall love your neighbor as yourself" (Matthew 22:37,39). This was in keeping with earlier Jewish prophets and sages who had sought to condense the legal code. Micah 6:8 had said, ". . .what does the Lord require of you, but to do justly, to love mercy, and to walk humbly with your God?" The great Hillel had taught a generation before Jesus that one should not do unto others what was hurtful to himself and declared that the remainder of the law was commentary. In the spirit of this declaration, Paul asserted that the entire law was fulfilled in one word, love (Galatians 5:14).

Jesus, then, changed the order of and motive for the observance of Judaism. The order was altered from Old Testament ritual and ceremonialism to New Testament worship in Spirit and in truth. The motive was changed from fear of death to love for the one who delivered from death. The demonstration of God's love through the sacrifice of his Son and the empowering of the believer with the resident Holy Spirit accomplishes the purpose of God's creation of mankind. He receives voluntary, spontaneous love from the creature, which he reciprocates bountifully. Man is now able to love as God loves, for "the love of God has been poured out in our hearts by the Holy Spirit" (Romans 5:5). The Holy Spirit which had been *with*

God's people in the Old Testament is now resident *in* believers, imparting God's love to them (John 14:17).

It is interesting that in order to establish a new system for Judaism following the destruction of the temple, rabbinic Judaism used some of the same premises that early Christian leaders had employed in their reformation of Judaism. The emphasis was changed from the temple cult to prayer, study, *tzedekah* (giving, performing good deeds), and the like. As the earliest church had appealed to the crucifixion and resurrection of Jesus as the vicarious atonement for sin and the means of salvation, early Jewish sages appealed to the binding of Isaac as a substitutionary sacrifice for all of Israel that was efficacious to all his descendants. Later this emphasis on the vicarious nature of Isaac's binding was diminished as the church came to teach Jesus' crucifixion as the fullment of the type of Isaac's binding. Rabbinic Judaism then became more and more a religion of emphasis on good works, with some thinking that good works balance the scales against bad works so that the judgment of God does not come upon the evil doer.

The New Testament order that Jesus brought to God's religion, Judaism, accomplished God's purpose. Through the vicarious atonement of Jesus, believers are restored to God and receive of his Spirit. They love God, keep his commandments, and freely worship him. Love fulfills all of God's moral code outlined in biblical Judaism.

God's plan of salvation, enacted from the foundation of the world, will reach its climax when Jesus returns, establishes his kingdom, rules over the world, destroys evil and death, and ushers in the eternal kingdom of the new heaven and the new earth. Then ten thousand times ten thousands of his saints will freely express their love for him in eternal praise and continual fellowship in his presence. Then there will be perfect righteousness, perfect holiness, total compliance with God's laws, for the earth will be full of the knowledge of the Lord as the waters cover the sea (Isaiah 11:9; Habakkuk 2:14). Love will have fully accomplished God's eternal purpose in the creation of mankind.

The Secret
of Fulfilling
the Law

MATTHEW 22:37-40

HEBREWS 7:12

Chapter 12
THE SECRET
OF FULFILLING THE LAW

From the very beginning of the New Testament era, the question of the proper relationship of the believer to the law of God outlined in the Hebrew Scriptures has been a subject of heated debate. Within the Christian community, there are two polarized extremities of thought concerning the law of God and its effect upon believers in Jesus Christ. These two diverse viewpoints are termed by each other as legalism (the strict observance of the law) and antinomianism (standing against the law).

The legalists, as they are called, maintain that the entire law of God remains in force even today. Some of them believe that without obedience to the laws of the Old Testament, one cannot be justified, and some are probably guilty of the Galatianism of which they are accused by the antinomians. They maintain that God's laws were not changed or repealed by Jesus and that their observance is necessary for our justification. In some circles, Remonstrants or Arminians, who believe that keeping the law is necessary after one's rebirth by faith in Jesus Christ, are referred to as legalists.

On the other hand are the antinomians who maintain that the law, including the Ten Commandments, was nailed to the cross of Christ. According to them, works of obedience are totally unnecessary for our justification. Many of this persuasion feel that the Old Testament Scriptures are useless in the "grace dispensation" and that Judaism is a worthless exercise in futility, very little different from heathen religions.

The debate of the legalists and the antinomians has raged for centuries. The real problem that perpetuates the irreconcilable differences between these two warring factions of Christianity is the fact that both sides of the argument have truth, both sides quote Scripture from the same Bible, and both sides stand unequivocally for their dogma. As is generally the case with polarized issues such as these, the truth lies somewhere between the two extremities. A proper restoration of first century Christianity represents a viable alternative to the two warring factions, a synthesis between the thesis of legalism and the antithesis of antinomianism.

THE "THOU SHALT'S" AND THE "THOU SHALT NOT'S"

Generally speaking, the question concerning observance of the law has not involved the "thou shalt not's" but has centered in the "thou shalt's." Few would advocate that one should now be permitted to steal, commit murder, bear false witness, or commit adultery. On the other hand, some would recommend that one no longer remember the Sabbath, observe the festivals, pay the tithe, and the like.

The fact is that God's law is composed of positive and negative commandments. In the Torah (Pentateuch) there are 613 commandments (*mitzvot*). Of these, 365 are negative commandments, the "thou shalt not's" of the Torah, a number which corresponds to the total days in a year. The remaining 248 commandments are positive "thou shalt's." John tells us that the transgression of any one of the 613 commandments of the law constitutes sin (1 John 3:4). James confirms to us that failure to observe the positive commandments is just as much sin as violating the negative commandments: "Therefore, to him that knows to do good, and does not do it, to him it is sin" (James 4:17).

The question is, what should we now do? How can we be sure that we fulfill the law in our lives? The answer is simply stated by Jesus, himself, in Matthew 22:37-40: "Thou shalt love the Lord thy God with all thy heart, and with all thy soul, and with all thy mind. This is the first and great commandment. And the second is like unto it, Thou shalt love thy neighbor as thyself. On these two commandments hang all the law and the prophets." These are the two "thou shalt's" of the New Testament. All of the requirements of the New Testament are summed up in one simple word– love, love for God and love for man. The law, then, is based in love, not in judgment.

The Decalogue was written by the finger of God upon two tablets of stone. The five commandments on one tablet governed one's conduct toward God and his parents. The five commandments on the other tablet governed one's relationship with his fellow man. These ten commandments became major categories under which all the remaining commandments of the law functioned.

LOVE FULFILLS THE LAW

If one truly loved God with all his heart, soul, and mind, he could never break one of the first five of the ten commandments. The motivating factor of complete love for God would cause the believer to make God's slightest wish his personal command. If one truly loved his neighbor as himself, he could never break one of the remaining five of commandments. This truth is brilliantly set forth by the apostle Paul in Romans 13:8-10: "Owe no one anything except to love one another: for he who loves another *has fulfilled the law.* For the commandments, 'You shall not commit adultery,' 'You shall not murder,' 'You shall not steal,' 'You shall not bear false witness,' 'You shall not covet,' and if there is any other commandment, are all summed up in this saying, namely, 'You shall love your neighbor as yourself.' Love does no harm to a neighbor; therefore love is the fulfillment of the law." If the law can be summed up and fulfilled in one word–love–then the law was a law of love, not of judgment and cursing, as some have suggested.

Paul repeats this theme in Galatians 5:14: "For all the law is fulfilled in one word, even in this: 'You shall love your neighbor as yourself.' " Perhaps he was taking his cue from his teacher Gamaliel, a disciple of Hillel the Great, who said concerning the law of God, "Whatever is hurtful to you, do not unto others. The rest [of the law] is commentary." When Paul discussed this theme of love for one's neighbor, he also delivered some sound advice concerning the nature of the New Testament calling and the believer's responsibility toward it: "For you, brethren, have been called to liberty; only do not use liberty as an opportunity for the flesh, but through love serve one another. . . . Walk in the Spirit, and you shall not fulfill the lust of the flesh" (Galatians 5:13,16).

A LIFE IN THE SPIRIT

The apostle to the Gentiles expanded upon this aspect of fulfilling of the law in Romans 8:2-4: "For the law of the Spirit of life in Christ Jesus has made me free from the law of sin and death. For what the law could not do in that it was weak through the flesh, God did by sending his own Son in the likeness of sinful flesh, on account of sin: He condemned sin in the flesh, that the righteous requirement of *the law might be fulfilled* in us who do not walk according to the flesh, but according to the Spirit." Because we have been freed from the law through the body of Christ, we can now fulfill the righteousness of the law by living a life in the Spirit. Our freedom is not a license to violate the commandments but an opportunity to realize the righteousness that they prescribed through the indwelling of the Holy Spirit. What the law could not do because of the weakness of the flesh, the Holy Spirit accomplishes so that we are now said to establish the law, rather than making it void (Romans 3:31).

This is the meaning of Hebrews 10:16,17: " 'This is the covenant that I will make with them after those days, says the Lord: I will put my laws into their hearts, and in their minds I will write them,' then he adds, 'Their sins and their lawless deeds I will remember no more.' " When the Holy Spirit becomes resident in the heart of the believer, the righteousness of the law that was completely fulfilled in Jesus Christ also becomes a part of his being. The righteousness of the law then is no more a bondage to works but a liberty of faith in Jesus Christ.

LOVE BRINGS UNCONDITIONALLY POSITIVE RESPONSES

When one walks in the Spirit and is not mindful of the things of the flesh, he has no problem in loving God and loving his fellow man; therefore, he has no difficulty in fulfilling the law. Since his spirit is fine-tuned to the needs and wishes both of God and of his fellow man, his selfish, lazy human spirit is overwhelmed by the Spirit of God and does what is pleasing to God and beneficial to his fellow man. The motivation is love, not selfishness, for he addresses himself to the commandments of God and to the needs of his neighbor with unconditionally positive responses.

In this kind of relationship with God and man, one has no difficulty in performing the worship that pleases God. One who walks in the Spirit will be attentive to the slightest wish of his Maker. If remembering days and seasons pleases God–and we have his Word that it does–he will volunteer to memorialize those times (Leviticus 23; 1 Corinthians 5:8). If being submissive to religious leadership pleases God, he will readily obey those who have rule over him in the Lord (Hebrews 13:17). If tithing and giving offerings please God, he will be anxious to do this work (Malachi 3:10; Matthew 23:23). If ministering to the physical, emotional, or economic needs of his neighbor pleases his neighbor and God, he will be careful to give special attention to those needs (Matthew 25:33-40).

The question of what we should do or should not do in respect to the law of God is simple when we live a life in the Spirit of God. The love of God which is shed abroad in our hearts by the Holy Spirit will build in us an overwhelming passion for pleasing God and helping our fellow man. The question then will not be, "How little (or how much) can I do and not incur God's wrath?", or "How little (or how much) can I do and still have the respect of my neighbor?", but "Where can I find an opportunity to do more for God and for my neighbor?" We will be consumed with the Jewish concept of *tzedekah* (righteous good deeds). And, after all, Jesus himself said that the church would enlighten the world and cause them to glorify God with "good works," not just faith (Matthew 5:16).

FINDING THE MIDDLE GROUND

Legalism and antinomianism are both extremities. The truth is in the middle, and this is where New Testament Christianity (or Judaism, if you please) comes into play. Jesus did not come to destroy either the law or God's religious system delineated in it. He rather put life into that ancient religious form by perfecting it forever with the new covenant. This is the faith or religion of Jesus Christ, the first step of which is our belief in him as our Lord and Savior. If we love him, we will certainly want to keep the ordinances of the New Testament and obey his commandments in all things (John 14:15).

By searching out those things of Judaism which Jesus perpetuated in a new and living way, we can learn what pleases him in our praise, worship, and service today, thereby ascertaining God's way for our lives. Biblical Judaism was the faith through which Jesus and the apostles expressed their devotion to God. As we search this ancient faith, we will find more and more that it will add depth to our praise, worship, and service of God.

How can we now fulfill the law? Love God, and love man, walking in the Spirit!

The Indwelling Holy Spirit

Chapter 13
THE INDWELLING HOLY SPIRIT
A UNIQUELY JEWISH EXPERIENCE

The great infilling of the Holy Spirit that occurred on the Day of Pentecost in Acts 2, along with the subsequent manifestations of that Spirit in the lives of believers, was merely a concentrated outpouring of something that had been periodically manifested in God's religious system for more than two thousand years before that Pentecost.

The supernatural has always been one of the identifying marks of the religion of Yahweh, the eternal God. Before the first century the indwelling of the Holy Spirit and the manifestation of its power to perform superhuman things through human instrumentality was a characteristic unique to Judaism and the Jewish people.

In the Hebrew Scriptures, we find abundant and continuing evidence of the supernatural. Who could forget the profound miracles worked through Moses parting the Red Sea, bringing forth water from a rock, and feeding more than a million people with manna? Or who does not remember Saul's speaking in *glossolalia* when the Spirit of God came upon him as he dwelt among the prophets? Or who does not recall Daniel's reading the unknown language written in the Babylonian temple by the hand of God? Or who could forget the deliverance of the Hebrew children from the fiery furnace? And, what of Elisha, who made an ax head float, gave the healing word to Naaman, the leper, and raised the Shunammite's son from the dead? Then there were Samuel, Jeremiah, Isaiah, and many others who prophesied the word of the Lord. These natural men, aided by the supernatural Spirit of God, foreshadowed good gifts that were to come in the New Testament era (Hebrews 10:1). Romans 12:6-8, 1 Corinthians 12:8-10, and Ephesians 4:11 delineate these gifts that were given bountifully to men following the ascension of Jesus Christ and his assumption of the role of High Priest for all believers (Ephesians 4:8).

Under the old covenant of God's religion, however, these supernatural events were at best occasional and in most times very rare, for it was difficult for the Almighty to find vessels who were worthy to demonstrate such power. Few men were willing to forsake the riches of Egyptian royalty to live in the desert or to remain fiercely loyal to the law of God in the face of execution or to suffer the rejection and ridicule of their peers and fellow countrymen. It remained for God to provide something better for us in the

New Testament era (Hebrews 11:39, 40).

THE HOLY SPIRIT IS GIVEN TO BELIEVERS

And, so it was that Messiah Yeshua, the reformer of Judaism, ushered in the better way through the introduction of a new covenant for God's ancient religion. Jesus introduced a new birth in which a believer could be born from above in a spiritual act that made him a new creation. Remission of sins was accomplished through the vicarious atonement provided by Christ's efficacious sacrifice on Calvary.

In a solemn promise to his disciples before his crucifixion, resurrection, and ascension, Jesus made an even greater provision for believers in his word."It is to your advantage that I go away . . . and I will pray the Father, and he will give you another Helper, that he may abide with you forever, even the Spirit of truth . . . *for he dwells with you, and will be in you* . . . you shall receive power when the Holy Spirit has come upon you; and you shall be witnesses to me" (John 16:7; 14:16, 17; Acts 1:8). The Spirit that had been *with* the Jewish people before this Pentecost now became resident *in* the believers.

When Jesus' promise was fulfilled, interestingly enough, it occurred on one of the major festivals of Judaism, the Feast of Pentecost. "When the Day of Pentecost had fully come . . . they were all filled with the Holy Spirit and began to speak with other tongues, as the Spirit gave them utterance" (Acts 2:1, 4).

Once before in recorded history such a profound event had occurred when the 120 priests officiated at the dedication of the temple in Jerusalem during the Feast of Tabernacles (2 Chronicles 5:12-14). The Holy Spirit so filled the temple with the smoke of his presence that the priests were unable to minister. This time, on the day of Pentecost, the Holy Spirit filled the hearts of 120 believers to such a degree that they appeared to be drunken and spoke in xenoglossy or languages with which they were not familiar (Acts 1:15; 2:1-15). On the first Old Testament Pentecost when the law of God was given at Mt. Sinai, 3,000 people died because of their idolatry (Exodus 32:28). On the first New Testament Pentecost when the Holy Spirit came to indwell believers on Mt. Zion, 3,000 people were saved when they repented and were baptized (Acts 2:41).

From that day throughout the book of Acts, the supernatural manifestations of the Spirit that had occurred occasionally in Old Testament Judaism became the hallmark of New Testament Judaism. The apostles went everywhere, healing the sick, exorcising demons, working miracles, and doing signs and wonders. The Holy Spirit which had been given to the children of Israel by measure was poured out without measure upon the New Testament believers, and they were filled with the Holy Spirit.

GENTILES RECEIVE THE SUPERNATURAL POWER

A few years later, the gift that had been unique and isolated to the Jewish people was brought to the Gentiles. Peter visited the house of Cornelius, the Roman centurion, at Caesarea by the Sea and explained the good news of salvation through Jesus Christ to those Gentiles. "While Peter was still speaking these words, the Holy Spirit fell upon all those who heard the word . . . . [and] they heard them speak with tongues" (Acts 10:44, 46). An experience that had been unique to Jews and Judaism was extended to the Gentiles and to the entire world.

After that time Jews and Gentiles alike, by the thousands, received the same experience that the 120 believers had received on the Day of Pentecost. They were filled with the Holy Spirit and through the operation of that Spirit proceeded to accomplish things that were beyond the power of natural man. Peter's shadow healed people. Paul sent cloths and aprons that he had touched to those who were sick, and they were healed. Agabus predicted the outcome of Paul's ministry. Philip experienced a physical translation from the Gaza to Azotus. Many other miracles and wonders were done through the power of the Holy Spirit.

THE GIFTS AND MANIFESTATIONS OF THE HOLY SPIRIT

The gift of the Holy Spirit brought many other manifestations into the lives of believers. Paul delineated some of these in 1 Corinthians 12:8, "To one is given the word of wisdom through the Spirit, to another the word of knowledge by the same Spirit, to another faith through the same Spirit, to another gifts of healings by the same Spirit, to another the working of miracles, to another prophecy, to another discerning of spirits, to another different kinds of tongues, to another the interpretation of tongues. But one and the same Spirit works all these things, distributing to each one individually as he wills."

These manifestations of the Spirit were given for the profit of the body. Through them the entire Church, both Jew and Gentile, received the witness of the supernatural Spirit of God that convinced millions of people to believe on the Messiah of Israel and the Savior of the world. The miraculous witness that had authenticated Yahweh's religion in the Old Testament was multiplied many times over through the outpouring of the Holy Spirit in the New Testament.

In Romans 12:6-8, Paul also detailed other gifts of the Holy Spirit: "Having then gifts differing according to the grace that is given to us," whether prophecy, or ministry, or teaching, or exhortation, or giving, or administration, or mercy. These gifts provided strength to the ongoing operation of the church in its mission and witness and enabled ordinary men and women to accomplish extraordinary tasks in the overspread of the gospel and the administration of the daily life and business of the church.

In Ephesians 4:11-16, the gifts which Jesus as High Priest gave to the church are said to include the ministry gifts of apostle, prophet, evangelist, pastor, and teacher (or pastor/teacher). It should be noted that these are not men but gifts which God gives to men to empower them for particular functions within the church. The purpose of these gifts is specific: ". . .for the equipping of the saints for works of ministry to the building up of the body of Christ" (literal translation). Ministry gifts are not ends in themselves, a means of exalting a professional clergy to fulfill all the works of ministry in the church. They are gifts of service designed to equip all believers so that they then can do the works of ministry that will build up the body of Christ. The duration of the church's empowerment with these gifts is also made clear: ". . .till we all come in the unity of the faith, and of the full knowledge of the Son of God, unto a complete man, to the measure of the stature of the fullness of Christ" (Ephesians 4:13, author's translation). Until such a time as the church comes to the unity of the faith and to complete maturity, all five of these gifts are so essential that the church can never perfectly function without each of them fully operational.

PROFESSIONALISM AND RATIONALISM REPLACE CHARISMATA AND FAITH

As the church denied its Hebraic roots, it more and more replaced faith and the operation of the Holy Spirit in the lives of believers with the rationalism of the Greco-Roman world. The development of a professional clergy was an immediate outgrowth of this change of emphasis. The elevation of that professional clergy to a higher state of holiness was a further result of emphasis on rationalism rather than faith and on professionalism rather than charismata. Ultimately the church was divided into the *ecclesia clerens* (teaching church) and the *ecclesia audiens* (listening church). The laity that was denied participation first in teaching ultimately was denied involvement in praise and worship so that the laity became spectators whose function it was to observe the performance of the clergy. Access to the Word of God was ultimately denied to the laity upon penalty of excommunication and even death. The result was a pitiful, weakened, ignorant, and superstitious populace that could easily be manipulated by political forces and the hierarchy of the church. The result was the clergy-laity gap that continues to weaken the church to this day.

The final and inglorious application of this emphasis on professionalism and rationalism was the development of the concept of sacramentalism in which the sacraments of the church were considered to be efficacious regardless as to the condition of the priest or the communicant. Sacramentalism led to a further diminution of the spiritual stature of the individual and militated further against the possibility of the Holy Spirit's ministering through individuals by means of his charismata and graces. In this environment of rationalism and professionalism, it was possible for men to know much *about* God and at the same time not *know* God. The fruits of the lives of some of the intellectual giants of the times were not those of the Holy Spirit. A clear and important truth is so obvious in this historical tragedy: if the church had not denied its Judaic heritage, it would never have ceased to be Holy Spirit led. Belief in and experience of the supernatural were essential to the biblical Judaism through which Jesus and the apostles expressed their devotion to Yahweh, the God of Israel. If this belief had been perpetuated, the church would not have exalted reason over anointing and professionalism over character and charismata.

The descent of the imperial church into the Dark Ages of the tenth and eleventh centuries is testimony to the degradation that is possible in what should be faith communities when cold professionalism and rationalism completely replace faith and the operation of the Holy Spirit in the lives of individual believers. It also produced the environment of such dogma and practices that precipitated the Reformation and the Catholic counter-reformation and their progressively developing emphasis on faith and personal relationship with God rather than the professionalism and rationalism of the past. Men came more and more to seek God for themselves and to find personal relationship with him, often manifest in the ecstatic, decidedly non-rational experiences that were documented in the various revivals that occurred in subsequent ecclesiastical history.

A SPIRITUAL RESTORATION

Various renewal movements were manifest in the fires of revival through the centuries. The Methodist awakening of the eighteenth century and the holiness revival of the nineteenth century brought spiritual renewal both to England and the United States. At the turn of the twentieth century a great spiritual revival was ignited from the embers of those renewal movements. Despite the fact that much of the church at that time posited a cessationist teaching that maintained that all the supernatural manifestations of the Holy

Spirit had ceased with the apostles and the canonization of the New Testament Scriptures, still many believers began to seek what most had thought unobtainable. They began to pray for the infilling of the Holy Spirit and its accompanying manifestations that characterized first century faith. And, in various ways at about the same time, men began to experience these manifestations again.

The operations of the Spirit which once had been unique to the Jews, then to the New Testament church, began to be manifest in the twentieth century among mostly humble, semiliterate people. While enthusiasm over the restoration of a New Testament experience brought forth many excesses and abuses, the obvious truth was that something had happened in the twentieth century that could not be explained away. The operation of the Spirit was at work. What was projected to be a century of the decline of Christian faith became one of the finest eras of explosive growth of the kingdom of God.

A WIDESPREAD OUTPOURING

In more recent times people of virtually every denomination have received the Holy Spirit and the manifestations of the gifts. The numbers have increased rapidly until they now reach into the millions. The largest identifiable segment of Christianity today are those who profess to be Spirit-filled. Again, enthusiasm over the restoration of a New Testament experience has brought forth excesses and abuses; however, the fact is that thousands of people are receiving the infilling of the Holy Spirit and are witnessing manifestations of the Spirit that have changed lives and matured believers.

Various renewal movements have produced a restoration of the New Testament order and degree of a uniquely Jewish experience in which ordinary men are moved by the Spirit of Yahweh, the God of Israel, to do supernatural things. The gifts of the Spirit were manifest in Judaism, perfected in the New Testament, and are being restored in our day.

Worship–
Man's Responsibility,
Man's Opportunity

Chapter 14

WORSHIP–MAN'S RESPONSIBILITY, MAN'S OPPORTUNITY

"Oh come, let us sing to the Lord! Let us shout joyfully to the Rock of our salvation. Let us come before his presence with thanksgiving; let us shout joyfully to him with psalms. For the Lord is the great God, and the great King above all gods. . . . Oh come, let us worship and bow down; let us kneel before the Lord our Maker" (Psalm 95:1-3, 6).

From the time that man was created in the image of the Eternal God, it has been both his privilege and responsibility to worship his Creator. The spark of divinity imbued into man by the breath of the Almighty has sought release in expressions of praise and devotion to the Creator. At the beginning, worship took the form of simple evening conversations as Adam walked and talked with God in the cool of the day. Since that time, God has always searched for men and women who would worship him with the concentrated intensity and consuming passion of the Holy Spirit and with the divine order of truth communicated through his Word.

In biblical history, God progressively communicated to mankind his Word and will, including the system of praise, worship, and service that he found pleasing. This system was designed to be a vehicle through which God's people could commune with their Maker. It included prescribed appointments, symbols, and rituals that would ever summon men from the routine of the mundane into intimacy with the Divine.

When he gave the law, God set forth a carefully delineated system of worship which was then required of those people who had agreed to covenant themselves with him to be his chosen nation. Complete observance of all the laws and ordinances of God was enjoined upon the children of Israel, often as a matter of life and death. When the people kept the commandments and worshipped God according to his prescribed formula, they were blessed with life and happiness. When they neglected their worship or rebelled against God's system, they were cursed with death and sorrow. Unfortunately, the worship of God carried out in this system often became largely ritualistic. The priestly leaders of Israel were careful to exact the letter of the law; however, their dedication was frequently more to ritual than to free worship. Mere ritualism is not complete worship, for the motive and attitude in which worship is carried out are more important than the outward form itself.

Repeatedly men have drifted away from God's design that his people commune with him in an intensely intimate, personal way. History records man's wavering between truth and apostasy, between intense worship and apathy toward God. Even the vehicles which God has designed to bring his people into intimacy with him have been perverted into lifeless rituals of vain repetition, allowing men the security of doing religious things when their hearts were far from God.

DEFICIENCIES IN ANCIENT WORSHIP

In John 4:22 Jesus evaluated the worship of both the Jewish people and the Samaritans, concluding that "salvation is from the Jews." Then he declared that the time was approaching when "true worshippers" would worship the Father in "spirit and in truth." With the coming of Christ and the New Testament, then, we find this new requirement for worship: "God is Spirit, and those who worship him must worship in spirit and truth" (John 4:24). Since Jesus came to reform and perfect God's religion for man, we may rightly expect that he would bring a better order to worship, itself. And, so he did. In the New Testament, true worship is required to have two dimensions. First of all, it must be carried out with spiritual depth. Then, it must also be rendered in proper scriptural order.

This is not to say that the worship under the first testament was bad or flawed. It is only to say that under the new covenant, there is a *better* system of worship based on a better covenant. For the apostles, the worship which became possible with the death and resurrection of Jesus was simply better than that which they had practiced in pre-Calvary times, for it completed and established what they had already experienced in their lives (Hebrews 9:23; Romans 3:31). The way in which the people of Israel had worshipped was *good*. The reformed way that Jesus brought was *better.*

In the old economy, many were often deficient in worship because they neglected this "spirit-and-truth" formula for worship. Both Jesus and Isaiah classified at least a part of the worship of official Judaism as vanity (Isaiah 1:13; Matthew 5:19). Again, the order of the reasons given for their failure was, *first*, deficiency of spirit and, *second*, lack of truth. They were worshipping mechanically through ritualism, and they lacked worship that came from the heart; therefore, they were not spiritual worshippers. Then, they were worshipping through human traditions, giving their own ideas preeminence over the Word of God; therefore, they were not worshippers in truth.

Judaism, the system which God himself designed and gave to his people, met with these divine indictments: "I hate your feasts" (Isaiah 1:14) and "You also transgress the commandment of God by your tradition" (Matthew 15:3). This was the case when men had perverted Judaism into a lifeless ritual. Christianity, too, experienced apostasy, degenerating into such an abysmal state in the Dark Ages that it warranted the prophetic denunciation of being "a cage for every unclean and hated bird" (Revelation 18:2). Both Judaism and Christianity have been victimized by Satanic attacks that seek to limit or divert the worship of God from its designed intent either through a loss of passion and fervency or through the introduction of heretical, non-biblical traditions.

The history of both Jewish and Christian worship underscores the fact that the "spirit-and truth" formula for worship is a "must" and as such is not optional. It is important, therefore, that we who have been adopted into sonship of God through Christ understand both the manner and motive of worshipping God in New Testament order. The body of Messiah must epitomize the fullest essence of biblical worship.

RECOVERING SPIRITUAL TRUTH

Despite the failures of both Christian and Jewish worshippers throughout history, the ever-searching God has always identified men and women whom he could call to renewal and restoration before the light of truth has been entirely extinguished. Such is the case in the world today. After centuries of Hellenization and Latinization that replaced the gold and jewels of divine truth on which the church was founded with the baubles and costume jewelry of human, even pagan, tradition, Christians by the millions are demanding the restoration of the Hebraic foundations of faith, practice, and discipline through which Jesus and the apostles expressed their devotion to God. A profound movement of renewal is restoring to God's people a passion for his Spirit and his truth. An over-Hellenized, over-Latinized Christianity is experiencing a re-Judaizing process that is reattaching Christian faith to its Jewish roots.

This is particularly true in the area of worship. Believers are being renewed in the Holy Spirit to a passion for intimacy that transcends merely knowing about God in traditional Greco-Roman rationalism and reaches the realm of knowing God in the richest traditions of Judaic thought and experience. This passion reflects a recovery for Christians of the Jewish concept of *kavanah*, the intense concentration on the Divine that transcends understanding and thrusts one into the realm of revering God. The past century witnessed the greatest, most far-reaching renewal of the Holy Spirit in all of human history.

At the same time, this revival has produced an attendant passion for truth, fulfilling the job description that Jesus gave for the Holy Spirit: leading "into all truth" (John 16:13). No longer content to follow blindly in the traditions of blind leaders of the past and consequently finding themselves in ditches of despair and confusion, believers are searching the Scriptures for themselves like the noble Berean Jews. God is revealing his Word in a clarity not witnessed since the first century as Christians are recovering the faith of Jesus and learning to be true worshippers by revering the Father in spirit and in truth, or in spiritual truth (as the *hendiadys* of John 4:24 can be translated).

ETYMOLOGY AND MEANING

Worship is commonly defined as "the act or feeling of adoration or homage; the paying of religious reverence as in prayer, praise, and so forth." It is derived from the Old English *worthship*, the act of ascribing worth to someone or to some thing. When we analyze the Hebrew and Greek words for worship, however, we gain a somewhat deeper meaning for the act of worship. The Hebrew word for worship, סָגַד (*segad*), means to bow oneself down, to fall down flat, to reverence, or to do obeisance, and it has the connotation of total submission to a superior (e.g., the king). The Greek translation of this word, προσκυνέω (*proskunéo*), means to prostrate oneself in homage or more graphically, to "kiss as a dog would lick its master's hand."

When we consider the absolute holiness of God and his complete transcendent otherness, we can but prostrate ourselves in awe in the presence of the Almighty who chooses to be immanent and to seek communion with man. Like the angels of heaven, we can but underscore his holiness by crying, "Kadosh, Kadosh, Kadosh," or "Holy, Holy, Holy," utterly holy, and wholly other, set apart beyond all human understanding.

Scriptural worship, then, is serious business, not something which is to be entered into with a lackadaisical attitude of superficiality. The true worshipper is one who approaches God with the proper attitude of submission, prostrated in spirit before the awesome holiness of Yahweh, the Almighty God. It is important, then, that we learn how to worship God.

REVERENCE AND HONOR–NOT ENTERTAINMENT

Worship of God is not entertainment for men. Far too often contemporary worship services (if they can be called such) have been designed around what is entertaining to those who are in attendance. While entertainment and things which please men are important in their own setting, they must never be confused with worship. Those meetings which are designed to appeal only to the excitement of the human spirit by doing things that are entertaining to men are failures as worship services. The important thing about worship is to discover the elements that please God and to employ them to their fullest in our worship. Worship is not simply what makes individuals or a congregation feel good, but what makes glad the heart of God. And, in order to accomplish this quest, we must learn from the Word of God what honors and pleases him.

Since worship can only be termed true worship when it has the proper blend of spirit and truth, we must elevate our spirits into the realm of his Spirit and our minds into the truth of his Word, and in that order. We must first be attuned to the Spirit of God, to its moving, to its flow. Our human spirits must be melted in sincerity, sobriety, and humility, standing in awe at the majesty of the Almighty. Then, our hearts and minds must be knowledgeable of the scriptural teachings concerning worship.

The first and foremost element of worship is the bowed head. "So the people believed; and when they heard that the Lord had visited the children of Israel, and that he had looked on their affliction, then they bowed their heads and worshiped" (Exodus 4:31). Reverence for God and for the place of worship is essential. While buildings certainly cannot contain the greatness of God, those places which are set aside, whether permanently or temporarily, for the worship of God demand respect. When God's people are gathered together for worship, whether it be in a home, in a sanctuary, or in the market place, the attitude of reverence should be the beginning of worship.

PREPARING FOR WORSHIP

The second element that is important to collective worship by the body of Christ is a structured approach, which is sometimes called a liturgy. Far too often ministers have concentrated all their energies on the preaching of the Word. Hours have been spent agonizing over a sermon, and the remainder of the worship service has been left to spontaneity and usually to confusion. The chance that the worship would interrelate with the sermon has been at best minimal. The "stream-of-consciousness" style of worship, like the "stream-of-consciousness" style of preaching begins nowhere, ends nowhere, and leaves nothing behind.

It is the duty of the individual who is entrusted with responsibility for corporate worship to develop a coordinated, cohesive liturgical order which will lead the worshippers progressively from the carnal, natural surroundings from which they have come, through the medium of thanksgiving, into the various media of praise and prayer, into personal communion with God in a higher dimension of worship, and finally into hearing the engrafted Word of God and altering their actions to conform to that Word.

In Luke 22:15-20 we find a classic example of a New Testament liturgy, one which was devised by our Lord, himself. The Apostle Paul enjoined the continued observance of this liturgy in 1 Corinthians 11:23-25: "For I received from the Lord that which I also delivered to you: that the Lord Jesus on the same night in which he was betrayed took bread; and when he had given thanks, he broke it and said, 'Take, eat; this is my body which is broken for you; this do in remembrance of me.' In the same manner also he took the cup after supper, saying, 'This cup is the new covenant in my blood. This do, as often as you drink it, in remembrance of me.' " In addition to this ceremony, Matthew 26:30 tells us that Jesus and the disciples sang a hymn at the conclusion of the meal. This hymn was probably Psalm 118, the conclusion of the *Hallel* Psalms that were a traditional part of the Passover celebration.

Liturgies can be as diverse as the gifted individuals who follow the leading of the Holy Spirit. Liturgy does not eliminate spontaneous, extemporaneous praise and worship. Rightly employed, it becomes a vehicle for such personal and individualized worship. Early synagogal Judaism was a prime example of this truth. The Jewish people were successful in holding the liturgical and the spontaneous in dynamic tension, with both being employed equally to the praise of God and the edification of the worshippers. Any liturgy which does not provide for the spontaneous is deficient; however, worship that is so extemporaneous that it is devoid of structure tends to become subjective and self serving and is often confusing and unproductive in bringing about life-changing experiences.

A JUDAIC SYSTEM WITH A NEW ORDER

As we evaluate the first of New Testament liturgies, the communion celebration that Jesus instituted, we find that the Old Testament observance was merely altered to incorporate the memorial of the new and perfect sacrifice of the spotless Paschal Lamb. Jesus brought a new and living dimension to the ritual of the Old Testament. The disciples continued to remember the same days, sing the same hymns, and carry out the same structure of their Judaic heritage; however, through Jesus they were brought a new order and motive in their worship. Passover was not abolished; it was given a new and living order for observance. The continuation of the Judaic system is also seen in the distinct, undeniable parallel between the earliest church's liturgies and those of synagogal Judaism. We see in this example an excellent pattern which we can employ in other transformed observances of the biblical festivals.

The diversity of conflicting Christian teaching and practice in the area of worship is resultant from the fact that leaders have not followed the example of Jesus and the apostles. They have set forth their own orders of worship on the basis of denominational tradition or personal preference. Many have made the mistake of thinking that the New Testament writings contained the system of worship for God's people; however, *the New Testament was written to reveal the new covenant for God's system, not the new system for God's covenant.* This is why many reject patterns, forms, and means of worship that are not found specifically in the Apostolic Writings. God's system, however, has always remained constant. The only change has been in the manner in which it was manifest. When we do not look upon the entire Bible as an organic whole, we open ourselves to gross misinterpretations. Without the New Testament, the Old Testament is incomplete. Without the Old Testament, the New Testament is without a foundation.

If we are to become successful worshippers, we must realize that God's system of worship was revealed in the truth of the Old Testament and perfected in the spirit of the New Testament. When we fully understand the forms of praise that pleased God in the Bible, we will employ singing, dancing, and ecstatic joy in our worship. We will employ altars in our sanctuaries on which to offer our prayers and the living sacrifices of ourselves to God. We will hear the preaching of the Word of God just as Israel of old heard the reading and expounding of the law. In short, we will maintain God's Judaic form of worship with a new emphasis and a new methodology.

COMMUNION WITH GOD

The third element essential to worship is fervency. Worship can have reverence and structure and still be ineffectual if it is not carried out with depth of commitment. The dimension of depth is necessary for experiential reality. We may observe and understand something that is real when it is represented in the dimensions of length and width; however, we can never experience reality unless the dimension of depth is also present. A fervent commitment to depth is also necessary to bring reality to our worship of God. Without this dimension, we deal only in the realm of superficiality, and we do not succeed in the real purpose for worship, which is *communication* and *communion with God.* The sages of Israel recognized this truth and discussed it as *kavanah* (the attitude of prayer and worship), which they said was more important than the practice itself. They declared that if any practice is carried out by rote without *kavanah*, it is worthless.

Quoting from Isaiah 29:13, Jesus described such ritualism, saying, "These people draw near to me with their mouth, and honor me with their lips, but their heart is far from me. And in vain they worship me, teaching as doctrines the commandments of men' " (Matthew 15:8-9). If one desires to ensure that his worship is not vain, he must do two things: teach the Word of God (not the doctrines of men) and come before God with full concentration and devotion to the worship that he is extending to the Creator. In effect, he is worshipping "in spirit" (*kavanah*) and "in truth" (the Word rightly divided). Worship is vain when it lacks the Spirit and when it teaches men's ideas.

REMEMBRANCE AND REENACTMENT

A great part of biblical worship is remembering and even reenacting the great acts of God in history. This is the reason God has set aside daily, weekly, monthly, seasonal, annual, and generational times to meet with his people. This schedule helps us to remember God's mighty acts that build our faith. Our acts of remembrance help us to sanctify time by setting it apart unto God. In this way we differ from the heathen who sanctify places rather than time.

When we remember the Sabbath by setting apart one day in seven for our families and God, we sanctify time. We remember that everything that exists was created by a personal God and did not simply come into being by happenstance or as the result of some impersonal cosmic force. We also remember that we have ceased from the labor of establishing our status before God by good works so that we could receive God's Sabbath, the person of Jesus Christ.

When the Jewish people celebrate the Passover, they teach their children what God did when "we were slaves in Egypt," emphasizing that not only were their forefathers delivered but also they, themselves, were saved by the hand of God. Each Jew considers himself to have been personally delivered from Egypt through this anamnesis, a yearly reenactment of the Passover. When Christians celebrate communion, they are, in effect, recalling vividly the crucifixion and resurrection of Jesus and sharing in that event for themselves as they discern the "body and blood" of Jesus in the bread and wine of communion. Though the body and blood of Jesus are not continually sacrificed in the Eucharist, believers do share in the communion of the body and blood of Jesus that was offered once upon the cross of Calvary. Remembrance and reenactment, then, are intrinsically involved in worship.

STUDY AS WORSHIP

In order to worship God effectively, then, it is important not only to be fervent in the Spirit but also to be accurate in the truth. In order to achieve this accuracy, we must "study" to show ourselves approved unto God, workmen who need not be ashamed because we are "rightly dividing the word of truth" (2 Timothy 2:15). At this point, we come to comprehend the Jewish concept that study is worship, for in studying the Word of God with all diligence, we actually submit ourselves to bow in God's presence and accept what he has said as the truth that must be practiced in our lives.

In prayer, we speak to God. In study, we hear from God as we listen to his words from the pages the Bible. Studying according to our Hebrew heritage means that we "meditate day and night" on the Word of God (Psalm 1:2). This meditation is far removed from Eastern Monism's meditation in order to "elevate the god within us" by chanting some mindless *mantra*. It is the process of repeating over and over the words of Scripture until those words are ingested and become a part of the very fiber of our being. This is the way in which study can become worship, for in it we hear God, and we hide his Word in our hearts.

For many centuries study has been at the very heart of the Jewish experience, so much so that much of Judaism has even considered study as the *highest* form of worship. Humbly submitting oneself to the wisdom of God revealed in the *Tanakh* (Hebrew Scriptures) was viewed as worship. The decision to study God's Word in order to *do* his Word is a meaningful act of submission and reverence–in short, it is worship. Study carried out with this motive is the very essence of Jewish learning. This is not study in order to understand; it is study in order to do. Abraham Joshua Heschel encapsulated this Jewish approach to study by saying that the Greeks study in order to understand while the Hebrews study in order to revere. God's Word and ways are ineffable: only by doing them does one understand them. This is the vision that keeps God's people from casting off restraint: "He that keepeth the law, happy is he" (Proverbs 29:18). Without the prophetic vision of the Word of God, people perish. With the understanding of rightly divided Holy Scripture, one can be taught, corrected, and instructed in righteousness, thereby becoming mature (perfect) and completely equipped unto all good works (2 Timothy 3:16, 17). It is then that the light of God's Word can shine through him so that men may see his good works and glorify the Father in heaven (Matthew 5:16). In this way, the wisdom and knowledge of God's Word become the source of our stability and the strength of our salvation (Isaiah 33:6).

Study is indeed the highest form of worship, for it is our subjection of our human reason to a conscious act of our human will to *believe* what God has said that manifests the faith that is credited to us for righteousness.

Though faith is generated in our hearts only by the grace of God, it is manifest only when we, like Abraham, decide to fulfill God's will in our lives by doing what he requests of us. When we believe God and act on our faith, we receive the imputed righteousness of Jesus Christ. When we study God's Word with a view toward obeying it, we become wholly submissive to God and can then walk in the spirit, not in the flesh. In such a state, there is no condemnation to us, for the law of the Spirit of life in Christ Jesus has freed us from the law of sin and death (Romans 8:1, 2). When we fully submit our lives to God's Word, when we study what he has said with complete devotion and intensity, we ascribe worth to him–we worship him. Study in order to do, then, is true worship.

BIBLICAL FORMS AND NORMS

As believers everywhere search for the Hebrew foundations of their Christian faith, they are rediscovering biblical patterns and means of worship. They are finding that all musical instruments can be used to "praise the Lord" (Psalm 150). They are reclaiming the arts which Satan and the world have polluted and corrupted. The biblical dance is reappearing throughout the land. Praying, praising, and singing in high praise are springing forth again. The singing of the Psalms and other parts of the Word of God is being restored, including the Hebrew minor mode of music that inspires reverence and awe. New Testament worship is being restored to the body of Christ as an important part of God's prophetic restoration.

While biblical means of worship are being restored, interestingly enough, the biblical concept of diversity in application is also being manifest. There are general outlines and concepts for worship that are scriptural; however, God makes room for every culture on the planet to add its own flavor and interpretation to the mix. It has never been God's intention to force all the peoples of the earth to become culturally Jewish, or British, or Indian, for that matter. It has been his will for all men to incorporate the eternal principles which govern the high praise of God into forms with which they have been familiar and comfortable. This is in keeping with the Judaic principle of unity in diversity which requires cohesion not uniformity.

REDISCOVERING BIBLICAL WORSHIP

Millions of Christians are exclaiming, "Enough!" They have had it with worship traditions inherited from Medieval Christianity with little, if any, reformation. They are no longer satisfied with performance/audience-based religion that is little different from the theatrical performances in ancient temples. They will no longer tolerate holy days and festivals that are little more than pagan celebrations with a thin veneer of biblical language and expression. And by the millions they are leaving traditional structured Christianity.

Increasingly, believers are reaching out for the God of the Bible. They are reclaiming their coinheritance with the People of the Book by restoring the Hebrew foundations of their faith. No longer satisfied with jejune ritual of Christianity past, now in the tradition of the Jewish forebears of their faith, they are hungry for more intimacy with God, more emotive expression of their love and passion for him. They want to do God's thing God's way. They want to worship him in words and forms which he has approved in his Word. They are discovering that this God of the Bible is a jealous God who seeks obedience more than sacrifice, who says, "If you love me, keep my commandments." Worship, then, is a matter of lifestyle, of absolute submission to the Word and will of God through the power of the Holy Spirit. It transcends the evanescent moment of religiosity in an all-too-short Sunday "worship service." It is an exercise that is practiced in the home, in the marketplace, in a library.

In the tradition of the Hebrews, study is worship, perhaps its highest form, for it is an act that prostrates the human mind and will before the Word of the Almighty with a view toward doing it. When one engages in the process of learning, he is being transformed by renewing his mind in what is merely a reasonable service of worship.

As one is reconnected with the Jewish roots of Christian faith, he comes to understand that work is a service of worship. (The Hebrew word *abodah* means both work and worship.) This truth underscores the biblical demands for ethics and morality in the workplace and for justice in the city square. It gives a sense of importance and fulfillment in simply being the priest and teacher in one's home, helping establish the fundamental unit of community, the family.

In true Jewish fashion, Christians are recognizing that the family, not the church, is the locus for spiritual development. They are assuming the responsibility of training their own children in the Word and ways of God, leading them in prayer, praise, study, and social interaction. No longer content to be emasculated, abdicating their God-given role of leadership and responsibility for training their children to a "church staff," fathers are taking their places alongside Abraham who God knew would teach his children his truth.

RESTORATION AND RENEWAL

Believers are demanding their rights, the entitlements of their status as fellow-citizens in the commonwealth of Israel. Israel's festivals, not Latin and Teutonic holidays, are their worship appointments, fused with profound meaning by the life, death, burial, resurrection, ascension, and parousia of Jesus, the Messiah. Israel's expressions of worship are increasingly becoming theirs. They now sing the Psalms and other biblical songs. They now dance Israeli dance, fulfilling God's instruction to praise him with the dance. They now celebrate *Yahweh Nissi*, the God of the banner, with visual stimuli toward worship. They are now restoring to the Christian worship experience the arts which have been so polluted by Satan but which have always been celebrated by the Jewish people. Like Israel of old, they have heard the command to awaken and "put on beautiful garments," the liturgical vestments that celebrate God and bring beauty and honor to the worship experience. The Sabbath is becoming more than a day on which one works hard at resting. It is a delight, a weekly sanctuary in time for celebrating God and one's family.

For those who have embraced Christianity's Jewish connection, traditional Christian worship patterns are taking on new meaning. The liturgy of the Word is far more meaningful to these restorers of ancient paths, for the Bible is interpreted in the light of its original language and its historico-cultural context. The liturgy of the Eucharist has become more intensely meaningful. No strange, exotic, mystical exercise, this communion! Instead, it is a continuation of the long-standing Jewish tradition that can be traced at least to Abraham's priest Melchizedek, a tradition of lifting the *Kiddush* cup in blessing to God and of breaking the bread that God brings forth from the earth. It is further the sharing of this same cup as the cup of redemption from Passover, recognizing in it the shed blood of the Lamb of God who takes away the sins of the world. It is a celebration of the Bread from heaven that was enfleshed in an earthen vessel to bring eternal life to all.

THE SEARCH IS ON

God is still seeking true worshipers, those who will worship him in the fervency of the Holy Spirit and in the system of the Word. As Christians everywhere are reawakened to the need for communion with God and to the value of their biblical heritage in worship, the high praises of God are being heard in the land. As the Hebrew foundations of Christian faith continue to be restored, increasing numbers will embrace the truth until the knowledge of God's glory covers the earth. In that day, all nations will come forth to worship the King, the Lord of hosts. May that day come speedily and in our lifetime!

Chapter 15

Yahweh's Liturgical Calendar

Passover	*Unleavened Bread*	*Firstfruits*	*Pentecost*
Death of Messiah	*Entombment*	*Resurrection*	*Holy Spirit*

Trumpets *Day of Atonement* *Tabernacles*
Day of Awakening *Israel's Salvation* *Return of Messiah*

Chapter 15
YAHWEH'S LITURGICAL CALENDAR
THE FESTIVALS OF ISRAEL AND THE CHURCH

Of all the elements of the biblical system of praise, worship, and service, probably none has been more generally neglected by the vast majority of the Christian community than God's liturgical calendar (the calendar prescribing times and programs of worship). While many elements of biblical Judaism have been perpetuated in most Christian churches (e.g., Bible readings, tithing, offerings), nineteen centuries of Gentile tradition have so obscured the calendar of events which Yahweh gave to his people as to render them essentially meaningless to millions of Christians.

The liturgical calendar of many Christian churches of the world today prescribes the observance of a wide range of days and seasons. In the past nineteen centuries, the church has set most of these times apart to memorialize some of the greatest events in the history of Christianity, and no doubt the intentions of those who established them were good. The truth is, however, that many of these days of memorial represent a departure–in some cases a radical departure–from the liturgical calendar that was outlined by God, himself, in the Hebrew Scriptures.

A grave inconsistency is found in this Christian teaching which relegates biblical festivals to meaningless obscurity by consigning them to the category of dreadful "legalisms" while at the same time exalting to sacrosanct and required status festivals of (at best) dubious and (at worst) outright pagan origin. Much of Christianity at least equals if not exceeds Judaism in its legalistic observance of its liturgical calendar, many days of which are but pagan festivals covered with a thin veneer of Christian tradition. While disavowing the importance of set-apart times when the question of biblical festivals is raised ("We observe every day alike," they say.), many churches still give preferential treatment to the times (days and seasons) that have become a part of Christian tradition, requiring their observance and prescribing certain practices while proscribing others.

THE NEED TO REMEMBER

Humans are prone to forgetfulness. It is simply impossible to remember everything all the time. For this reason God has set apart daily, weekly, monthly, seasonal, and generational times of remembrance. The only one of the ten commandments which concerns time begins with the injunction:

"Remember. . ." Since the Bible is a record of the events of God's dealing with man in history–a recounting of those times when God and man met–it is a call to remembrance for men of each generation to recall and even reenact in their lives what produced communion between God and man in other eras. David declared it: "I will remember the works of the Lord; surely I will remember your wonders of old" (Psalm 77:11). He further expanded upon this call to remembrance and its purpose: "These things I remember, as I pour out my soul . . . I went with the throng and led them in procession to the house of God, with glad shouts and songs of thanksgiving, a multitude keeping festival" (Psalm 42:4).

Though Christians celebrate his birth and his resurrection at Christmas and Easter, respectively, Jesus commanded his disciples to celebrate only one event in his life–his death. ". . . this do . . . in remembrance of me. For as often as ye eat this bread and drink this cup, ye proclaim the Lord's death till he come" (1 Corinthians 11:25, 26). The celebration of the Eucharist is a continuing remembrance of the death of the Messiah that provided atonement for man's sins and the expectation of the resurrection unto eternal life. This is the reason for Paul's exhortation to Gentiles at Corinth: "For indeed Christ our Passover also has been sacrificed: *therefore let us keep the feast* . . ." (1 Corinthians 5:7, 8). It is through sanctifying time that we remember. And, because man tends to forget, God has established markers in time, appointments on his own calendar, for man to remember and be drawn closer to his Maker.

SANCTIFYING TIME

Time is uniquely and integrally involved in human existence. It is a dimension that permeates the whole of creation as a part of the tri-universe that is wholly composed of energy, space, and time. Yahweh God, who exists beyond all time, initiated time when "in the beginning" he created. From the dawn of the creation, he ordained that the "lights in the dome of the sky" would serve to "separate the day from the night" and would be "for signs and for seasons and for days and years" (Genesis 1:14). While there are those throughout the community of man who minimize and even disparage special times, days, and seasons, the truth is that God has always had them. The Holy Scriptures contain a virtual plethora of incidences in which God visited and/or performed special works on the times which he had appointed in his Word.

Judaism and Christianity are religions which celebrate the great events of history. Much of the worship of both communities is focused on remembrance of God's mighty acts in history. It could be said, then, that they are religions of history and, therefore, of time. While the deities of the pagans were always associated with places and things, Yahweh has always been the God of events. While the ideal of Greek philosophy was to escape time and while the hope of Eastern Monism is to escape existence, Yahweh's religion is one of time and events and the hope of resurrection. Those who would engage themselves in Yahweh's religion must learn to appreciate and set apart time in order to remember what he has done and from those examples anticipate what he will do.

The reason for the continuing celebrations in remembrance of history is the fact that for Judaism and Christianity, time is not cyclical and causal–it is linear and covenantal. The religions outside the Judaeo-Christian tradition think of time as cyclical and causal, with the mindless wheel of fate and *karma* moving forward in never-ending repetition in which one event becomes the cause of the next which precipitates the next, *ad infinitum.* Judaism and Christianity perceive time as linear and covenantal–it starts somewhere (with divine creation) and ends somewhere (with the Messianic Age), and it is wholly dependent upon God's unilateral covenant(s) with his chosen people. We cannot function in the present or understand what we are to do in the future if we do not understand and celebrate the past.

AN APPOINTMENT CALENDAR

Centuries ago, Yahweh outlined in the *Tanakh* (Holy Scriptures of the Old Testament) an appointment calendar of the times on which he desired to meet with his people. It was on these times that he prescribed certain acts of divine service which were to be carried out by his people in praise and worship of him. This was God's liturgical calendar, an outline of special occasions on which his people were to meet with him and on which he would meet with them.

The festivals which God has outlined in his liturgical calendar are called *mo'edim,* the Hebrew word for appointments. "Let the children of Israel also keep the passover at its appointed time [*mo'ed*]. . . . But the man who . . . ceases to keep the Passover . . . shall be cut off from among his people, because he did not bring the offering of the Lord at its *appointed time* . . ." (Numbers 9:2, 13). Obviously God considered the appointments on his calendar to be important to his people, for the penalty for willful neglect of his *mo'edim* was separation from Israel.

It is nothing short of amazing that people in today's world who are so conscious of time and appointments should ignore and even disdain appointments that God, himself, has set. If one were granted an appointment to meet with the monarch, president, or prime minister of his nation, he would make extensive preparations to ensure the fact that he was prepared and on time. How much more important is God, the Creator of the universe, than a temporal political figure! Should not believers exercise as much caution in meeting with God at the times that he has charted on his appointment calendar?

If man's evaluation of God's calendar relegates it to relative insignificance, Yahweh's intention concerning it was perfectly clear at the time at which he implemented it among his people: "So this day shall be to you a memorial; and you shall keep it as a feast to the Lord *throughout your generations*. You shall keep it as a feast by an everlasting ordinance" (Exodus 12:14). Since God himself left little doubt that his days of memorial would be observed by his people throughout their generations, *forever*, those who are Bible believers should certainly be searching the Word of God to discover the timing of God's days of memorial and the proper New Testament method of observing those days.

REHEARSALS

The convocations that Yahweh enjoined upon Israel were also called *miqrot*, which means rehearsals. This also underscores an important truth about the days and seasons on the biblical liturgical calendar. They are both historical and prophetic. They were events of history, and they are propaedeutic of things to come. This is the definitive truth that Paul established in Colossians 2:16, 17: "Therefore let no one judge you in food or in drink, or in regarding a festival or a new moon or sabbaths, which are *a shadow of things to come*, but the substance is of Christ."

All holy days and sabbaths were shadows or pictures of greater things to come. Their reality is manifest in Christ. It is no mistake, then, that they are called rehearsals, which by nature are practices in preparation for the real performance. All of the biblical holy days are predictive of Jesus and are fulfilled in him. Until he came, they were rehearsals. When he came, the reality came on the world stage. After his manifestation of the reality, those festivals which he fulfilled become remembrance practices for believers. Those which remain to be fulfilled continue to be rehearsals for the time when the world stage will be set for the return of the Messiah.

MARKERS IN TIME

The first marker in time that God established for his people was a daily reminder, the hours of prayer. Coupled with the Judaic practice of reciting blessings to God for the occurrences of each day (over one hundred are possible), the hours of prayer give believers in God an opportunity to "re-joice always" and to "pray without ceasing, in everything give thanks" (1 Thessalonians 5:16-18). There are three hours of prayer: morning, noon, and evening. The morning hour of prayer (*Shacharit*) concurred with the morning sacrifice in the temple at 9 a.m. The Jewish people believe that Abraham introduced this prayer time. The noon hour of prayer (*Mincha*) is believed to have been introduced by Isaac. The evening (afternoon) hour of prayer (*Ma'ariv*) coincided with the evening sacrifice in the temple and is believed to have been introduced by Jacob.

David declared the times of prayer: "Evening and morning and at noon will I pray, and cry aloud, and he shall hear my voice" (Psalm 55:17). Daniel is famous for his faithful commemoration of these hours of prayer: "Now when Daniel knew that the writing was signed, he went home. And in his upper room, with his windows open toward Jerusalem, he knelt down on his knees *three times* that day, and prayed and gave thanks before his God, *as was his custom* since early days" (Daniel 6:10). The Holy Spirit was given during the morning hour of prayer: "For these are not drunk, as you suppose, since it is only the third hour of the day [9 a.m.]" (Acts 2:15). The hours of prayer were a continuing part of the lifestyle of the apostles: "Now Peter and John went up together to the temple at the hour of prayer, the ninth hour [3 p.m.]" (Acts 3:1); "Peter went up on the housetop to pray, about the sixth hour [12 noon]" (Acts 10:9); Cornelius saw in a vision "about the ninth hour of the day" [3 p.m.] an angel who said to him . . . 'Send men to Joppa, and send for Simon whose surname is Peter. . ." (Acts 10:3, 5). The importance of the hours of prayer, however, did not limit prayer and worship to those times, for David praised God "seven times a day" also (Psalm 119:164).

The second marker in time was weekly, the Sabbath. It was God, him-self, who set apart the Sabbath when at the conclusion of six days of cre-ation, he rested on the seventh day (Genesis 2:2). God rested in order to establish a principle for the creation even though by his very nature he is indefatigable. One day in seven is needed for rest and restoration of what is expended in the six days of work. When he enjoined the remembrance of the Sabbath upon Israel, God's intent was that on that one day in seven his people would remember that their God had created the universe: "Remem-ber the sabbath day, to keep it holy. . . . For in six days the Lord made the heavens and the earth, the sea, and all that is in them, and he rested the seventh day" (Exodus 20:8, 11). It was also a remembrance of Israel's re-demption from slavery in Egypt: "And remember that you were a slave in the land of Egypt, and that the Lord your God brought you out from there by a mighty hand and by an outstretched arm; therefore the Lord your God commanded you to keep the Sabbath day" (Deuteronomy 5:15).

While the rest of the world trusted in their own labors and worked seven days a week, Israel was to trust in God by working six days and setting the Sabbath apart as a day of fellowship with family and God. Israel honored the God of creation and redemption. The church, by setting apart one day in seven, also honors the God of regeneration through the Messiah, who is the believer's rest, and it also underscores its expectation of the Messianic kingdom's millennium of rest (Hebrews 4:9). While we recognize the fact that the "Sabbath was made for man" (Mark 2:27) and not vice versa and we underscore the fact that Jesus is "Lord of the Sabbath" (Matthew 12:8), we do understand that Sabbath is a memory device which confronts us weekly with the importance of setting one day in seven apart for interaction with God and our families.

The third marker in time was the new moon, which spoke to Israel of new beginnings each month and directed their attention to God as the source of everything that they enjoyed throughout the month.

The fourth marker in time was the seasonal festivals. These included Passover, Pentecost, and Tabernacles. These gave the people opportunity to honor God at the important times of their harvest season.

The fifth marker in time was the Sabbatical year. For six years the land was to be cultivated; however, every seventh year, it was to lie fallow. This again was a statement of Israel's dependance upon God, not upon the land or upon themselves.

The sixth marker in time was the year of jubilee, which occurred after the cycle of seven Sabbath years (49 years) was complete. It was the fiftieth year that signaled the release of all slaves, the settlement of debts, and the return of land to its original owners. Again, this was a symbol of Israel's dependence upon God and of God's intention that freedom reign among his people.

Perhaps a seventh marker in time should be considered also—the Sabbatical Millennium, which the New Testament, particularly the Apocalypse, predicts as a time of rest for God and man during the Messianic Age of the kingdom of God.

All of these markers in time are parts of God's liturgical calendar for praise, worship, and service from his people. They represent important opportunities for man to meet with God at his *mo'edim* (appointed times).

THREE TIMES A YEAR

The primary events on God's liturgical calendar are set forth in Exodus

23:14-17: *"Three times you shall keep a feast to me in the year*: You shall keep the *Feast of Unleavened Bread* (you shall eat unleavened bread seven days, as I commanded you, at the time appointed in the month Abib, for in it you came out of Egypt; none shall appear before me empty); and the *Feast of Harvest*, the firstfruits of your labors which you have sown in the field; and the *Feast of Ingathering* at the end of the year, when you have gathered in the fruit, your labors from the field. Three times in the year all your males shall appear before the Lord God."

There are, quite simply, only three festivals in each year which God specifically calls his "*Feasts.*" The Hebrew word *chag* (feast) is employed only in reference to these three festivals: Passover (*Pesach*), Pentecost *(Shavout)*, and Tabernacles (*Succot*). Originally these were called Unleavened Bread, Harvest, and Ingathering, respectively. While there are other times of celebration throughout the biblical year, there are in reality only three Feasts of Yahweh. This fact certainly does not limit the application of the term *feast* to other times of memorial; however, it does underscore the relative importance of Passover, Pentecost, and Tabernacles.

Throughout the Bible, God continually emphasized these three annual festivals. "The Feast of Unleavened Bread you shall keep . . . And you shall observe the Feast of Weeks, of the firstfruits of wheat harvest, and the Feast of Ingathering at the year's end. *Three times* in the year all your men shall appear before the Lord, the Lord God of Israel" (Exodus 34:18, 22, 23); *"Three times* a year shall all your males appear before the Lord your God in the place which he chooses: at the Feast of Unleavened Bread, at the Feast of Weeks, and at the Feast of Tabernacles" (Deuteronomy 16:16).

In each of these Pentateuchal references, God clearly establishes and reiterates the requirements that all the males of Israel appear before the Lord three times each year. When the worship to God was established in the Temple in Jerusalem, this same liturgical calendar was employed by King Solomon: "Then Solomon offered burnt offerings to the Lord on the altar of the Lord . . . [on] the three appointed yearly feasts–the Feast of Unleavened Bread, the Feast of Weeks, and the Feast of Tabernacles" (2 Chronicles 8:12, 13). This confirms the fact that God continued to place importance of Israel's observance of these three feasts: Passover, Pentecost, and Tabernacles.

It is perfectly fitting that three festivals should have prominence in the liturgical year. The numerical parallel is seen in the universe is actually a tri-universe composed entirely of energy, space, and time. It is also repeated in the three colors of light–red, yellow, and blue. It can be demonstrated in the three dimensions of space–length, width, and depth. And, of course it is a reflection of the three persons of God–Father, Son, and Holy Spirit.

THE THREE FEASTS OF YAHWEH

The three Feasts of Yahweh have often been termed Jewish festivals; however, this is a misnomer. The ownership of the feasts is clear. They are not Jewish feasts; they are Yahweh's feasts. "The feasts of the Lord, which you shall proclaim to be holy convocations, these are *my feasts*" (Leviticus 23:2). Much of the church has used the term "Jewish festivals" as a means of relegating these feasts to inferior status or relative insignificance. The truth is that they are Yahweh's feasts. If the church is God's church, then God's feasts should be the church's festivals.

Since Israel was an agrarian society, it was only natural that God would establish his times of memorial in accordance with the agricultural seasons. The first festival, Passover, occurred in the first month at the beginning of the agricultural year, the beginning of spring. The second festival, Pentecost, was celebrated at the end of spring and the beginning of summer. The third festival, Tabernacles, occurred in the seventh month at the end of the agricultural year in autumn. The timing of this sequence concurrent with the agricultural events, however, was not borrowed from some fertility rite of the Canaanite world. God chose Nisan (March-April) as the first month because it marked the timing of Israel's deliverance from Egypt. And, he chose the seventh month to end his liturgical year because seven is the number of perfection or completion.

The first of Yahweh's feasts is *Pesach*, the Feast of Passover, which occurred on the fourteenth day of Abib (Nisan), the first month of the Jewish religious calendar, followed immediately by the seven-day Feast of Unleavened Bread. Initially, both Passover and Unleavened Bread were grouped under the heading of "Unleavened Bread" (Exodus 23:15; 34:18). This was a spring festival that occurred around the time of the vernal equinox. (The name of the month *Abib* means "ears"–referring to the earing of the ripening barley harvest.) During this time the Israelites removed all the leaven from their houses and partook of unleavened bread for eight days (seven days in addition to the day of Passover). As time progressed this entire festival came to be known as *Pesach*, the Feast of Passover. By the time of Ezekiel, it was described in this way: "In the first month . . . you shall observe the *Passover, a feast of seven days*; unleavened bread shall be eaten" (Ezekiel 45:21). This was especially true in the time of Christ: "Now the Feast of Unleavened Bread drew near, which is called the Passover" (Luke 22:1). The entire spring festival came to be included under the term *Passover*. Passover was the day for killing the lamb; however, it came to encompass also the seven days of unleavened bread.

The second of Yahweh's feasts was *Shavuot*, the Feast of Harvest. In other places in the Scriptures, this festival was called the Feast of Harvest (Exodus 23:16). In reality, it was a fifty-day festival which celebrated the counting of the *omer* from the day after the Sabbath that followed the Passover until seven weeks were complete. Then, on the next day (the fiftieth day of the counting) the firstfruits of the wheat harvest were offered before God. Over time, this festival came to be known as the Feast of Pentecost, the name which is applied to it in Acts 2:1. The word *Pentecost* is the Greek term meaning the fiftieth (day).

The last of the three Feasts of Yahweh was *Succot*, the Feast of Tabernacles, called the Feast of Booths and the Feast of Ingathering. This festival was an autumnal event celebrating the completion of the harvest. At this time the Israelites lived in booths made of tree limbs and leaves, both recalling their bondage in Egypt and looking for the sign of the coming of the Messiah. This was the feast which Jesus observed at the temple in John 7. Tabernacles was called the Feast of Ingathering because it celebrated the end of the agricultural year when the entire harvest had been reaped.

There are, then, three Feasts of Yahweh, those three festival times which he made prominent in his liturgical calendar. The observance of Passover, Pentecost, and Tabernacles was enjoined upon Yahweh's chosen people on a perpetual basis, forever. It is for this reason that these three feasts might be called the "forever feasts" of the Lord.

SEVEN FESTIVALS IN THREE

In the events which were scripturally prescribed to occur at or around the times of the three Feasts of Yahweh, seven distinct individual memorial times were singled out by God to be a part of his liturgical calendar. These seven times are often called the seven feasts of the Lord.

The seven festivals are outlined in Leviticus 23, which serves as a complete delineation of God's liturgical calendar: "These are the feasts of the Lord, holy convocations which you shall proclaim at their appointed times. [1] On the fourteenth day of the first month at twilight is the Lord's Passover. . . . [2] And on the fifteenth day of the same month is the Feast of Unleavened Bread . . . [3] When you come into the land which I give to you, and reap its harvest, then you shall bring a sheaf of the firstfruits of your harvest to the priest. . . . [4] And you shall count for yourselves from the day after the Sabbath, from the day that you brought the sheaf of the wave offering: seven Sabbaths shall be completed. Count fifty days to the day after the seventh Sabbath . . . You shall bring from your habitations two wave loaves . . . They are the firstfruits to the Lord. . . . [5] In the seventh month, on the first day of the month, you shall have a sabbath-rest, a memorial of blowing of trumpets, an holy convocation. . . . [6] Also on the tenth day of this seventh month shall be a day of atonement . . . [7] The fifteenth day of this seventh month shall be the Feast of Tabernacles for seven days to the Lord" (Leviticus 23:4-6, 10, 11, 15-17, 24, 27, 34).

THE FEAST OF PASSOVER

The Passover was instituted as a yearly memorial and anamnesis of Israel's deliverance from Egypt, which was effected when the Lord passed through Egypt, destroying the firstborn of each family that had not applied the blood of the paschal lamb to the door posts and lintels of their houses. This was the last of the ten plagues which Yahweh had inflicted on Egypt, and it was the event which caused Pharaoh to relent and release the people from the bitter slavery they had endured for so many years. The complete story of this event is recorded in Exodus 12:3-13, 21-27.

For centuries after that time the Jewish people obeyed the commandment of God and observed the Feast of Passover on the fourteenth day of Abib, the first month of the religious year. Under the full moon, each member of the nation of Israel remembered the supernatural deliverance wrought by Yahweh and considered himself personally to have been delivered from Egypt. In an unbroken line from the first Passover (over 3400 years ago), the Jewish people have kept the commandment that God gave them to observe in perpetuity.

Since he was a devoted and observant Jew who diligently obeyed the commandments of God, Jesus maintained the tradition of Passover observance throughout his life. Indeed, in each of the three years of his ministry, he observed the Passover (John 2:23; 6:4; 13:1). Then on the night of his last celebration of the Passover, Jesus instituted a new memorial for the observance of Passover among his disciples. Since Jesus was the Lamb of God (John 1:29) who was to be offered on the very day of Passover to deliver the people from the bondage of sin and death (Matthew 26:2), he introduced a new celebration for Passover, commanding his disciples to recognize his body and blood in the unleavened bread and wine of the Passover and to partake of them in remembrance of his death until his return. It was the *matzah* of the Passover that Jesus used to demonstrate his broken body, and it was the third of the four cups of Passover wine, the cup of redemption, that he used to demonstrate his shed blood. This ceremony was outlined in Luke 22:17-20 and confirmed in 1 Corinthians 11:23-26.

Jesus was the Passover Lamb (1 Corinthians 5:7) who was slain from the foundation of the world in the eternal plan of God's salvation for man (Revelation 13:8). In the killing of an animal to cover the sin and nakedness of Adam and Eve in the Garden of Eden (Genesis 3:21), God had demonstrated the necessity for the shedding of blood for the remission of sins (Hebrews 9:22) and foreshadowed the time when the Lamb of God would be offered for the sins of the world (Hebrews 9:25-28; 10:10-14). In order to fulfill the Passover type, Jesus had to be spotless, free from sin, (Hebrews 2:17,18; 4:15), something which was accomplished in him through the things that he suffered (Hebrews 2:10).

The continuing observance of Passover was enjoined upon the church by Jesus, himself: "Do this in remembrance of me" (Luke 22:19). Paul further urged Passover observance upon the church, including the Gentiles, in his exhortation in 1 Corinthians 5:7, 8: "Christ our Passover has been sacrificed for us. Therefore let us keep the feast . . . with the unleavened bread of sincerity and truth." Even after the separation of the church from the matrix of Judaism around the end of the first century, a large part of the church (among them Polycarp and Melito of Sardis) continued to observe Passover with communion on the fourteenth day of Abib, a fact which earned for them the appellative *Quartodecimans*, or "fourteeners," which the more Hellenistic Christians heaped upon them in derision. This observance of Passover continued in the Western church until 325 C.E. when the Roman Emperor Constantine proscribed the celebration of Passover with communion in his effort to purge the church of its Judaic heritage. It continued in the Eastern church until the eleventh century.

THE FEAST OF UNLEAVENED BREAD

The Feast of Unleavened Bread began on the fifteenth day of Abib, immediately following the day of Passover and continued for seven days. During this time the people of Israel removed and kept leaven out of their houses, remembering the fact that when they were delivered from Egypt, they had not had time to allow for the leavening of their bread. Hence it was called "the bread of haste." The first day of Unleavened Bread also celebrates the actual deliverance from Egypt which took place on the fifteenth day of Abib (Numbers 33:3).

By the time of the prophets, and particularly by the time of Christ, the Feast of Unleavened Bread had become so interconnected with the Feast of Passover that the entire eight days of unleavened bread came to be called the Passover, with the paschal event becoming the focus of the entire week of devotion to Yahweh.

The Feast of Unleavened Bread symbolized the complete work of Christ that removes sin from the lives of believers. Leaven in the New Testament is symbolic of sin and false teaching (e.g., the leaven of Herod and of the Pharisees [Mark 8:15], the leaven of malice and wickedness [1 Corinthians 5:6-8], the leaven of legalism [Galatians 5:9]). The interconnection of the Feast of Unleavened Bread and the Passover clearly demonstrates the need for atonement which removes sin from the lives of believers. The fact that the removal of leaven is both an event of one day and of seven additional days helps us to understand that believers in Christ initially have sin removed from their lives by the shed blood of the Passover Lamb and that the purification process is one which extends through time in a sanctification process which is manifest in obedience to the Word of God (John 17:17; Ephesians 5:26).

The traditional Jewish ceremony of the removal of leaven in each home is a good example of how God removes sin from the lives of believers in Jesus. After the house is completely cleaned and all dishes and utensils have been boiled or passed through fire, the father hides ten pieces of leavened bread in the house and encourages the children to find those pieces. The children, however, are not permitted to touch the pieces of leaven when they discover them but bring their father to remove them from the house. The father takes a feather and a wooden spoon and gently removes the leaven from the house and later burns it with fire (usually at the synagogue). God, our Father, encourages us, his children, to examine ourselves to see if we are in the faith (1 Corinthians 11:28; 2 Corinthians 13:5) and to discover the secret sin in our lives (Psalm 19:12). We, however, may not remove the sin. Only our Father can remove it and cast it into the lake of fire, never to be remembered against us. And, he does so with extreme gentleness, for "if we confess our sins, he is faithful and just to forgive us our sins, and to cleanse us from all unrighteousness" (1 John 1:9).

The New Testament church's celebration of the Feast of Unleavened Bread emphasized the purification of the inner man, the removal of sin and unrighteousness from the lives of those who had received the Passover in Christ. This is the clear message of 1 Corinthians 5:8: "Therefore let us keep the feast . . . with the unleavened bread of sincerity and truth."

THE FEAST OF FIRSTFRUITS

The third of the seven feasts is the Feast of Firstfruits. This was the time for celebration of the firstfruits of the barley harvest in the land of Israel. Details of the commandments for observance of this festival are found in Leviticus 23:9-14. At this time of the year, according to tradition, the high priest went into the barley field in the evening as the first day of the week immediately following Passover began and plucked up a sheaf of the barley. (The timing of this event was at sundown on the Sabbath, since the Hebrew day begins at sundown, with each day recognized as "the evening [first] and [then] the morning" as in Genesis 1:5.) This sheaf was then kept in the temple until the time of the morning sacrifice on that same first day of the week, at which time the high priest waved the sheaf before the Lord as a firstfruits offering of thanks for the harvest.

The rich symbolism of this yearly Judaic festival is readily demonstrated in the resurrection of Jesus Christ. There can be no doubt that Jesus was resurrected sometime between the end of the Sabbath (sundown Saturday) and sunrise on Sunday, for when the women came to the tomb at sunrise on the first day of the week "while it was yet dark" (John 20:1), they found that the tomb was already empty. While there is no concrete evidence in the scriptural record to establish the fact that Jesus resurrected at a particular time of day, the shadow of the events in the Feast of Firstfruits surely gives us a suggestion that the Lord Jesus could well have resurrected at the time at which the high priest plucked up the wave sheaf of the barley harvest from the field. When the risen Lord appeared to Mary Magdalene on the following morning, he would not permit her to touch him, saying, "I have not yet ascended to my Father" (John 20:17). No doubt, Jesus ascended to the Father in order to wave the firstfruits of the resurrection before him at the hour of the morning sacrifice when the high priest waved the sheaf in the temple.

Perhaps it is more than a coincidence of the language of Scripture that Jesus is called by the apostle Paul "the firstfruits" of the resurrection in 1 Corinthians 15:23 when he speaks of the order (perhaps chronological) of the resurrection. The historical fact that Jesus was resurrected (witnessed by over five hundred people, many of whom accepted martyrdom rather than deny their testimony) stands as a firstfruits symbol of the bounty of the resurrection in which all believers will be resurrected at the end of the age. Just as the wave sheaf represented the bulk of the harvest to come, so the resurrection of Jesus represents the resurrection which is come.

There is evidence that at the time of the crucifixion of Jesus, some of the saints who had died were resurrected (Matthew 27:52). This, no doubt, was emblematic of the event which occurred during the time of Jesus' entombment when descended into the heart of the earth, to *hades* or *sheol* (Hebrew), and led captivity captive (Ephesians 4:8, 9) by preaching to the spirits who were imprisoned in the grave (1 Peter 3:19), those over whom death had reigned supreme (Romans 5:14), and delivering them from the power of death when he ascended. Perhaps it was not only himself but also these whom he led captive into the heavenlies that Jesus waved as the new Melchizedek High Priest before his Father in heaven.

THE FEAST OF PENTECOST

The Feast of Pentecost was celebrated fifty days after the spring festival season, hence its name. It was a festival which began on the morning after the Sabbath after Passover and concluded on the morning after seven additional Sabbaths had passed, or fifty days later. The day of Pentecost (the fiftieth day) was "fully come" (Acts 2:1). It was a festival of celebration for the wheat harvest, which featured a firstfruits offering of two loaves of bread that were waved before the Lord.

There is much controversy as to the date of the celebration of the Feast of Pentecost, also called the Feast of Weeks or the Feast of Harvest. The Sadducean party maintained a literal rendering of the Pentateuchal references to Pentecost by saying that the first day of the Feast of Weeks was the morning after the weekly Sabbath after Passover (Leviticus 23:11). The Pharisees, who were the founders of Rabbinic Judaism, believed that the first day of the fifty days was on the morning after the first day of Unleavened Bread or the morning after the annual Sabbath of the first day of the Feast of Unleavened Bread. Others (notably the Samaritans) believed that the first day of Pentecost should be on the morning after the last day of Unleavened Bread. Still others believed that it should occur on the morning after the weekly Sabbath after the entire Feast of Unleavened Bread. In all likelihood, the position of the Sadducees was more accurate scripturally, so that the day when "Pentecost was fully come" (Acts 2:1), was always on Sunday, fifty days after the Sunday following the weekly Sabbath after Passover.

Pentecost has been historically celebrated by the Israelites as the anniversary of the giving of the law. It was surely in this time frame that Moses ascended up into the mountain and received the tablets of the law. Since the people of Israel so loved the Torah of Yahweh, Pentecost became a time for rejoicing in the covenantal provision of God for their order and well being.

It was only fitting, then, that when another of the great events in the lives of believers in Jesus as Messiah occurred, it coincided with the day of Pentecost. "When the Day of Pentecost had fully come . . . they were all filled with the Holy Spirit and began to speak with other tongues, as the Spirit gave them utterance" (Acts 2:1, 4). The great enduement of the Holy Spirit which was to empower the believers for service both as witnesses to

Christ and as overcomers and fulfillers of the law of God was poured out upon the church on the day of Pentecost. The law of the Spirit of life in Christ came on the anniversary of the giving of the Torah law.

The purpose of the Holy Spirit was to empower the believers to gather disciples to form the church. The rich symbolism of the loaves of bread that were offered as firstfruits of Pentecost is readily seen in the fact that the church is recognized as one bread (1 Corinthians 10:17), millions of particles of flour baked together into one loaf. The fact that there were two identical loaves in the offering of Pentecost indicates that God would make the one offering of the church from two bodies of people, Jews and Gentiles (Ephesians 3:6).

That the early church continued to observe the Feast of Pentecost is seen in the determination of Paul to be in Jerusalem for Pentecost (Acts 20:16) and in his reckoning his travel schedule by Pentecost (1 Corinthians 16:8). No doubt, this was a celebration of the great event that had occurred on that first New Testament Pentecost when the Holy Spirit was given.

THE FEAST OF TRUMPETS

The Feast of Trumpets occurred on the first day of the month of Tishri, the seventh month of the Jewish religious calendar and the first month of the civil calendar. This day is considered the New Year for Jews throughout the world (*Rosh HaShanah*–meaning literally, "head of the year"). Trumpets also signaled the end of the agricultural harvest season, when all of the fruits and grains of the field had been harvested. It heralded the beginning of the second great time of festivity in the nation of Israel, a season which came exactly six months after the Passover season.

The day of the Feast of Trumpets was a new moon, a time of the "memorial of blowing of trumpets" and a "holy convocation" of the people (Leviticus 23:24). The purpose of the Feast of Trumpets was to call all of Israel to attention in preparation for the forthcoming Day of Atonement, the highest and holiest day of the Jewish year, which followed ten days later. Israel took this time as a ten-day period of introspection and evaluation of individual conduct over the preceding year.

The theme of the blowing of trumpets is a recurring *leitmotif* that is seen throughout the Bible. Joel 2:1: "Blow the trumpet in Zion," 1 Corinthians 15:52: ". . .the trumpet will sound, and the dead will be raised incorruptible," and Revelation 8:6: "The seven angels who had the seven trumpets prepared themselves to sound," along with many other passages of Scripture, reveal the continuing work of the blowing of trumpets in the midst of God's people throughout the ages.

The biblical trumpet was the shofar, the ram's horn. At each occasion when the shofar was blown, it called Israel's attention back to the *Akedah*, the binding of Isaac, and the substitutionary ram that God provided to be sacrificed in his place. The principles of vicarious atonement and substitutionary righteousness that have always been foundational to Judaism and Christianity have been underscored with each soul-piercing blast of the shofar.

While there is no specific reference to the observance of the Feast of Trumpets in the New Testament, the fact that Jesus participated in the Feast of Tabernacles celebration is indicative of the fact that both he and the nascent church continued to honor this biblical ordinance. No doubt, the gospel theme of the call to repentance and restitution was an appropriate message for this time of self-examination and repentance in Israel.

THE DAY OF ATONEMENT

The Day of Atonement was and is the highest and holiest day of the biblical liturgical calendar (Leviticus 23:27). The events of that day are detailed in Leviticus 16:7-16, 29, 30. The fact that the Day of Atonement was celebrated on the tenth day of Tishri is strikingly parallel to the fact that the Paschal lamb was set apart on the tenth day of Abib in the Passover season. The unique sacrifice which was offered on this day involved two goats, one called the Yahweh goat and the other the scapegoat. Of the two, one was chosen by lot to be the blood sacrifice to Yahweh for the sins of the high priest and all of the nation of Israel. The other goat became the scapegoat, the one upon which the sins of the people were confessed by the high priest. In laying his hands upon the head of the goat, he transferred the guilt of Israel to the goat, which was subsequently sent into the Judaean desert, bearing the sins of the people outside the camp of Israel.

While the sacrifice of Jesus took place on Passover, there are still profound similarities between his offering of himself for the sins of all mankind and the ceremony which took place on the Day of Atonement. Jesus was both the Yahweh goat who provided the blood of atonement and the scapegoat who bore the sins of all the world upon himself and took them outside the camp of the peoples of the earth into *sheol* itself (Hebrews 13:12). Since Jesus is the once-and-for-all-time atonement (Hebrews 9:26), his death forever fulfilled the sacrificial elements of the Day of Atonement. There is no need for another sacrifice, for the offering is complete in the body of Jesus.

THE FEAST OF TABERNACLES

The Feast of Tabernacles is the climax of Yahweh's liturgical calendar.

It was called the Feast of Ingathering, for it was the time of rejoicing over the completion of the harvest in Israel. The fact that this festival began on the fifteenth day of the month of Tishri (at the full moon) is also parallel with the beginning of the Feast of Unleavened Bread on the fifteenth day of Abib (at the full moon). Both the Feast of Unleavened Bread and the Feast of Tabernacles began their celebrations on the two days of the year when night and day are equal, for they were on the day (and night) of the full moon at the time of the vernal equinox (Unleavened Bread) and the autumnal equinox (Tabernacles).

The Feast of Tabernacles is discussed in Exodus 23:16 and in Leviticus 23:39-43. Historically Israel dwelt in booths, brush arbors constructed of tree limbs and other foliage, that served as reminders of their deliverance from the bondage of Egypt. Tabernacles was also remembered as the time on which Solomon dedicated the Temple of Yahweh in Jerusalem, one of the most celebrated events in Jewish national history.

Some have suggested that Jesus may have been born at the time of the Feast of Tabernacles. It is commonly held that the ministry of Jesus was of three and one-half years in duration (calculated according to the number of Passovers which Jesus celebrated), and that it began at the time of his thirtieth birthday. Since it is certain that Jesus was crucified at Passover, if he were thirty-three and one-half years old at his death, then it follows that he was born around the time of the Feast of Tabernacles, six months before the Feast of Passover. Tabernacles may well have been the fullness of time (Galatians 4:4) at which the Lord Jesus chose to become *tabernacled* with men (John 1:14).

It has also been suggested that since the temple of Solomon was dedicated at the Feast of Tabernacles, the establishment of the church with the ordination of the twelve apostles also occurred during the time of the Feast of Tabernacles. It would certainly be appropriate that two parallel events would have occurred within the same time frame on Yahweh's liturgical calendar.

THE FEASTS REVEAL GOD'S SALVATION PLAN

One of the clear statements of Holy Scripture is that the festivals (holy days) foreshadowed events of the New Testament era. Colossians 2:16, 17 tells us that holy days and Sabbath days are "shadows of things to come, but the substance is of Christ." Coupled with Hebrews 10:1: ". . . the law [has] a shadow of good things to come. . .", this Pauline statement should help us to understand that the festivals of Judaism are very much a part of the Christian heritage and speak profoundly to us of the Jewish Rabbi whom we recognize as Messiah and Lord. Quite simply, the Jewish festivals are pictures (shadows) that help us to understand the life, ministry, death, resurrection, ascension, and second coming of Jesus more clearly. The three major feasts, Passover, Pentecost, and Tabernacles, speak to us of the comprehensive plan of God for the New Testament era.

Just as the liturgical calendar is divided into three segments of time for celebration, so the New Testament era is divided into three prophetic times. The profound conjunction of these prophetic events with the order of the liturgical calendar can be no accident. That they are a part of the divine purpose is readily apparent. It is exactly as Paul and the writer of Hebrews teach: the Sabbaths and festivals of the Torah are prophetic symbols which adumbrate the reality that is seen in Christ and the church.

The Passover season was celebrated with three interrelated festivals– Passover, Unleavened Bread, and Firstfruits. Pentecost is the festival that stands alone is in the midst of the agricultural year. The Tabernacles season is celebrated with three interrelated festivals–Trumpets, Day of Atonement, and Tabernacles. It is no coincidence that the greatest events of the New Testament era are found at its beginning and at its ending, with a long period of time interposed.

The New Testament time began with the offering of the Paschal Lamb, Jesus Christ, on the cross of Golgotha to provide atonement–a means by which God, himself, could pass over the sins of mankind and allow those who believe to live. The fact that Jesus died on the day of Passover is confirmation that the event which signaled the beginning of the New Testament was the Passover, just as it had signaled the beginning of the Old Testament era with Israel's deliverance from Egypt. The accompanying fulfillments of the two adjunct festivals are also seen in the work of Christ. First, the removal of leaven (Unleavened Bread) from the one bread of God's congregation (the church) was accomplished through his offering of himself. Secondly, his resurrection from the grave on the day of Firstfruits signaled the confirmation of the hope of resurrection and the means of resurrection in him: "I am the resurrection and the life. He who believes in me, though he may die, he shall live" (John 11:25).

Then, literally fifty days after the resurrection of Jesus, the church was endued with the power of the Holy Spirit on the very day of Pentecost, a fact that was witnessed by Jewish people from many nations of the world who had gathered at Jerusalem for the feast. This was the empowerment which enabled the church to go forth to witness of Christ's resurrection and to build up the body of Christ, his church (Acts 1:8). This work has continued to this day with the church still laboring to complete the "harvest" of souls that will signal the prophetic fulfillment of the Feast of Pentecost. While Pentecost ends literally fifty days after the Feast of Firstfruits, the theme of harvest continues until the time of the Feast of Tabernacles; hence this time interposed between Passover and Tabernacles represents the gathering of the church.

Since Tabernacles marks the end of the harvest, it can be expected that this season should mark the end of the spiritual harvest. Jesus rightly said, "The harvest is the end of the age" (Matthew 13:39). The harvest is at the culmination of the era of divine grace, the time when Jesus will return to establish his Messianic Kingdom on earth. It is the time of the consummation of all things. Just as Passover had three interrelated festivals that were fulfilled in the beginning of the New Testament era, so Tabernacles has three interrelated festivals that will be fulfilled at its end. These events are clearly set forth in the eschatological teachings of both the *Tanakh* (Old Testament) and the New Testament.

The first work that must be accomplished near the end of the age is the Feast of Trumpets, the awakening of the church, the kingdom of God, and the nation of Israel both spiritually and prophetically to the nearness of the *eschaton*. The trumpet will be blown both in the church and in Israel ("Blow the trumpet in Zion."–Joel 2:1). It will be a time for awakening the sleeping kingdom of God (Matthew 25:6). All the people of the earth will be urged to make preparation for the impending return of the Lord Jesus in what will be a heart-rending time of universal trouble and conflict the likes of which the world has never seen. The nations of the world will be called upon to repent, and they will be judged of God by the manner in which they react to the church and to the people of Israel.

The second great prophetic work which will be accomplished in this time near the end of the age will be the salvation of the nation of Israel, a national day of atonement for those who are God's chosen people according to the flesh. In this time the promises of God to Abraham and the patriarchs will be fulfilled when the fountain that cleanses from sin is opened to the entire house of Israel (Zechariah 12:10; 13:1, 6), an event which Zechariah predicts as an immediate antecedent of the coming of the Lord (Zechariah 14:1). In Romans 9:27 and 11:26, Paul predicted the salvation of all of Israel, the remnant that remains in the land at the time of the return of Christ. They will look upon him who was pierced and mourn for him as for an only son (Zechariah 12:10). Again, this event will occur during great tribulation. The great irony of the wisdom of God will be manifest at this time when he will use the Gentile church to stand with Israel and in effect bring his mercy to Israel to provoke them to receive Messiah (Romans

11:11, 31).

Finally, the Feast of Tabernacles will be fulfilled when Jesus, himself, returns from heaven to establish his Judaic kingdom on earth for a millennium. This is the reason that the great festival which will be celebrated throughout the world during the reign of Christ is the Feast of Tabernacles, the feast that has been designed for both Jews and Gentiles (Zechariah 14:16). The second coming of the Messiah, the seal of his prophetic promise, will be memorialized annually at Tabernacles throughout the duration of his reign.

Tabernacles is also called ingathering. The prophetic significance of this event is noted throughout the New Testament. The coming of Messiah represents a time of ingathering of all the righteous harvest of the earth into God's barn, for "the harvest is the end of the age." He is the one like the Son of man on the cloud who will "thrust in [*his*] sickle and . . . reap for the time has come . . . to reap, for the harvest of the earth is ripe" (Revelation 14:14, 15). The reapers are the angels (Matthew 13:39) to whom Jesus gives the order at the culmination of this age to "gather together his elect from the four winds, from one end of heaven to the other" (Matthew 24:31). This is the explicit reason for the return of our Lord: "If I go . . . I will come again, and *receive you unto myself*" (John 14:3).

The coming of Jesus signals that event for which we who are believers and, indeed, all of creation has sought: the resurrection and the change (Romans 8:22, 23). "The dead in Christ will rise first. Then we who are alive and remain will be caught up together with them in the clouds to meet the Lord in the air. And thus we shall ever be with the Lord" (1 Thessalonians 4:16, 17), and "the dead will be raised incorruptible, and we shall be changed" (1 Corinthians 15:52). This is the event which Paul describes as "the coming of our Lord Jesus Christ, and our gathering together to him" (2 Thessalonians 2:1). It is the event that takes place "in the dispensation of the fullness of the times" when he will "gather together in one all things in Christ, both which are in heaven, and which are on earth . . . " (Ephesians 1:10).

Since Tabernacles is the end of the agricultural year, it symbolizes the end of the gospel era, the time when all the righteous of the earth, both Jew and Gentile, will be resurrected to stand with the Messiah upon the mountain of the Lord (Zechariah 14:4). Subsequently, every nation of the earth will be required to commemorate the Feast of Tabernacles annually (Zechariah 14:16, 19).

The Jewish people have long believed that the Festival of Tabernacles is for both Jews and Gentiles. This season gives every Christian an excellent opportunity to join with Jewish friends in celebrating God's overthrow of the evil of human slavery. We can take this time to pray for men and women who even today are viewed as subhuman and are dominated by unrighteous political systems that exploit and enslave them. We can also celebrate the fact that we have been delivered from an even more onerous slavery, the bondage to sin, through the emancipation that occurred for us when we received God's perfect sacrifice for sin, Jesus the Messiah. And, we can join with the Jewish people in anxious anticipation of the coming of the Messiah and the age of peace that he will bring. Indeed, we can exclaim, "Maranatha!", and we can say with John, "Come, Lord Jesus" (Revelation 22:20).

FESTIVALS AND THE MENORAH

An excellent mnemonic device that will enable everyone to remember the seven festivals as being divided into three time frames under the heading of three feasts is to superimpose them upon the Menorah, which has three divisions: three lamps on one side, one lamp in the middle, and three lamps on the other side. There are three festivals in the beginning of the agricultural year: Passover, Unleavened Bread, and Firstfruits. Then, there is one festival in the middle of the agricultural year: Pentecost. Finally, there is a total of three festivals and holy days in the end of the agricultural year: Trumpets, Day of Atonement, and Tabernacles. (Interestingly enough, one could extend the analogy by adding the Jewish festival of Purim to one side and the festival of Hanukkah to the other, and the result would be a nine-branched Hanukkah candlestick, the *hanukkiah*!) Again, the seven festivals and holy days can be seen witnessed in the seven colors of the rainbow, the seven days of the week, the seven notes of the musical scale, and others. Seven is the number of perfection or completion; therefore, it is altogether appropriate that Yahweh's liturgical calendar should feature seven holy days.

FESTIVALS IN THE APOCALYPSE

The uniqueness of this parallel is established in the fact that it is clearly seen in the one great document which is described as a panorama of the New Testament era, the Book of Revelation. John was told by Jesus that he was to "write the things which you have seen, and the things which are, and the things which will take place after this" (Revelation 1:19), three categories of events which make up the new dispensation. The things that John had seen were witnessed by John in his gospel: the life, death, burial, and resurrection of the Lord Jesus. He talked briefly about them in Revelation 1:5-8. Interestingly enough, when Jesus appeared in his post-resurrection splendor to John on Patmos, he was seen "in the midst of seven golden candlesticks." Perhaps the positioning of the Son of Man in the middle of the Menorah was emblematic of the fact that three of the branches represented the things which "you have seen," the one candlestick in which he was standing represented "the things which are," and the three candlesticks on his other side represented "the things which will take place after this" (Revelation 1:19). At the time at which Jesus appeared to John, the prophetic program of God was indeed in the middle of the fourth candlestick, the fourth feast, Pentecost. Chapters 2 and 3 of Revelation deal with the call of the church to right relationship with God and to reconfirmation of its commission in the earth as the body of Christ. The observant reader could rightly expect to find the remainder of the Book of Revelation to be a description of the events of the final three branches of the candlestick or the final three festivals. And so it is!

There is no more detailed and complete description of the events of the "last days" than that of John's apocalypse. While hints of these truths are seen throughout the entire Bible, John's revelation is a digest of eschatological truth. It is no coincidence that the entire Book of Revelation represents instant replays in various settings of the same prophetic scenario. It begins with trumpets (also seen as seals and vials), and it ends with the bodily return of Jesus Christ and the establishment of his earthly kingdom. Interposed in these scenarios is national Israel passing through a time of trouble along with the church (Revelation 7, 12, 14), including the sealing of 144,000 of Israel (the Day of Atonement fulfillment). The end result of the apocalypse is the proclamation of the kingdom of God, "Behold, the tabernacle of God is with men" (Revelation 21:3), a clear parallel with the prophetic fulfillment of the Feast of Tabernacles. It is readily apparent that if one lays the seven feasts of Yahweh across the Book of Revelation, there is a perfect match, beginning with Passover and ending with Tabernacles.

Can there be any doubt, then, that the liturgical calendar of Yahweh's feasts that has been commemorated for centuries is in reality a prophetic appointment book that reveals in chronological order the events of the New Testament era, which both begins with a Jewish feast and ends with a Jewish feast? Could it be that the revival throughout the Christian community of interest in the restoration of the Judaic roots of the gospel is merely preparation for the return of the Jewish Messiah and the establishment of the Judaic kingdom of God upon earth? In the end, all the nations of the world will celebrate the Feast of Tabernacles each year in commemoration of the return of the Lord of glory to reign with his church over the whole earth!

NEW TESTAMENT OBSERVANCES

While most Christian theologians have posited that God's remembrance system was destroyed in Christ, this was never Paul's contention. As a matter of fact in 1 Corinthians 5:7, 8 we find him encouraging Gentile believers to celebrate the festival of Unleavened Bread (Passover) because "Christ our Passover has been sacrificed for us." This statement, coupled with Colossians 2:16, 17 (where Paul declares that holy days and Sabbath days are "shadows of things to come, but the substance [reality] is of Christ") should help us to understand that the festivals of Judaism are very much a part of the Christian heritage.

The Feasts of Yahweh were perpetual, eternal observances. With the advent of Jesus Christ and the introduction of the New Testament, God did not abandon his liturgical calendar. On the authority of his Word, it was to remain in force forever. The worship of God, however, was taken out of the remembrance of physical deliverance and thanks for physical sustenance and was placed in the realm of the spiritual. In the New Testament era the Feasts of Yahweh served both as times of memorial on God's liturgical calendar and as shadows of the reality of grace.

The spring festival of Passover was obviously fulfilled in Christ. The festival of Pentecost was fulfilled in the giving of the Holy Spirit to empower the church to herald the gospel into all the world. We can now celebrate the fulfillment of those festivals in the same manner in which Jesus and the apostles honored them.

When we come to the fall festivals, however, there is much room for speculation. We still are rehearsing for their fulfillment. Many believe that they tell us much about the advent of the Messianic Age. But, beyond the eschatological speculations, the Jewish holy days, *Rosh Hashanah*, *Yom Kippur*, and *Succot* can teach Christians great lessons that will enhance their faith. What Christian could not profit from a yearly call to repentance that *Rosh HaShanah* signals with the clarion call of the shofar on the first day of Tishri? And, what Christian would count of little value the opportunity to share with the Jewish people in the ten "Days of Awe," the time for introspection to see if they have sinned against God or man? Could not the Day of Atonement be a time for Christians to renew themselves in repentance that is the product of Godly sorrow? At the very least Christians could use this season as a time for praying for the peace of Jerusalem and the well being of the international Jewish community. Then, Tabernacles can be a time for Christians to join with the Jewish people in remembering that Yahweh is a God who delivers from slavery and brings "joy unspeakable and full of glory" to his people, both Jew and Gentile. Since Zechariah 14:16-19 predicts that all the nations will celebrate this festival in the Messianic Age, could we not get a head start on this celebration and join with our Jewish brothers and sisters in remembering God's deliverance and his abundant provision?

A CALENDAR FOR ALL PEOPLE

The most frequently asked questions concerning biblical festivals and Christian faith are, "Should Christians observe the biblical feasts, and, if so, how?" The answers are quite simple: if Jesus and the apostles observed God's liturgical calendar and if it is pleasing to God that his people do so, there is every reason for their observance, and the method of observance should be the same way in which the first century church honored them. In 1 Corinthians 5:7, 8, Paul instructed Gentile Christians to "observe the festival" of Passover. Then in 1 Corinthians 11:23-26, he gave them a very basic liturgy for observance. It is a simple biblical and historical fact that the earliest church observed the Passover with the celebration of communion and continued to do so well into the fourth century. In Acts 1 and 2, we find the church observing Pentecost, not in the traditional agrarian order, but with prayer, worship, teaching, preaching, and the receiving of the Holy Spirit. While historical observances may be meaningful and provide understanding of Messiah Jesus and his salvation, spiritual celebrations like those of the earliest church are more meaningful for Christians.

Christians have been denied a great legacy through centuries of ecclesiastical Judaeophobia, anti-Judaism, and anti-Semitism. Is it not time that we reclaim our rightful Judaic heritage that we have inherited as heirs of God and joint heirs with Jesus Christ, our Jewish Lord and Messiah? If you have been thinking about restoring the Hebrew foundations of your Christian faith, along with a right and biblical relationship with the international Jewish community, why not begin by examining the liturgical calendar which the earliest church used to express its worship to God and to understand more clearly their Savior and Lord?

Koinonia–
Communion with
God and Man

Chapter 16
KOINONIA–COMMUNION WITH
GOD AND MAN

When one is born again through faith in Jesus Christ, he becomes a partaker of the New Covenant. His agreement to accept the Lordship of Jesus Christ brings upon him the glorious privileges and the awesome responsibilities of the new covenant. In such an agreement every believer assumes the privilege of sonship, the right to address the Eternal God as "Father," but he also assumes the responsibility of maintaining the proper relationship to God and to his brothers and sisters in the kingdom.

The mutually supportive relationship between God and the believer and between the believer and all other believers is called *koinonia* in the Greek New Testament and is translated both as communion and fellowship in the Authorized Version. The word *koinonia* literally means partnership and comes from the word *koinoneo,* which means to have in common or to share.

The partnership between God, the believer, and his brothers and sisters in Christ is the subject of the introduction to John's first epistle. "That which we have seen and heard we declare to you, that you also may have fellowship [*koinonia*] with us; and truly our fellowship [*koinonia*] is with the Father and with his Son Jesus Christ. . . . if we walk in the light as he is in the light, we have fellowship [*koinonia*] with one another, and the blood of Jesus Christ his Son cleanses us from all sin" (1 John 1:3, 7).

The apostle John was reemphasizing the concept of fellowship that had characterized the administration of the new covenant since the day of Pentecost. On that day the *koinonia* (communion) between God and the believers was maximized in an overpowering manifestation of divine glory with men of faith and worship for God. The believers were filled with the Holy Spirit and communed with God as none before them had done. They experienced the ultimate *koinonia* with God, as they were elevated from the temporal into the eternal, from the earthly into the divine.

COMMUNION WITH GOD BRINGS COMMUNION WITH MAN

The immediate residual benefit of this depth of communion with God was the strengthening of the believers' relationships with one another, and particularly so with the leadership of the infant church. "And they were continuing steadfastly in the teaching and fellowship [*koinonia*] of the apostles, in the breaking of bread, and in the prayers. And the ones believing had all things common together, and they sold their properties and possessions and distributed them to all, according as anyone had need. And from day to day, continuing steadfastly with one mind in the temple and breaking bread from house to house, they shared food in gladness and simplicity of heart, praising God and having favor with all the people. And the Lord added the ones being saved from day to day together" (Acts 2:42, 44-47, literal translation).

There is something about genuine communion with God which awakens one's need for communion with his fellow man, and particularly so with his brothers in Christ. The sharing of every aspect of life with fellow believers is as important as communion with God. The walk of the believer in the New Testament is more than just a ritual for worship. Commitment to the new covenant is commitment to a way of life. Indeed, the movement that developed within Judaism in the first century which came to be known as Christianity was first called *The Way*.

This is why it was important that those who were initially filled with the Spirit had an overriding mutual concern for one another that caused them to do whatever they had to do including selling their possessions to minister to the needs of those who were a part of the communion or fellowship of believers in that day. The sharing of emotions, of spiritual experiences, and of the needs of daily living is what true *koinonia* or fellowship is all about.

TRUE CHRISTIANITY IS A SHARING EXPERIENCE

Far too often Christianity has been represented as a religion in which people come together once a week to share only in worship. In too many churches communicants are not bound together in the *koinonia* of the church as a total community socially, materially, and spiritually. Christianity today needs to experience true communion and make this experience dominant in every phase of life. Like the early church, Christians need to eat food together, share material resources together, worship together, pray together, and maintain their fellowship with spiritual leadership.

Too many Christian leaders have dwelt heavily upon the idea that ministers should be "fishers of men," not "keepers of the aquarium." While it is important that ministers concern themselves with winning unbelievers to Christ, it is equally important that they be found strengthening the relationships of those believers in their care both to God and to one another. When the apostle Peter was counting fish, Jesus challenged his love by asking him to "feed my sheep." Ministers cannot afford to become so engrossed in fishing for men that they allow the sheep to become divided, separated, and starved for communion with God and their fellow believers.

It is through scriptural communion that we are able to manifest the two attributes which Jesus said were the completion of God's religion for mankind: the love for God and the love for our neighbor. When the love of God is perfected in us, we reach out for communion and fellowship with God and with man. As we share our love with God and man, we become more completed and fulfilled individuals because we gain more than we give. In reality, it is fair to say that the level of our maturity, spiritually and socially, is determined by the extent of our fellowship and communion with God and man, for love is the bond of maturity (Colossians 3:14).

THE MANDATE OF THE NEW COVENANT

The instrument which mandates communion with God and man in the life of the believer is the new covenant. When one accepts Christ, he commits himself to his covenant. In reality, he is joined to Christ through this covenant: "Therefore, my brethren, you also have become dead to the law through the body of Christ, that you may be *married* to another, even to him who was raised from the dead" (Romans 7:4).When we enter into this covenantal relationship with Jesus, we become "members of his body, of his flesh and of his bones" (Ephesians 5:30). The communion of Christ and the believer is as real as the communion of husband and wife when they are joined by a covenant to become one body. In the eyes of God the body of Christ is one in the Spirit.

The unique characteristic of the new covenant is that all those who are partakers in that agreement become members one of another: "For as we have many members in one body, but all members do not have the same function, so we, being many, are one body in Christ, and individually members of one another" (Romans 12:4, 5). When believers fully realize that they are indeed covenantally joined together in the church, they will seek the *koinonia* which will be manifested in this manner: "That there should be no schism in the body, but that the members should have the same care for one another. And if one member suffers, all the members suffer with it; or if one member is honored, all the members rejoice with it" (1 Corinthians 12:25, 26).

The covenantal relationship which joins the members of the body of Christ together is not a human device or idea. The adoption of believers into sonship of God brings them into covenantal relationship with God and consequently with all the members of the body of Messiah. Recognition of and fellowship with other members of the church is not, therefore, a matter of choice for the believer. The status is a sovereign act established on divine initiative. The failure of the believer to recognize what God has done can only bring a debilitating loss of the spiritual benefits that precipitate from communion with fellow members of the body.

COVENANTAL RELATIONSHIPS FORESHADOWED IN ISRAEL

The covenantal relationship and its accompanying *koinonia* in the New Testament era were foreshadowed in the Old Testament with the nation of Israel. From the time that the Israelites made their covenant with God in Exodus 19:5-8, they had a covenantal responsibility to maintain the proper relationship with God and with their fellow members of the nation of Israel. All those who were born in Israel or who accepted the terms of the covenant became related socially, economically, and spiritually to the whole of Israel.

Unfortunately, this relationship which was a part of their covenant fostered in much of Israel a spirit of exclusivity and eventually developed a kind of xenophobia, or fear and disdain for those who were not Israelites. For believers, however, the Spirit of God that becomes resident within them at their rebirth causes them to reach out in love to those who are not a part of God's covenant and to share with them the right of access to the *koinonia* of God and the body of Christ. There should be no introversion in the personality of the church.

A SYSTEM FOR PRESERVATION

In the congregation of God in the wilderness, Moses employed a system that he developed on the advice of his father-in-law as a means of reinforcing the importance of the covenant and of the fellowship which it produced. This system is revealed in Exodus 18, where Moses established rulers over tens, fifties, hundreds, and thousands. This system worked in addition to the fellowship of the family, the clan, and the tribal units, and it was designed to provide leadership and protection to all of Israel.

This kind of arrangement foreshadowed fellowships which developed in the New Testament church that made for greater communion among the believers. It is through these relationships that individual members of the body of Christ receive their strength from the body as a whole. And, this kind of *koinonia* is what preservation is all about, the keeping of the individual by means of association and strength derived from the whole.

The Judaic system which God authored for the preservation of his people in the Old Testament was fulfilled in the similar Judaic system of the New Testament church: ". . . from whom all the body, nourished and knit together by joints and ligaments, grows with the increase which is from God"

(Colossians 2:19); "From whom the whole body, joined and knit together by what every joint supplies, according to the effective working by which every part does its share, causes growth of the body for the edifying of itself in love" (Ephesians 4:16). The proper growth and maturity of the body of Christ, then, is contingent upon the covenantal relationships of its members in communion with God and with one another.

This example from ancient Judaism is most appropriate in our day when mega-churches tend to make Christian fellowship impersonal and unaccountable. Small groups foster greater support for individuals in a loving community, and they provide for the accountability that every believer needs. The small groups can take many forms; however, they should be patterned after the biblical example.

INDIVIDUALISM VS. COMMUNITY

In much of Protestant Christianity, the emphasis has been placed upon individual salvation to such an extent that the idea of corporate salvation has been virtually lost. "Each man stands before God for himself," we say, and rightly so. One does not become a part of the redeemed community simply because he was born into a Christian family in the same manner as one becomes a Jew by being born into a Jewish family. In the New Covenant, one must be "born again [from above]" (John 3:3), "begotten again by the word of God" (1 Peter 1:3). The spiritual rebirth must be the result of a conscious act of one's will to believe upon Jesus Christ as God's resurrected sacrifice for sin (Romans 10:10). Coupled with the Western ideal of individual freedoms guaranteed by society as a whole, the truth of individual redemption under the New Covenant has diminished the traditional Jewish ideal of corporate salvation, of a redeemed community. As is so often the case, we tend to exalt one concept (which is true) at the expense of another (which is also true). And, to the extent that it has divorced itself from this part of its root system, Christianity has been impoverished.

Israel had no such difficulty. Each individual thought of himself as a part of the corporate whole, of the Israel of God that was redeemed (saved) by the grace of God from Egyptian bondage and called out to be his people. Virtually all the prayers of the *Siddur* (the Jewish prayer book) are prayed in the first person *plural* (e.g., "*We* are your people . . . you have called *us.*")

Christians would have a better feel for this concept of corporate salvation if only they remembered the Lord's Prayer: "*Our* Father . . . give *us* this day *our* daily bread . . . forgive *us* our sins . . . lead *us* not into temptation. . . deliver *us* from evil." With this kind of mind-set, one is more conscious of the fact that he needs those who share in the covenant with him and that his actions affect the whole of his community. One does not tend to withdraw into some isolationist mentality expressed in the once-popular tune, "Me and Jesus got our own thing going; we don't need anybody to tell us what it's all about!" Just as each individual Jew manifested faith to place the blood of the Passover lamb on the door frame of his house, so each individual must accept the fact that Christ our Passover is sacrificed for us (1 Corinthians 5:7); however, just as God summoned Israel corporately to Sinai in order to enter into a covenant with them, so he has summoned the church to Calvary in order to establish the New Covenant with the redeemed community. As Israel was called out corporately, so the church is called out corporately. Indeed, this is the meaning of the word *church*– "the ones called out."

When we fully realize the fact that as believers in Messiah Yeshua, we are a part of one corporate community, we understand that our actions affect everyone else in that community. We can no longer cloister ourselves in the ghettoized mentality of separatism and denominationalism, further perpetuating the scandal of a divided church. We are one community. We must have fellowship (*koinonia*) with one another and fully recognize and acclaim one another as members of the body of Christ.

It is true that one can choose his friends; however, it is equally true that one cannot choose his family. So it is with the church. Everyone who has believed upon Jesus Christ has become a child of God. If believers are children of God, then they are all siblings. They have no choice in the matter, for the same God has adopted them all into sonship. The church would do well to learn from the Jewish people, who even though they may disagree vehemently about many issues, nevertheless affirm one another's Jewishness. They understand the need to underscore their relationship as a community.

OUTWARD SYMBOLS OF KOINONIA

There are two scriptural ceremonies which bring vividly to our attention the proper communion that we are to have with God and with our fellow members of the body of Christ. The first of these is the communion, celebrated with the elements of unleavened bread and wine which remind us of the communion of the body and blood of Christ which we receive by partaking of his Word and Spirit. This ceremony is a part of our *koinonia* with God.

The second is the ceremony of the breaking and sharing of the loaf of bread which reminds us of the fact that we are all particles of wheat that have been baked together with the fire of the Spirit into one loaf. Many are finding this a meaningful, mutually affirming expression of the oneness of the body of Messiah. Whether it is merely the sharing of food from house to house as the church did in Acts 2:42, or the formal breaking and sharing of a loaf in corporate worship, sharing bread with one another affirms the inherent unity of the church. This material expression is a meaningful part of our *koinonia* with one another.

RESTORATION

The Holy Spirit is at work today to bring about the restoration of the communion and fellowship that characterized God's system in Judaism and in the earliest church. It is time that the church resolve to fulfill the prayer of Jesus "that they all may be one" (John 17:21). This can be accomplished only if the previous part of his prayer is answered: "Sanctify them through your truth. Your word is truth" (John 17:17). We must be restored to the biblical foundations of our faith, for only then can we be set apart (sanctified) by the truth of the Word of God. Only when we understand that our salvation is both individual and corporate can we fully recognize our mutual responsibilities to one another as members of the body of Christ. And only then can we have true fellowship that is not conditioned upon anything except the one covenant of grace that we all share equally.

As God works to bring restoration to the community of faith in this time of preparation for the coming of Messiah, let us work to restore long-broken relationships, by establishing true *koinonia* in the body of Christ. Let us be found diligently "serving the Lord" and in love "serving one another," for this is the true *koinonia* which was foreshadowed in the Judaic system of the old covenant and was perfected in the body of Christ in the new covenant.

What's
in a
Symbol?

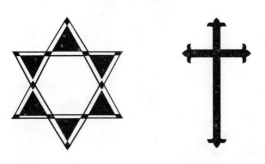

WHAT'S IN A SYMBOL?

Symbols have always been controversial. What means one thing to one person or to one culture may mean an entirely different thing to another. A symbol that inspires devotion and reverence among certain people may bring abhorrence and revulsion to another. Such is the case with symbols of the Scriptures that have been applied to the religion of the God of the Bible. While we must be concerned about the impact of our symbols upon our fellow man, in the end, of course, we must be most concerned with pleasing God, himself, and with things that honor him and represent his truth.

Both the Magen David (Star of David) and the cross have been centers of controversy, primarily because they have attained prominence as symbols of Judaism and Christianity. To the Jewish people, the cross is a revolting symbol that brings to mind the centuries of unrelenting and systematic persecution heaped upon them by the church and "Christian" autocrats. For some Christians the Star of David is a symbol of what they consider to be anti-Christ Judaism.

TAINTED SYMBOLS

It has been argued that the Star of David is a symbol of the occult that was developed in the idolatrous cultures of the Middle Eastern empires that predated the kingdom of Israel. It is true that the Star of David has been an object of magic and sorcery in the conjuring up of spirits, necromancy, and other practices forbidden in the Scriptures. For this reason, many teachers recommend that believers in Christ have nothing to do with this symbol because of the manner in which it has been used.

The same line of reasoning is used concerning the use of the cross as a symbol of Christianity. Some scholars say that the cross originated as a symbol for Tammuz and was first used in the pagan worship of Babylon and Egypt. Because of this association, therefore, they urge all believers to shun the use of the cross as an emblem of Christianity.

This idea of not using anything that at some time had been looked upon with disfavor was adopted in the church. Beginning in the second century, the church more and more felt that it had to distance itself from Jews and Judaism. By the time of Constantine the Great, things Jewish were proscribed by imperial or ecclesiastical edict. In like manner, following the

Reformation, many Protestants felt that everything Roman Catholic had to be totally rejected.

WHAT TO KEEP, WHAT TO DISCARD?

The truth is that if blasphemous abuse of symbols, names, and liturgy of biblical faith were sufficient grounds for believers to discontinue their use, very little would be left for us to employ in our identification with and worship of the Eternal God. We could not use the personal name of God, Yahweh, for this name has been used in the magical incantations of sorcerers for centuries. We could not use the biblical dance in worship of God, for this manner of physical expression has certainly been carried to detestable excess in nearly every culture in the history of mankind. We could not sing, use musical instruments, find a suitable day of worship, we could not preach, teach, or, in short, do practically anything!

What is a reasonable solution to the dilemma of the use/abuse debate? A practical answer is found when we remember that the various elements of all heathen religions and the occult have been merely perverted forms of the one religion of the eternal God. In the beginning, there was only one God and one religion. When Satan fell from heaven, he did not become the creator or originator of anything. But, he did become the polluter of everything sacred and holy. Since he was responsible for the worship of Yahweh in heaven (Ezekiel 28:12-15), it was only natural that in his fallen state he would profane worship and direct it toward himself. Because Satan perverted certain objects or practices is no reason for Christians to believe that they became evil *per se.*

LEARNING TO SEPARATE THE TRUE FROM THE FALSE

When we look at the practices of heathendom in this light, we begin to realize that our task is not simply to discard everything that has some remote connection with pagan worship or the occult, but to separate the true from the false. Far too often when people come to the understanding of some biblical truth, they go to extremes and find themselves out of balance in another direction. In a fit of hyper-spirituality they begin to eliminate what is true. Then, they become exalted in their own minds because of their knowledge and form an elitist attitude that almost immediately becomes judgmental toward others. When others do not share their views, they go up in a puff of holy smoke!

In order to avoid such extremism, we must learn to extract the true from the false and exalt it. We are far more effective when we are *for* something rather than *against* everything. This is in context with Paul's advice to the church: "Test all things, hold fast what is good" (1 Thessalonians 5:21). Ascetic withdrawal from the world has never been the Judaic model or in keeping with the teaching of our Lord who prayed that we should not be removed from the world but protected from the evil of the world (John 17:15).

THE MENORAH–GOD'S SYMBOL

Of all the symbols devised to demonstrate truth, the menorah is the only one that was designed by God himself. It was employed before the throne of God in heaven from eternity past. That is where Moses saw it when he was instructed to "make [all things] according to the pattern which was shown you on the mountain" (Exodus 25:40). That is also where John saw it in Revelation 4:5. The seven-branched candlestick is a perfect revelation of God's plan to bring the light of the world to all men through his Son Jesus Christ and through the church.

The twelve foundations of the menorah are not mentioned in Scripture; however, they are vividly portrayed in the menorah carved in the arch depicting Titus' parade into Rome following the destruction of the temple in 70 C.E. The base of this menorah features a two-tiered hexagonal base, making a total of twelve sides. The menorah's base reveals the twelve tribes and the twelve apostles, the foundation of the church's light.

The menorah's seven lamps of fire were reflected in the seven priests who carried the ark of the covenant (Joshua 6:4). They are also seen in the seven men chosen to carry out the ministry of the church in Acts 6:3. These seven lamps of fire are symbolic of the seven spirits of God (Revelation 1:4; 4:5), which are actually seven channels through which the one Holy Spirit flows to bring light and power to the church.

The menorah also has seventy decorations including its branches. These are a reflection of the seventy elders of the people who received the spirit of Moses and prophesied in Numbers 10. They are also seen in the seventy whom Jesus commissioned in Luke 10 to go before him and prepare the way for the kingdom of God.

The golden candlestick, then, is a depiction of both Jesus and the church as the light of the world. It is through human instruments that the oil of the Holy Spirit flows to bring light both to God's people and to a "crooked and perverse generation" among whom the church stands as a light (Philippians 2:15). Since we are the light of the world, we should place our light upon a candlestick so that it will give light to all (Matthew 5:15). By maintaining a biblical lifestyle that is reflected in the pattern of the menorah, we let our light shine before men so that they see our good works and glorify the Father in heaven (Matthew 5:16).

It is no coincidence that God said he had ordained a lamp for his anointed ones (Psalm 132:17) and that he declared that he would not rest until his salvation will go "forth as a lamp that burns" (Isaiah 62:1). Jesus is the light of the world, and he was revealed from the midst of seven lampstands (Revelation 1:12, 13). If the church is the light of the world, it will also be revealed in the menorah.

The menorah is the one symbol which has generally escaped pollution and misuse. Perhaps this is because it was designed by God himself and has been protected by him. More than any other symbol, it is appropriate for the church to use the menorah in its worship.

THE MAGEN DAVID STAR

The six-pointed Star of David is a symbol both of Judaism and of the Jewish people. The origin of its use to signify Israel is uncertain. It has been asserted that there is a connection between the Star of David and God's promise to Abraham in Genesis 15:1, "Fear not, Abram, I am your shield." The *Q'uran* speaks of the Magen David as the "Seal of Solomon," and oral tradition claims that it was used on the shields of David's mighty men and thereby acquired the name *Shield of David*. Regardless as to its antiquity, however, the Star of David is today the preeminent symbol for Jews, Judaism, and Israel.

Because it is a hexagram, the Star of David has been associated with pagan ritual and with the occult. This, however, is simply a reflection of evil's attempt to pervert good and use it for its own ends. While it may, indeed, have symbolism for things satanic, it still manifests truth. The Star of David represents the Trinity of God (Father, Son, and Spirit) reaching down to and being superimposed over the trinity of man (body, soul, and spirit) through the atonement of Christ and the giving of the Holy Spirit. Only when God enters the heart of man is light manifest. The Star of David speaks to us as believers that Jesus, the day star, has arisen in our hearts (2 Peter 1:19) and that through him we have the opportunity of shining as stars forever by turning many to righteousness (Daniel 12:3).

Regardless as to its historical use, the Star of David was certainly sanctified as a symbol for the Jewish people when six million of their number wore that emblem to their deaths in the death camps of Nazi Germany during the Holocaust.

THE CROSS—SYMBOL OF REDEMPTION

The cross is meaningful and important in God's religion, for there is no other symbol that so clearly manifests the message of redemption. It represents to us the power of God unto salvation, the divine act of unfathomable love for mankind through which the Father gave his only begotten Son so that fallen man might be restored to God and have eternal life (John 3:16). It represents the physical instrument that made possible the lifting up of the Savior so that all men may be drawn unto him (John 12:32).

The cross is the one symbol that demonstrates the New Testament which Jesus brought to Yahweh's religion. It reveals the redemptive work of Christ on Calvary and as such represents completion of Judaism's symbolism. Without the sacrifice on the cross, the Magen David and the menorah are incomplete. It is for this reason that we, as Paul, can glory in the cross of Christ, not because of the suffering exacted on that cruel instrument, but because of the glory that came through the risen Savior (Galatians 6:14) and the salvation and eternal life that came to believers through the sacrifice accomplished on that instrument.

LIVING EMBLEMS–OBJECTS OF REVELATION, NOT WORSHIP

Symbols have their place of importance, not as objects of worship, but as objects of revelation. In Romans 1:20 Paul tells us that God is revealed through material things. We can understand God and his workings much more clearly when we consider the symbols that he has given us or that men have made in order to honor him. It is altogether fitting and proper, then, that the menorah, the Star of David, and the cross should be used in Christian symbolism, for they demonstrate the religion of the Eternal God and help us understand his divine truth.

What's in a symbol? Different things to different people, but only one thing to God!

"This Is My Name Forever"

Chapter 18
"THIS IS MY NAME FOREVER"

"What is your name?" These passionate words of Moses as he sought divine confirmation of his commission to stand before Pharaoh and demand the release of the enslaved Israelites have echoed from the hearts of countless men and women of faith through the centuries. Who is the God of the universe, the one God who is supreme and utterly unique? By what name should men describe him and in what name should they seek his favor and blessing?

The name or title by which one refers to Deity has been a subject of interest to mankind from time immemorial. While various titles, including God, Lord, the Great King, the Almighty, and the like have been applied to the Creator, he must certainly have a personal name, a name which expresses his nature and being.

Prior to Moses' experience, God was not known by his personal name (Exodus 6:3). When the time came for the exodus, God equipped Moses with an infallible witness for his authority to organize such a momentous event when he revealed to him the meaning of his secret name, the name by which he was to be known forever. Listen to God's answer to Moses' question in Exodus 3:14, 15: "And *Elohim* [God] said to Moses, *Ehyeh Asher Ehyeh* [I AM WHO I AM.] . . . and *Elohim* said again to Moses, Thus you shall say to the children of Israel, *YHWH* of your fathers, the *Elohim* of Abraham, the *Elohim* of Isaac, and the *Elohim* of Jacob, has sent me to you. This is my name forever, and this is my memorial to all generations."

THE NAME AND ITS PRONUNCIATION

The name *YHWH* has been called the tetragrammaton because it is composed of four Hebrew letters, ה/ו/ה/י (*yôdh, heh, waw, heh*). YHWH in English cannot be pronounced because it has no vowels. On this technicality of the usage of vowels and their placement within the tetragrammaton, there is much controversy; however, the consensus of scholarship concludes that the most likely pronunciation is Yäh´-wêh.

CAUTION AND RESPECT

God's statement in Exodus 3 regarding his name, Yahweh, has a very noteworthy ring of finality: "This is my name for ever." The prophet Hosea reconfirms Moses' account of God's name: "Even Yahweh is Elohim of hosts; Yahweh is his memorial [*name*]" (Hosea 12:5). Isaiah corroborates this: "I am Yahweh, that is my name; and my glory I will not give to another" (Isaiah 42:8). Jeremiah adds his confirmation: "They will know that my name is Yahweh" (Jeremiah 16:21). Amos says, "Yahweh is his name" (Amos 5:8). Zechariah declares: "In that day there will be one Yahweh, and his name one" (Zechariah 14:9). Considering the explicitness of this evidence and the repeated use of the name by the Hebrew prophets and wise men, why would anyone wish to discontinue the use of the name of the Supreme Deity?

Over time, the Jewish people developed a sensitivity to possible misuse of the name *Yahweh*. Part of this was a result of their supreme respect for God. It was also borne out of their fear of violating the third commandment ("You shall not take the name of the Lord your God in vain."). Ultimately, Jewish people became very reluctant to use the name at all. By the time of Christ, it was used only once a year by the high priest on the day of atonement and then only in such hushed tones that it was virtually lost in the chanting of the priests. Fearing an unwitting violation of this commandment, early Jewish sages substituted the word *Adonai* (Lord) for the name *Yahweh* in their reading of the Scriptures.

Where the Tetragrammaton is used in the Hebrew text of Scripture, it is vowel-pointed thus יְהֹוָה, using the vowels of the word *Adonai* (Lord), so that it may be pronounced, "*Adonai*." The Talmud says, "It is written *yothe hay* [*Yahweh*] but it is pronounced *aleph daleth* [*Adonai*]." This time-honored tradition that shows ultimate respect for the personal name of God by not permitting its use was respected by Jesus himself in his use of "kingdom of heaven" instead of "kingdom of God" (substituting "heaven" as a euphemism for "God"), just as all Jews do, using "*Adonai*" for the Tetragrammaton, and as many do, using "*HaShem*" (The Name) instead of "God." Today, יְ is commonly used among the Jewish people to indicate the Ineffable Name as it is used in writings in Hebrew.

When the Hebrew Scriptures were translated into the Greek of the Septuagint, this emphasis was maintained so that Yahweh was translated *Kurios*, which means Lord. Subsequent translations of Holy Scripture have respected this same Jewish tradition of not pronouncing the name YHWH and offering instead a substitute rendering. It is primarily for this reason that we have the present-day representation in English translations, which is "LORD" in most cases. Unfortunately, a conscientious Jewish reason for not pronouncing and transliterating the name יְהֹוָה (Yahweh) has caused the understanding of God's personal name to be lost to the vast majority of the Christian community.

It is important, however, that Christians understand the fact that God does have a personal name. That name is YHWH. A close, yet inaccurate translation/transliteration of this personal name has appeared as *Jehovah*. This rendering repeats the mistake made by the late Renaissance Christian Hebraists when they saw *yôdh*, *heh*, *waw*, *heh* in the Masoretic Hebrew text with the *nekudot* (vowel pointing) of the Hebrew word <u>A</u>d<u>o</u>n<u>a</u>i (Lord) supplied (vowels emphasized). Since in German the letter "y" corresponds to "j" and "w" corresponds to "v," the transliteration became *Yehowah* or *Yehovah*, which came into English as *Jehovah*. Though Jehovah is etymologically incorrect, it is a cultural English (or other language) equivalent of *HaShem* that can (some would argue, should) be used by Christians to avoid pronunciation of the Tetragrammaton.

MEANING OF THE NAME

The Hebrew name *Yahweh* can be compared with the Hebrew word for being, *hayah*, to gain the full significance of its meaning. *Ehyeh* (first person singular of *hayah*) means "I am." Yahweh means, "I am because I am, I am that I am, or I cause myself to be." It is a formation of the causative (*hiphil*) conjugation of the verb and is intended to reveal the cause of existence. Yahweh's choice of this name to express his being then, was highly accurate, for he alone possesses the quality of aseity–he is the cause of his own existence. It is also an accurate expression of the fact that God alone is the cause of all existence. "Without him was nothing was made that was made" (John 1:3). The name *Yahweh* has also been translated, "I will be what I will be," which is a statement of God's immutability, a characteristic which he alone possesses. This name can also be translated, "I will be there," a statement of his eternal presence. When the Jewish people think of the ineffable name, it means to them, "He is," or "He was."

THE SON OF GOD AND HIS NAME

When the Son of God was brought into the world in the role of Savior, he maintained the name of divinity by which he had previously revealed himself to Moses and other patriarchs of Israel in his pre-incarnation Christophanies. The name which the angel Gabriel instructed Joseph and Mary to call him was ישוע (Yeshua), which simply means Yah in the role of Saviour. Jesus was the *Memra* (*Logos* in Greek), the Word of God who existed with the Father from eternity past and shared the name *Yahweh*. It was only fitting, then, that when he became man, he should maintain that name together with the expression of his role. Some have even suggested that the name *Yah* was more emphatic in the Saviour's name. The Emphatic Diaglott says, "For *Isoua* among the Hebrews is salvation, and among them the son of Nun is called *Joshua*; and *Iasoue* is the salvation of Jah."

The English word by which we refer to the Son of God is Jesus, which is a transliteration of the Latin *Iesus*, which comes from the Greek *Iesous*, which in turn is a direct transliteration of the Aramaic *Yeshu* (with a final sigma [s] added to indicate the nominative case), which transliterated the Hebrew *Yeshua* (with final ayin [ע] omitted).

Some have supposed that the word *Jesus* is a translation of Zeus, the king of the Greek gods. It is totally inconceivable that the scholars who translated the Hebrew into the Greek for the Septuagint Version would have used the name of a pagan deity in reference to their national hero, Joshua, who was called Yeshua in the Hebrew but was called *Iesous* in the Greek. This is the reason why Joshua is called Jesus in Acts 7:45 and in Hebrews 4:8 of the King James Authorized Version. We are certainly at liberty to use Jesus as the name of our Saviour as a proper transliteration of his Hebrew name, Yeshua.

The name *Yahweh* was understood by the early Christian scholars. Clement of Alexandria (212 A.D.) gave *Iaove* (a transliteration of Yahweh) as God's name. Origen (253 A.D.) gives *Iae* as God's name, a transliteration of Yah, the abbreviated form of Yahweh. Epiphanius (404 A.D.) and Theodoret (457 A.D.) give *Iabe*.

A BALANCED APPROACH TO USING THE NAME

One might well question the importance of learning the proper name of Deity. After all, in most versions of the Holy Scriptures, this name does not appear. The Authorized Version occasionally refers to God's name as Jah or Jehovah. Most often it names him as "the LORD." When one reads the Hebrew Scriptures, however, the continued and repetitive use of Yahweh in reference to Deity is unmistakable. This personal name *Yahweh* appears approximately 6,800 times in the Hebrew Bible. If the Heavenly Father was careful enough to give Israel his proper name, it would seem that we who honor and worship him should want to understand that name for ourselves.

On the other hand, it is certainly not so utterly distasteful for believers to refer to Yahweh by the various titles which rightly apply to his Being that he would cut them off for worshipping false gods, as some have mistakenly suggested. Using such titles and names to refer to Deity could not be construed as violation of the third commandment, for one would have to take or use the name *Yahweh* in vain, not use another name or title in sincere reference to the Eternal. Indeed, Jesus taught his disciples to pray, "Our Father," not, "Our Yahweh." While the names of Deity are important, it should be remembered that all names are merely words designed to reveal the qualities of the bearer. Though Yahweh and Yeshua are the proper names of Deity, it is appropriate to say, "The Eternal," or "The Savior."

Too often God's people lack balance. This has been the case with the name *Yahweh*. The Jews were so afraid of violating the third commandment by pronouncing the name that they avoided its use and may well have lost its original pronunciation. Some Christians have rediscovered and restored the use of the name and have taken the other extreme, believing that failure to use the name exclusively is a violation of the third commandment. We must remember that God speaks English, Chinese, and Spanish, as well as Hebrew and that we can use terms and names that communicate with one another and with the public our understanding of God.

We must use wisdom in conversing with unbelievers in the language with which they are familiar. By isolating ourselves totally to the use of biblical Hebrew surnames of God, we severely restrict the effectiveness of our witness. While understanding the name of God is important for information's sake, understanding the authority and meaning of the name is more essential to the believer today.

Christians must also be sensitive to the concerns of the Jewish people for respect and honor of the Ineffable Name. Attempting to pronounce the name or to transliterate it from Hebrew is particularly offensive to most Jews and is considered blasphemous by many. If Jesus respected the tradition of using substitute terms or euphemisms for the Tetragrammaton, surely Christians can mirror their Lord's respect for Jesus' people.

RESTORATION

Biblical names in Hebrew forms, transliterated into the world's languages, are a part of the restoration of Christianity's Jewish foundations. Believers should gain this knowledge and enrich their relationship with God by understanding his nature revealed in his proper name, Yahweh.

The need for restoring the knowledge of God's name by the believers today is readily discernible in the fact that those who are called his elect are referred to in Revelation 14:1 as "having his Father's name written in their foreheads." Surely those who will be called by his name should want to know his name. Moses did!

Understanding God's personal name is but another part of the great heritage of Judaism that is being restored in our day. It is a part of the better way of recognition and worship of the Eternal God. While Christians should honor the Jewish people's sensitivities concerning the use of the Ineffable Name, they should certainly come to understand what God's name is and what it means.

Biblical Ecumenism–
God's Challenge to
Today's Church

Chapter 19
BIBLICAL ECUMENISM:
GOD'S CHALLENGE TO TODAY'S CHURCH

The final prayer that Jesus made in behalf of the congregation (church) that he had established was this: "Sanctify them by your truth. Your word is truth. . . . I do not pray for these alone, but for those who will believe in me through their word; *that they all may be one,* as you, Father, are in me, and I in you; that they also may be one in us, *that the world may believe that you sent me*" (John 17:17, 20, 21). Unfortunately, our Lord's prayer has gone largely unanswered and unfulfilled. For the centuries that have ensued since Jesus prayed this prayer, the church has been the epitome of division and conflict rather than of unity and harmony.

From the earliest controversy that arose between the Hellenists and Hebraists in Acts 6, Christianity has been characterized by internecine strife and fratricidal carnage. Like Pogo in the comic strip, we have met the enemy, and he is us! The church has channeled more energy and resources into fighting against itself than it has in battling against the archenemy of everything that is of God, a very real and subtle Satan. Much of the division that has occurred has resulted from political intrigue, pitting brother against brother in a struggle over power, resources, and money. Often questions about dogma have drawn battle lines that have resulted in personal invective, excoriation, anathematizing, and excommunication. The landscape of history is littered with broken bodies and psyches, casualties of this ongoing, multifaceted "Christian" civil warfare.

How can a religion that is founded on love be so filled with hate? How is the church ever going to escape the treadmill of self-inflicted trauma and get on the road toward fulfilling Christ's prayer? Is the vision for Christian unity an "impossible dream," or can we discover the reasons for historical divisions, come to an understanding of the nature of biblical unity, and begin an earnest quest for facilitating that unity?

Unity in Christianity, however, represents a massive paradigm shift, for the church has been characterized more by schism than by efforts toward unity. First, there was the great proto-schism in the second and third centuries that ripped the church from its Jewish matrix and its relationship with Judaism and the Jewish people. Then there was the great schism in the eleventh century which separated Roman Catholicism from Eastern Orthodoxy. Other divisions were interspersed around these great schisms, and more followed. Corruption in the church forced the Reformation; however, the reformers often carried their rhetoric and zeal too far. Some made unfair and inaccurate caricatures of Catholic faith. They began to fight not only the Roman church but also one another. Rarely has a reformer had the spiritual maturity to employ Christ's advice in the last of the Beatitudes and "rejoice" when they were persecuted and defamed. Rather than seek rapprochement, they entrenched themselves behind ever-growing denominational walls, hurling epithets and personal invectives at their "enemies," all the while bringing violent division to the church and dishonor to the name of their Lord.

LOGOMACHY, THE BANE OF THE GREEKS

Cicero, the great Roman orator and statesman who lived just before the time of Christ, made the following observation about Greek society in his own day: "Mere logomachy is the poison of these pitiful Greeks, who thirst for contention rather than for truth." One could not ask for a more picturesque and apropos diagnosis of one of the major reasons for division in historical Christianity and in the church today. Fighting over words to no profit has been the church's sport and folly for virtually all of its existence.

Instead of a never-ending, unquenchable thirst for the truth of God's Word, Christians have sought to become more verbose, more adroit in their rhetoric, more advanced in polemics. Most ministers and laymen have been so entangled in denominationalism, so enslaved to organizations, that they would hardly lend an ear to the exposition of biblical truth. Instead of coming together to reason as the Lord admonished in Isaiah 1:18, most Christians are content rather to fortify the denominational barriers that so separate and alienate God's people. Instead of examining the Word of God in search of truth, theologians and church leaders read their Bibles in search of even the smallest scintilla of scriptural evidence to lend credence to their already preconceived notions and theories. Prooftexting has become a virtual bibliolatry in the church, with people worshipping the Bible of God more than the God of the Bible. Choosing to ignore texts that demand love for and submission to one another, they boast that they are "defenders of the faith." They align themselves on one side of controversial and often paradoxical issues, all the while ignoring or explaining away (to their own satisfaction) the evidence offered by others for their differing understanding.

Polemics has been the focus of much of Protestant Christianity as members of various denominational persuasions have characterized one another as less than Christian and often consigned one another to the pits of hell because they did not see eye to eye on matters of doctrine and polity. Then, trumpeting such texts as, "Can two walk together except they be agreed?" (Amos 3:3), to justify their divisive words and actions, they have reveled in driving inextricable wedges between believers, ever widening the chasm of division. Men of sterling debating skills but questionable character have been celebrated as champions of "doctrinal purity."

It is apparent that Paul foresaw the grave danger of logomachy upon the church. He admonished Timothy: "Remind them of these things, charging them before the Lord not to strive about words [logomachy] to no profit, to the ruin of the hearers. Be diligent to present yourself approved to God, a worker who does not need to be ashamed, rightly dividing the word of truth" (2 Timothy 2:14-15). Paul instructs the church not to engage in logomachy, connecting this practice with the "vain babblings" of Hymenaeus and Philetus, whose words ate like gangrene at the very fabric of the church (2 Timothy 2:17). A great lesson for the church today is contained in these words. Mere logomachy is unprofitable and even threatens the welfare of the Christian community with the voracious appetite of gangrene.

Paul also elaborates more expansively on the danger of logomachy in 1 Timothy 6:3-5: "If anyone teaches otherwise and does not consent to wholesome words, even the words of our Lord Jesus Christ, and to the doctrine which is according to godliness, he is proud, knowing nothing, but is obsessed with disputes and arguments over words [*logomachia*], from which come envy, strife, reviling, evil suspicions, useless wranglings of men of corrupt minds and destitute of the truth, who suppose that godliness is a means of gain. From such withdraw yourself." What a graphic and accurate description of the church throughout its history! Logomachy has produced untold envy, strife, character assassination, and perverse disputation, all of which have often come from men of corrupted minds who were destitute of truth. No wonder Paul enjoined Timothy to "withdraw" from such persons!

Logomachy was and is the deadly poison of the Gentiles that prevents the church from unifying itself into an irresistible force for Christ in the world. The church has been too much like the Athenians and strangers at the Areopagus who "spent their time in nothing else but either to tell or to hear some new thing" (Acts 17:21). Here is another poison to the church: theologians and leaders like nothing better than to initiate some new theory rather than to accept and practice the truth of God's never-changing Word. O that church leaders would imitate Paul, who declared in 1 Corinthians 2:4, "My speech and my preaching was not with persuasive words of human wisdom, but in demonstration of the Spirit and of power, that your faith should not be in the wisdom of men, but in the power of God." Paul was not confessing a vocabulary deficiency or some lack of erudition. He instead reminded the people that his preaching did not rely on the "persuasive power of words of human wisdom" (as the Greek is more accurately rendered). His confidence was in God's power! His religion was that which was fulfilled in "believing all things which are written in the law and in the prophets," the very essence of biblical Judaism (Acts 24:14).

When will the church stop drinking from the cup of this poison? When will leaders realize that even if they have the truth, it is not their job description to lead and guide people into truth? When will we stop usurping the role of the Holy Spirit to "reprove the world of sin" and to " lead and guide into all truth" (John 16:8, 13)? When will we cease fighting over words and making a brother an offender for a word (Isaiah 29:21)? When will we realize that "only by pride comes contention" (Proverbs 13:10), take a deep look into our individual and corporate souls to see the pride and its horrible effect, and rid ourselves of this debilitating malady? O that Christian leaders today were at least as wise as the pagan Cicero!

THE CENTRAL/PERIPHERAL THEOLOGY QUESTION

Most Christians have always had a difficult time discerning the difference between what is central to their faith and what is merely peripheral. Their not being able to separate that which is of consequence from that which is less significant has left far too many Christians like those hypocrites among the Pharisees of old whom Jesus derided for straining at gnats and swallowing camels (Matthew 23:24). Inability to discern what is important has contributed greatly to the divisions in Christianity.

In Christian faith, there are certain fundamental beliefs which are essential to the faith without which it cannot stand. These are the theological non-negotiables which are considered central theology. In order to be firmly established in the faith, it is important for believers to have a solid understanding of these teachings and that they be elevated above all other beliefs to an area of primary importance.

Some of the central theological concepts of Christianity include belief in one God, Creator of heaven and earth; in the doctrine of the fall of man, the inherent sinfulness of mankind, and in the need for a Savior; in Jesus Christ as the only begotten Son of God, who for the salvation and reconciliation of the human race to God came from heaven and became incarnate by the Holy Spirit in the womb of the virgin Mary; in both the absolute deity and the absolute humanity of Jesus; in the vicarious atonement in which Jesus lived a sinless life, was crucified for the sins of the human race, was resurrected, and ascended to heaven to intercede for mankind with the heavenly Father; in the indwelling of the Holy Spirit in the hearts of believers who receive Christ through faith; in the coming resurrection of the dead; and in the coming of Jesus to judge the living and the dead in his everlasting kingdom;. These are the areas of theology which are central to our faith. Of course, there are other doctrines about God and the Lord Jesus Christ that are important and should be understood by believers; however, the simple statements above form a focal point with which we can have clear vision in our Christian walk.

Other scriptural teachings fall into the area of peripheral theology. The further they are removed from conveying direct knowledge about God and Christ, the further they go into the periphery and the less clear they become. While it is possible for a person to have above 180 degrees of natural peripheral vision, it is also a fact that the further objects are removed from the central focal point of the eyes, the less clear they are. Such is true with peripheral theology.

As long as we Christians keep the central and the peripheral in proper perspective, it is possible for us to have the confidence that comes from being able to view both; however, we will always find ourselves in trouble when we attempt to focus on the peripheral. As with natural vision, in order for us to focus on something in the periphery, it is necessary for us to remove our eyes from the central. And, when we remove the focus of our attention from the Lord Jesus Christ, like Peter of old, we find ourselves sinking in the maelstrom of uncertainty.

This distinction between central and peripheral is true of much speculation about yet unfulfilled prophecy. One clear rule for interpreting prophecy is this: "No prophecy of the Scripture can be fully understood until *after* it has been fulfilled." Much of the confusion that exists in Christianity over eschatology would have less effect upon Christian fellowship and unity if everyone could use Paul's wisdom: "Now we see through a darkened mirror . . . but then face to face" (1 Corinthians 13:12, author's translation). If everyone would admit that his own understanding of future prophecy is not perfect and that it is often a matter of subjective, rather than objective thinking, we would be more tolerant of one another in this area of teaching.

It has often been said that Christians do not disagree so much on what the Bible says as they do on what it does not say. This true statement applies to the central/peripheral theology question where many of the controversies and conflicts that divide Christianity are founded in various interpretations of matters on which the Scriptures are not definitive. To

manifest dogmatic tenacity in clinging to concepts which are not defini-
tively set forth in the Scriptures and to force those concepts on others as a
test of fellowship is to exert an aura of divine authority that goes beyond
scriptural commissions. It is to arrogate to oneself the position of the voice
of God in the earth, the sole repository of his truth. And, it certainly leaves
one dangerously open to the deception of heresy.

THE SERVANT LEADERSHIP MODEL

One of the reasons for division in the church is the fact that its leaders
too often have ignored our Lord's admonition, "You know that the rulers of
the Gentiles lord it over them . . . Yet it shall not be so among you . . . whoever
desires to be first among you, let him be your slave" (Matthew 20:25-27).
Jesus never intended that a professional clergy elevate itself above the rest of
the church to form an elite ruling class. The system in which he, himself, had
been reared and in which the apostles had functioned was synagogal Judaism,
an egalitarian exercise which featured the interaction of a multitude of counse-
lors, the model in which the safe exercise of leadership can be found (Proverbs
11:14). Plurality of eldership and collective decision making were the norm in
the earliest church (Acts 6:3; 15:6; Galatians 2:9).

When church leaders in succeeding generations neglected the servant
leadership paradigm which Jesus demonstrated, they began to model their
leadership styles after the autocratic political and/or business systems of
their societies. Leaders became increasingly turf-protective, seeking to pre-
serve and extend the aegis of their dominion. Sects within the church became more and more elitist and parochial. Increasingly, the church became
a *quasi*-political organism, and leaders competed for political and economic
power. Monarchial bishops assumed control over the church in geographic
areas. Finally, the bishop of Rome sought to establish his primacy over the
entire church, an effort that culminated in the establishment of the papacy,
producing subsequent abuses of power and precipitating the East-West
schism. Christianity became Christendom.

When the Reformation came, leaders adopted the models of govern-
ment common to their societies. Nationalism produced state churches and
an ever-increasing sectarianism, as movements crystallized into entrenched
bureaucracies. Unfortunately, these denominations escalated the infight-
ing and strife within Christianity. Still others arose seeking reform from
newly entrenched structures; however, their efforts produced other crystallized movements, fostering still more divisions in the universal church.

When men seek for dominion within self-serving bureaucracies rather
than sacrificing their egos to submit themselves one to another in a humble

search for truth, they have allowed demonic strongholds to be erected in their lives that bind them in pride, conceit, and arrogance and produce abusive behavior that wounds and weakens the members of the body of Christ. When the church departs from the servant-leadership principle espoused and employed by Jesus and the apostles, it treads dangerous ground.

It should be noted that Jesus ascribed abusive exercises of power as being typical of Gentiles, implying that such conduct was not the norm in Hebrew society in which the disciples had been reared. This was especially true in the religious life of the Israeli people. Though the priesthood and the temple order remained important, the daily religious practices of the people had centered in their synagogues since the time of the Babylonian captivity. Synagogal Judaism was the first grand experiment in the democratization of religion. It was this model, rather than the Gentile examples, that the apostles were to employ in their exercise of leadership over the reformed congregation of Jesus.

Here is the biblical description of servant leadership: ". . . a servant of the Lord must not quarrel but be gentle to all, able to teach, patient, in humility correcting those who are in opposition, if God perhaps will grant them repentance, so that they may know the truth" (2 Timothy 2:24, 25). Whoever is the chiefest in the churches, let him employ this kind of conduct in providing oversight for God's people.

Surely the church can now return to that model that was manifest in its earliest years. When leaders learn to serve rather than "lord it over" God's heritage, they will be able to avoid the attitudes that have promoted division. When they are submitted to one another in love, they can promote the unity that the church so desperately needs.

CONSERVATIVE IN DOCTRINE, LIBERAL IN PRACTICE

It is very possible to maintain complete loyalty to one's doctrinal persuasions while at the same time making allowances that others may well understand those issues differently and, therefore, have practices that differ from one's own. Traditionally, most Christian denominations have considered such a flexible position to be "compromise" and have excoriated as unprincipled those who would be so exercised.

This principle, however, is one of the keys to promoting Christian unity. We must have the wisdom to understand that we are not infallible in our understanding and that we must have tolerance for others. It is important that we respect one another's otherness. We cannot continue to consider other Christians who do not share our doctrinal positions to be less than Christian or even second-class Christians. We must gain a healthy appreciation for diversity within the body of Christ, understanding that there are different callings and giftings as well as different concepts. We need not compromise our own beliefs in order to maintain a diplomatic, magnanimous attitude and demeanor. We can, indeed, be staunchly conservative in our doctrine while at the same time being liberal in practice. In this way we are able to fulfill the means by which we can walk humbly with God: doing justice and loving mercy (Micah 6:8).

In seeking to reclaim our biblical Hebrew heritage, we must be careful that we do not establish a new elitism that brings judgment and condemnation upon those who do not understand these concepts. If we are to adopt a truly Judaic mind-set, we will maintain tolerance for others, and we will shun the development of yet another creed that establishes another orthodoxy and further divides the body of Christ. Such tolerance is truly Judaic and represents the mind of Christ as well.

FLEXIBILITY–A CURE FOR EXCLUSIVITY AND ISOLATIONISM

Much of the spirit of exclusivity and isolationism in Christian denominations is the product of the intransigence of bureaucrats in crystallized organizations whose *status quo* was threatened by the insight of reformers, causing them to respond with excommunication and persecution. It is unfortunate, however, that the manner in which many of the reformers responded to persecution from traditionalists has proven nearly as damaging to Christianity as their restored truth has proven beneficial.

Persecution, whether verbal or physical, causes people to make clear distinctions between allies and enemies. Those who are friendly become strong allies; those who are unfriendly or even apathetic become enemies. And, the battle lines are drawn. If reformers are not balanced in their understanding of a new concept, persecution is likely to force them beyond their original progressive idea into egotism, egocentricity, or even megalomania. These personality traits of leadership, then, are translated into masses of people as exclusivity and even a kind of xenophobia.

The only way to avoid these consequences in religious reformations is for reformers to have an unusual degree of love and Christian maturity. Indeed, one's level of maturity can be measured by the manner in which he handles criticism and persecution. Unfortunately, too many reformers have not had the ability to "rejoice" when persecuted and slandered (Matthew 5:11, 12).

When a movement becomes too rigid and crystallized in its exclusive thinking, it is probable that it will elevate secondary ideas to the level of primary truths, trying to bring the periphery into focus with the central. When this happens, a sect or even a cult develops, and fanciful scriptural interpretations or fleshy ideas gain prominence. Christians become even more divided, fighting against one another in implacable anger.

The secret to avoiding such intransigence and crystallization is to maintain flexibility. Intransigence must give way to flexibility. Crystallization must be melted down by love for God and for men into viscosity and malleability. And flexibility is achieved only by repeatedly being stretched, almost to the breaking point. This is true in terms of the human body, and it is true also in the body of Christ. Believers must stretch themselves beyond their traditional ideas and comfort zones to be inclusive and accommodating to others who have different views and priorities. When we learn this lesson of flexibility, we will find the church moving toward true unity.

WISDOM JUSTIFIED OF ALL HER CHILDREN

The approaches to ministry that Jesus and John the Baptist took could not have been more different. The one thing that they had in common was the fact that both of their ministries brought forth fruit unto righteousness in people's lives. Jesus expressed a profound truth when he noted that John "came neither eating bread nor drinking wine," and Israel's religious leaders said that he had "a demon." Jesus, on the other hand, came "eating and drinking," and the same leaders said that he was a "glutton and a winebibber, a friend of tax collectors and sinners!" Then, he offered this great word of wisdom: "But wisdom is justified of all her children" (Luke 7:33-35). It is demonstrably true that men can take different approaches to ministry, with different emphases and different focuses and at the same time both be right. The determining factor is the results that their ministries produce. This is not to say that the end justifies the means and is certainly not an endorsement of consequentialism. It is to say that wisdom is manifest in producing righteousness and holiness in the lives of people.

Paul continued to emphasize this need for pluriformity and tolerance in the church with his argument in Romans 14 that those who preferred a vegetarian diet should be considered equally by those who did not and those who do not observe one day above another should be considered on equal footing with those who chose to memorialize special days. Paul's words of wisdom are, "Let each be fully convinced in his own mind" (Romans 14:5). It has been said that a man convinced against his will is of the same opinion still. We must allow every man to stand before God for himself and to give emphasis to those things of which he is personally convicted by the Holy Spirit. God's requirements upon believers are not entirely uniform. Often he may require something of one individual in order to deal with a weakness in his life that he may not demand of another person because he does not have that same weakness. We must learn the wisdom of allowing the Holy Spirit to impart his gifts and graces, to lead into truth, and to bring conviction as he wills. Then, we can gain the benefit and strength that comes from accepting one another, not on the basis of what we believe but on the basis of whom we believe–the living Christ.

UNITY IN DIVERSITY

In order to come to unity, we must understand what it is. Historically, the church has thought of unity as uniformity, and it has sought to force a uniform approach to doctrine and polity through credalism. Denominations have insisted that all their constituents believe and practice the same things. Men have been excommunicated for daring to adapt church worship and polity to follow the leading of the Holy Spirit and minister to God's people. The safe feeling of uniformity has demanded that everyone look and act alike.

True biblical unity, however, is not uniformity. It is as impossible for the body of Christ to be completely uniform as it is impossible for the entire human body to be an eye. There are many different functions within the body, and each is vital to health and well being. So it is in the church. There are diversities of callings, of giftings, of administrations, but each is important to the community of believers.

Unity is cohesiveness in the midst of diversity. Just as the diverse organs and functions of the human body are joined together cohesively by the blood that flows to every part, so the church in all of its diversity is united through the blood of Jesus that both gives life and removes impurities from the body. Each part of the body must appreciate the otherness of the other parts, for it is through the diversity within the body that all of its functions are fulfilled and the body remains healthy.

Those who understand biblical principles of unity in diversity never hold to the possibility of the emergence of one monolithic organization that will eventually bring all Christians under its aegis. The Roman Catholic Church has tried that, declaring, *"Extra ecclesiam nulla salus"* ("outside the [Roman] church there is no salvation"), and scores of other denominations have made the same proclamation; however, it has simply not worked even when promoted on the edge of the sword. Just as Judaism has always been and still remains organized into a myriad of locally autonomous bodies, so Christianity must maintain and respect the integrity of its various groupings.

CHRISTIANITY'S JEWISH ROOTS AND ECUMENISM

One of the factors that has contributed most to the division in the church is its denial of its Hebraic heritage, its severing itself from the Jewish roots of faith from which it grew. The unconscious result of this separation has been the ongoing tendency of the church to read into its self-evaluation the various traditions of the cultures into which it expanded. Since it was taken from the biblically Judaic matrix and transplanted into foreign soil, the church has been defined by virtually every culture possible. Leaders have even read their own cultural and religious ideas into Holy Scripture rather than exegeting Scripture in the light of the Hebrew language and the Jewish culture in which it was written. Is it any wonder then, that there are so many divisions in the church? The real wonder is that there are not many more divisions!

Greater unity in the body of Christ will be achieved only when the church rediscovers its biblical Judaic identity. Having been torn from its mother's arms at a tender age, it suffers from an identity crisis and consequent immaturity. It is essential to the health of the church that it restore its Jewish connection, recovering its Hebraic foundations. When believers of various denominations around the world recognize the truth about the Jewish roots of their faith, they discover that they have far more in common than they ever thought possible. Controversial doctrinal issues are often resolved by a simple understanding of the historical and biblical matrix from which those issues emerged. When we get back to the Book and to the mind-set of the people who wrote the Book, we will find answers to most of the issues that have so long divided us.

While schism has been the norm for Christianity, it has been largely missing from Judaism. Variety, rather than schism, has been the spice of Jewish religious life throughout the Christian era (with the lone exception of the Karaites). Though Jews have always been divided into various overlapping groups (e.g., ancient Pharisees, Essenes, and Sadducees and the modern Orthodox, Conservative, and Reform), they have never lacked a sense of interrelationship and interdependence. They have always recognized one another as fully Jewish. This is a great lesson that Christians can learn from Judaism. Despite our different approaches to the worship of the one God, can we not view one another as fully Christian, brothers and sisters in the family of God?

A NEW UNITY OF THE SPIRIT

As we continue the quest for Christian unity, we must understand that the unity which we seek is not produced by a spirit of unity but by the unity of the Spirit. It is the unity of which the Holy Spirit is the agent and facilitator. This is the clear first step toward ultimate unity in the body of Christ which Paul outlined in Ephesians 4:1, 3: ". . . walk worthy of the calling with which you were called . . . endeavoring to keep the unity of the Spirit in the bond of peace." One of the historical problems in ecumenical efforts of the past has been that they have been motivated largely by a spirit of unity. But, labor unions have a spirit of unity, as do sports teams and political parties. A spirit of unity will never bring unity to the body of Christ. The only thing that can unify Christ's body is the Holy Spirit of God. It is only through the agency of the Holy Spirit that God's love is "shed abroad in our hearts" (Romans 5:5) drawing us together in fellowship and mutual submission. Christian unity is cohesiveness generated by the agency of the Holy Spirit.

As we yield ourselves to the agency of the Holy Spirit, we present the possibility that we can destroy barriers of fear, indifference, and hostility that have kept us from encountering one another with full knowledge of and concern for one another. Perhaps one of the most important factors in this new move of the Holy Spirit that will bring true unity in cohesive interaction among diverse elements in the body of Christ will be the recovery of the Jewish roots of our faith. Indeed, one of the primary job descriptions of the Holy Spirit is to "lead and guide into truth." As we come together to rediscover this ancient truth of the inherent Jewishness of Christian faith, we will find ourselves flowing together into cohesive relationships forged by the unity of the Spirit, true biblical ecumenism. We become networked for translocal fellowship without the constraints of a new denominational rigidity. We are made an organic one by the Holy Spirit, not by a contrived, manipulated, and forced human mechanism. Our unity then compares with that of Jesus and the Heavenly Father, a sublime cohesiveness that is manifest in our compliance with the will and Word of God.

Lion or Lamb? The Messianic Question

Chapter 20
LION OR LAMB?
THE MESSIANIC QUESTION

At the time of the birth of Jesus, the spirit of Messianism was everywhere in Israel. The Hebrew prophet Daniel's predicted time lapse between the reconstruction of the temple and the coming of Messiah neared completion. During that pivotal time in human history, some sixty men arose in Israel or thereabouts, claiming to be the promised Messiah.

From the fall of man the expected appearance of the promised Deliverer had sprung up in the hearts of each succeeding generation. This was especially true of the Israelites after Jacob declared of Judah, "The scepter shall not depart from Judah, nor a lawgiver from between his feet, until Shiloh comes; and to him shall be the obedience of the people" (Genesis 49:10). Balaam, the prophet for hire who was commissioned to curse Israel, saw the Messiah instead: "I shall see him, but not now . . . a Star shall come out of Jacob; a Scepter shall rise out of Israel . . . out of Jacob One shall have dominion" (Numbers 24:17, 19). Even the great Moses, the founder of biblical Judaism, predicted in Deuteronomy 18:15 that God would raise up a "prophet like me from your midst" and that "him you shall hear."

As time passed, the expectation of the Jewish people increased, reinforced by the ever-unfolding prophetic identity of this promised Messiah. Both the promise and the lineage were more firmly established in God's oath to David, "I will set upon your throne the fruit of your body" (Psalm 132:11). Centuries later, another Hebrew prophet pinpointed the place where the Messiah was to be born: "But you, Bethlehem Ephrathah, though you are little among the thousands of Judah, yet out of you shall come forth to me the One to be Ruler in Israel. . . ." (Micah 5:2). Knowing that the Messiah was to come out of Judah, the Jews expected him to be like Judah of old, of whom Jacob said, "Judah is a lion's whelp . . . He bows down, he lies down as a lion" (Genesis 49:9). They looked forward to his coming to deliver them from the scourge of Roman occupation. They expected Messiah to devour all the enemies of Israel.

THE SUFFERING MESSIAH BRINGS SPIRITUAL LIBERTY

Unfortunately, however, most Jews neglected to observe all that God had said about this coming Messiah. They overlooked Daniel's prediction: "And after sixty-two weeks, an anointed one shall be cut off " (Daniel

9:26). Though some of Israel's sages came to expect the coming of two Messiahs, Messiah son of David (the king) and Messiah son of Joseph (the suffering servant), most Jews hoped for the coming of the Lion of Judah. In their longing for deliverance from physical oppression, they neglected to anticipate the coming deliverance that Messiah would bring that would be of far greater consequence than mere physical and political freedom. The great work that Messiah was first to accomplish was the deliverance of his people–and, indeed, of the whole world–from the bondage of sin.

How was this to be accomplished? Messiah was to be cut off, not for himself, but for the sins of man. This was the message of the prophet Isaiah: "But he was wounded for our transgressions, he was bruised for our iniquities; the chastisement for our peace was upon him, and by his stripes we are healed. . . . He was led as a lamb to the slaughter, and as a sheep before its shearers is silent, so he opened not his mouth" (Isaiah 53:5,7).

It was fitting, then, that the Lamb of God that was slain to liberate men from the bondage of sin should have been offered on the day of Passover, just as the lamb had been slain some fifteen hundred years before on the very first Passover to bring about the liberation of the children of Israel from Egyptian bondage. Liberation from sin required the shedding of blood (Leviticus 17:11). Just as men's paschal lambs had provided the blood of redemption for Israel of old, so God's Passover Lamb shed his blood and redeemed the entire world from the power of sin and death. Again, the Hebrew prophets made the issue clear. According to David, the Messiah's hands and feet would be pierced (Psalm 22:16). Zechariah predicted that the Messiah's Jewish brethren would share responsibility for this sacrifice (Zechariah 12:10; 13:6).

Before the Messiah could liberate Israel physically, he had to liberate them spiritually. What value would physical liberation have if one were in bondage to sin? This is why Messiah came first as a lamb–indeed, the Lamb slain from the foundation of the world.

THE RESURRECTION PREDICTED

But, would the death of the Messiah as a sacrificed Lamb be the end of this profound personality? Again, the prophets of Israel predicted the truth: "When you make his soul an offering for sin, he shall see his seed, *he shall prolong his days. . . .*" (Isaiah 53:10); and "For you will not leave my soul in Sheol, nor will you allow your Holy One to see corruption. You will show me the path of life. . . ." (Psalm 16:10,11).

This is exactly what occurred when the Messiah was offered as a sacrifice for sin. History documents the fact that Jesus of Nazareth was resurrected from the grave and that he ascended into heaven, events witnessed by over five hundred people. Just as David had predicted in Psalm 2:7, God said of him, "You are my Son. Today have I begotten you," a fact confirmed by Peter in Acts 2:34, 35. And, as David had further prophesied in Psalm 110:1, "The Lord said to my Lord, 'Sit at my right hand, till I make your enemies your footstool.' " Jesus now sits enthroned at the right hand of the Father in heaven awaiting the time when he will return "to execute vengeance" upon the ungodly (Jude 15), to dash the nations in pieces (Revelation 2:27), and to establish the Messianic Kingdom of righteousness upon the earth.

Many of the leaders of Judaism have interpreted these passages differently, applying them to all of Israel. They have asserted that Christians have no right to use the Hebrew Scriptures to reveal Jesus as the Jewish Messiah. These "Christian" interpretations, however, were all made by Jews, both Jesus and the apostles, at a time when there was no monolithic Judaism whose interpretation was considered authoritative for all Israel. Christians of all nationalities have based their faith on Jewish interpretations of the Hebrew Scriptures that established the faith of the earliest Jewish church in Jesus as Messiah and Lord.

COMING AS THE LION OF JUDAH

The coming of the Messiah as the Lion of Judah will be that to which Zechariah 14:2-4, 11 refers: "For I will gather all nations to battle against Jerusalem; the city shall be taken . . . Then the Lord will go forth and fight against those nations, as he fights in the day of battle. And in that day his feet will stand on the mount of Olives, which faces Jerusalem on the east . . . The people shall dwell in it; and no longer shall there be utter destruction, but Jerusalem shall be safely inhabited."

When Messiah Yeshua (Jesus) came the first time, John the Baptist declared, "Behold the Lamb of God who takes away the sins of the world" (John 1:29). When he comes the second time, he will appear as John the Revelator described him, "the lion of the tribe of Judah, the Root of David" (Revelation 5:5).

The enigma of a personality that could be manifest first as a lamb and then as a lion has baffled thousands of people, including a majority of the Jewish people; however, the Hebrew prophets predicted that such would be the case, and the Jewish Messiah of the first century manifestly fulfilled their predictions. This is the scandal of the good news of God's salvation: he who was to be king of the world became a servant. He who was sinless took upon himself the sins of us all, for which he suffered and died. But, again in consonance with the Hebrew prophets, he resurrected to ascend to the Father as the Lamb worthy to open the book (Revelation 5:8, 9). And, even when he comes to sit in his kingdom as the Lion of Judah, he will still be the Lamb of God who takes away the sins of the world (Revelation 22:1). Messiah is not, then, either lion or lamb, nor are there two Messiahs. He is one Messiah, both God's king and sacrifice, lion and lamb.

Israel's
Divine
Appointment

ISRAEL'S
DIVINE APPOINTMENT

"And so all Israel will be saved, as it is written: 'The Deliverer will come out of Zion, and he will turn away ungodliness from Jacob" (Romans 11:26). The promise of this passage of Holy Scripture goes beyond the salvation of individual Jews and beyond the grafting in of the Jewish branches into their own olive tree. It predicts the salvation of the entire nation of Israel.

This is in keeping with the prophecies of Zechariah, chapters 12 through 14. The prophet declared that in the last days God would make Jerusalem a cup of trembling and a burdensome stone for all people (Zechariah 12:2, 3). From the time that the atrocities of Nazi anti-Semitism burdened the consciences of the nations of the free world to the extent that they permitted the formation of the State of Israel, this tiny Middle Eastern nation has been spotlighted in world news. With the grip of the oil-rich Arab nations on the economies of the industrialized nations of the world, Israel has indeed been a burdensome stone and a cup of trembling.

The situation will continue until the time when a great political and economic upheaval will overwhelm the earth in the years immediately prior to the return of Jesus Christ. Then the nations of the world will come under the leadership of a charismatic dictator (the other horn of Daniel 7:20), and they together will seek to destroy Jerusalem, the Jews, and true Christians, trying to obliterate the nation of Israel, Judaism, and Christianity from the face of the earth.

In this time of tragedy, however, there is hope for Israel. God told Zechariah, "*In that day* . . . I will pour on the house of David and the inhabitants of Jerusalem the spirit of grace and supplication. They will look upon me, the one they have pierced, and they will mourn for him as one mourns for an only child, and grieve bitterly for him as one grieves for a firstborn son" (Zechariah 12:9,10). God further explained that this supplication would be heard: "In that day a fountain shall be opened for the house of David and for the inhabitants of Jerusalem, for sin and for uncleanness . . . and one will say to him, 'What are these wounds between your arms?' Then he will answer, Those with which I was wounded in the house of my friends" (Zechariah 13:1, 6).

The fulfillment of this passage of Jewish prophecy is rather obvious. Israel as a nation is destined to return to their God, whose heart many have pierced by their infidelity to his Word and will. The nation of Israel will recognize the Messiah whom they have long awaited to be he whose hands were pierced in the house of his friends (Psalm 22:16; Zechariah 13:6). As that takes place, they will find that the fountain that cleans away sin that was opened by a Roman spear two thousands years ago will again be opened to the whole house of Israel (Zechariah 13:1).

IRREVOCABLE ELECTION

The Scriptures clearly show us that God's covenant with Abraham and his children is a unilateral covenant contingent only upon God's grace. The expansion of that covenant to become the national constitution for Israel is also a unilateral covenant, and since it is a divine covenant, it is especially irrevocable. Paul confirms this truth in Romans 11:26, 27, 29: "The Deliver will come out of Zion, and he will turn away ungodliness from Jacob; for this is my covenant with them, when I take away their sins' . . . for the gifts and the calling of God are irrevocable."

The preservation of the Jewish people is a matter of supreme importance, for it is proof of God's immutability. "I am Yahweh, I do not change: therefore you are not consumed, O sons of Jacob" (Malachi 3:6). The continuation of the Jewish people as an identifiable entity despite centuries of unrelenting persecution and slaughter defies all the laws of history for the assimilation of conquered peoples. God, and God alone, has ensured their survival and their continued identity as his chosen people. He even devised the means by which they would be preserved. His law (Torah) has been and will continue to be a guardian assigned to supervise and protect the Jewish people until they are brought by that law to their divine appointment with their Messiah (Galatians 3:24). The law of God will remain in place until it has fulfilled this, its primary function. No amount of infidelity on Israel's part has obviated God's faithfulness and his continued grace toward his people or ever will do so.

Christians should remember that it was also an act of God's grace that brought partial blindness to Israel (Romans 11:25) so that the Gentiles could be saved. It was the same God who hardened Pharaoh's heart who also partially hardened Israel (Isaiah 6:10). Likewise, it is God who will use the Gentiles as instruments in his hand to bring about Israel's provocation (Deuteronomy 32:21; Romans 11:11), and it is God who will remove the veil that is upon Israel's eyes–and upon the whole world, for that matter (Isaiah 25:7)–when Israel turns to the Lord (2 Corinthians 3:16). Israel will never be provoked to anything but anger and disdain by a Christian church that seeks to "convert" Jews to a Christianity that voids the commandments of

God and replaces the Judaic concepts and practices of biblical faith with pagan traditions.

Christians should also remember that only God can draw his chosen people Israel to himself. And, only the Holy Spirit can open eyes of understanding. There is no room in the church for proselytization through unethical and deceptive tactics. All Christians are called to witness to the entire world; however, that witness must be exercised in this manner: "Sanctify the Lord God in your hearts, and always be ready to give a defense to everyone who asks you a reason for the hope that is in you, *with meekness and fear*" (1 Peter 3:15). Too many Christians have approached Israel with a militant spirit and a trophy mentality, trying to "convert" the Jews for their own glory. Or, they have "loved" the Jews because of some eschatological scenario that required them to love Israel in order to have their own expectations fulfilled. The job of the church today is to replace the arrogance and belligerence of the Christian past with genuine love and unconditional support for the international Jewish community and the nation of Israel, to share their faith in honesty and integrity, and to leave the future in the hands of the God who is able to bring his will to pass. Only God can save, and we have his word on it: he will save Israel. It is based on his immutability, it is his irrevocable election, and it is inevitable!

The church must resolve to support in word and in deed the right of all Jewish peoples to exist as Jews with complete self-determination, free from political, economic, social, or religious coercion, intimidation, or persecution. Christians also must profess determination to stand with the international Jewish community against any individual or corporate threat.

A TIME OF TROUBLE

Throughout history, the Jewish people have fallen victim to the blind hatred of the world's anti-Semitic political powers. Surely Zechariah's prophecy has been fulfilled in crusades, pogroms, and the Holocaust: "And it shall come to pass in all the land, says the Lord, that two-thirds in it shall be cut off and die, but one-third shall be left in it" (Zechariah 13:8). This prophecy will be culminated in the coming time of world trouble that Jesus called the "great tribulation" (Matthew 24:21, 22) which God, himself, will truncate so that the entire human race will not be destroyed. This may well be the culmination of Jacob's trouble predicted by Jeremiah the prophet, "Alas! For that day is great, so that none is like it; and it is the time of Jacob's trouble, but he shall be saved out of it" (Jeremiah 30:7). The key to Zechariah, however, is not the persecution and slaughter of the Jewish people, but that "one-third shall be left therein" to be refined as gold so that they will say, "The Lord is my God," and God will say, "It is my people." And, the key to Jeremiah's "time of Jacob's trouble" (regardless as to when that time may be or may have been) is that Israel "shall be saved out of it." Frankly, Israel has already had enough persecution and slaughter at the hands of the Gentiles to have fulfilled all these prophecies many times over. Now it is time to look for their return to their God, saying, "The Lord is my God," and for their salvation out of the trouble that the prophets predicted.

The time of great trouble upon all the world will be concluded when all nations will be brought against Jerusalem for battle, whereupon the Lord, himself, will "go forth and fight against those nations . . . in that day his feet shall stand upon the mount of Olives . . . and the Lord will be king over all the earth" (Zechariah 14:3, 4, 9). In that day Israel will be saved and will sit down with Abraham, Isaac, Jacob, and David in the kingdom of their Messiah.

"ALL ISRAEL SHALL BE SAVED"

This salvation of national Israel is the great spiritual event with which the New Testament writers concerned themselves. Paul referred to this prophetic work in Romans 9:27,29: "Isaiah also cries out concerning Israel: 'Though the number of the children of Israel be as the sand of the sea, a *remnant will be saved* . . . And as Isaiah said before, 'Unless the Lord of Sabaoth had left us a seed, we would have become as Sodom, and we would have been made like unto Gomorra.'"

The Greek word for remnant in this passage of scripture means "those who are left alive." This is the remnant of Romans 11:5: "Even so then, at this present time there is a remnant according to the election of grace." Both the prophets and the apostles of Israel predicted the time when a remnant of Israel according to the God's choosing would remain alive upon the earth. And, they declared that those Jewish people would unanimously acclaim their Messiah.

From all indications of the Scriptures, Paul's prediction in Romans 11:26, "All Israel shall be saved," will happen literally when the entire nation of Israel will turn collectively to God. He then will save them all with an everlasting salvation and will punish all the nations and people who have been their tormenters.

Don't Let
Anti-Semitism
Ruin Your Health

Chapter 22
DON'T LET ANTI-SEMITISM RUIN YOUR HEALTH

From the time that God chose the nation of Israel above all peoples of the earth and revealed to them his chosen system of worship, the forces of evil have concentrated themselves in the spirit of anti-Semitism, the hatred for and aversion to Jews and things Jewish. The root of anti-Semitism is antipathy toward Yahweh, the God of the Bible. The satanic element in the world is positioned against God and against whatever he is doing on planet earth; therefore, the primary target for Satan and his minions has been the one major visible symbol of God and his sovereign election, the Jewish people.

The spirit of anti-Semitism first manifested itself in the heathen peoples of the Middle East who resented the establishment of the nation of Israel in their midst. Israel constantly defended itself against its neighbors whose love for their gods necessitated their hatred of the God of Israel. These inhabitants of the land could simply not submit themselves to God's choosing and his awarding the land of Israel to the progeny of Abraham. They hated the Jews and tried repeatedly to destroy them.

Israel's strategic location at the confluence of what was then the earth's three known continents, the land bridge between Europe, Asia, and Africa, made it a natural target for conquest-minded sovereigns of many nations. Land, however, was not the only motivation, for each of these competing empires had its own pantheon of gods and philosophies that were set forth in contradistinction to Yahweh and the Hebraic world view.

Anti-Semitism, then, was a primary motivation for Babylon, Assyria, Egypt, and other Middle Eastern empires. Their religions exalted the sun god and sought the destruction of Jerusalem and the Jews' religion. A succession of these kingdoms conquered and enslaved the Jewish people, but they could not destroy Judaism. Babylon, the bastion and source of polytheism, conquered Jerusalem and carried most of the people to Babylon. Again, Babylonian anti-Semitism could not destroy Judaism. While in Babylon, the Jewish people began what would eventually be one of the preserving elements for Judaism, the synagogue, small corporate worshipping communities that perpetuated the knowledge and worship of God. The effort to destroy Judaism failed, and the Jews were returned to their land by Cyrus the Mede, who helped them rebuild the temple and restore the worship of Yahweh.

In the kingdom of Persia the ugly head of anti-Semitism was reared and personified in Haman, the prime minister of King Ahasuerus. Only the valiant, self-sacrificing stand of a young Jewish girl saved the Jewish people. With all of the Jews of the world living in the kingdom of Persia, Haman's proposed slaughter of "all the Jews that were throughout the whole kingdom of Ahasuerus" (Esther 3:6) would have resulted in genocide, obviating of God's covenants with Abraham and Israel; therefore, God raised up Esther "for such a time as this."

Later anti-Semitism was focused in Antiochus Epiphanes. This Seleucid king subjected the Jewish people to tortures and slaughter, trying to force them to recant their faith in Yahweh and Judaism in favor of the polytheism of Greece that was directly descended from Babylonianism. Antiochus was defeated by the Maccabees only after he had profaned the temple in Jerusalem with pagan worship and had heaped atrocities upon the Jewish people. Once again, Judaism prevailed as the temple was rededicated. In a way, Antiochus' anti-Semitism was even more subtle than what had preceded him because it sought to replace the Jews' monotheistic religion with the polytheism of the Hellenic world or to syncretize their faith with Greek philosophy.

In later years, anti-Semitism found an effective vehicle in the Roman Empire, whose egomaniacal emperors could not countenance the arrogance of a people who so staunchly defended their religion and their right to self-determination in Israel, their land. Rome could not tolerate the passionate independence of the Jews and their devotion to the one God of the Bible. While Judaism was officially recognized by the Roman Empire as a legitimate religion, the intelligentsia and the patricians had nothing but disdain for this "primitive" people and their "invisible" God. They called the Jews "infidels" because they did not believe in the pantheon of deities that Romans worshipped. So, successive, bitterly fought campaigns were launched against the Jews in an effort to subjugate them and their religion. The greatest of these occurred in 70 C.E. when Titus conquered Jerusalem and destroyed the temple. Later Hadrian built a Roman city on the ruins of Jerusalem after he had suppressed the Bar Kochba rebellion, and he forbade Jews and Jewish Christians to enter the city upon penalty of death.

Initially Rome's extermination program was also turned against the Christians, the new sect that had arisen among first century Judaism that recognized Jesus of Nazareth as the Jewish Messiah. Perhaps millions of these Christians were slaughtered by the Romans. The message of the Christians, however, was not envisioned as exclusively for the Jews and was extended to all men. Subsequently masses of Gentile believers in this re-formed kind of Judaism were brought into the church by the disciples of Jesus.

As with most new movements, the passage of time brought a diminishing of the zeal and fervor of the original faith and the gradual increase of institutionalism. As the congregation (or church) that Jesus had founded began to grow among the Gentiles, it gradually compromised its teachings, blending the Judaism of the primitive church with the Hellenistic concepts that were prominent in the Greco-Roman world.

The more the Christian church accepted the concepts of the heathen religions and the more they minimized the Jewish practices in the church, the less persecution came to the church and the more it became accepted by the political powers of the day.

ANTI-SEMITISM CONQUERS CHRISTIANITY

A sad and tragic event was occurring, for the anti-Semitism of the Gentile world was gradually being transferred to the Christian church which had been born out of Judaism in the first century. It began as Judaeophobia, a fear of Jews and things Jewish. Early Christian leaders who had replaced faith and power with rationalism and professionalism were hard-pressed to compete with Jewish rabbis and the synagogues. They began to inculcate fear of Jews and Judaism as a means of maintaining their converts' loyalty to the church. (A prime example of this is the "sermons" of John Chrysostom in the late fourth century.)

As years turned into centuries, Judaeophobia was replaced by anti-Judaism as the church began to stand against the religion of the Jews. Finally, the church took on more and more antipathy for the Jews themselves as well as for the system of Judaism. Anti-Semitism became entrenched in the church, producing an environment where it was not only acceptable but also applaudable for Christians to hate and persecute Jews in the name of Christ. Jews came to be characterized as bloodthirsty Christ killers, and the Christian religion that had been characterized by love came to be dominated by hate. Thousands, perhaps millions, of Jewish people were tortured and slaughtered through the subsequent centuries under the sign of the cross. Even today, the cross is a symbol of hatred and murder to millions of Jews throughout the world and for good reason!

The Crusades, launched by frenzied Christians to liberate the "holy land" from the Moslem "infidels" in the eleventh through the thirteenth centuries, became events of terror and death for the Jews when the cry went out, "Why should we go thousands of miles to kill the Moslem infidels when these infidel Jews live among us?" Countless Jewish men, women, and children were herded into synagogues and were immolated. Untold numbers of Jews were slaughtered under the banners of the crusaders. So many Jewish women were raped by "Christians" that the rabbis were forced to reckon Jewishness as being born of a Jewish mother rather than by the centuries-old patrilinear system.

Then, in the fourteenth century a pandemic plague nearly decimated the population of Europe and parts of Asia. The Black Death (bubonic plague), carried by fleas that infested the rats that were everywhere in the filthy cities, killed nearly half of the population in the West. Jews seemed exempt from this plague (probably because they kept their homes clean); therefore, the Jews were accused of poisoning wells, and thousands more were slaughtered.

In the fifteenth and sixteenth centuries, Jews were murdered by the thousands by emissaries of the church in the Inquisition. Anti-Semitism enjoyed one of its most bloodthirsty seasons, as synagogues were destroyed, Jews were burned. An all-out effort was launched to destroy the Jews and their religion from the face of the earth. Spain, Portugal, and England expelled Jews, confiscating most of their land and possessions and adding them to royal treasuries.

Then there were centuries of pogroms in eastern Europe which forced resettlement of Jews and brought them torment, torture, and death. This was especially so in Russia where the czars were intensely anti-Semitic and often blamed the Jewish people for the ills of society, unleashing hordes of tormenters upon them. These state- and church-sponsored persecutions continued into the twentieth century, as Jews were continually persecuted and slaughtered in the name of the Christian religion, out of the czars' fervor to support and defend the Russian Orthodox Church.

The obvious question must be asked: Why would a religion that purported itself to be from Yahweh, the God of Israel, seek to slaughter God's chosen people and their God-given religion? The answer must be equally obvious: The powers of evil (not the ministers of righteousness) were at work to obliterate the true knowledge of God from the earth. Romanism and Orthodoxy at their worst were at work to destroy the monotheism of Judaism in the name of preserving the Christian faith.

Miraculously, God preserved the Jewish people and their religious system. Though it was tainted by the traditions of the fathers and though it failed to recognize the true work of redemption wrought on Calvary by Messiah Jesus, Judaism was, nevertheless, a much clearer reflection of God's system of praise, worship, and service than what was offered by the

Latin or the Greek churches.

PROTESTANTISM FAILS TO REPUDIATE ANTI-SEMITISM

At the beginning of the sixteenth century, God started a restoration of the Christianity of the first century, when the idolatry and sacramentalism of the official church were replaced in various reformed communities by faith in God and in the vicarious atonement of Jesus Christ. Both the Protestant Reformation and the counter-reformation within the Roman Catholic Church sought a return to the principles of earliest Christianity.

The one thing that was tragically overlooked in the reformation, however, was the spirit of anti-Semitism which its leaders failed to purge from their midst. The fathers of Protestantism simply failed to restore their reformed Christianity to its inherent Jewish ideals.

The reformers espoused a restored faith that was founded on "*sola scriptura*" (Scripture only) and "*sola fide*" (faith only), and they promoted a return to the grammatico-historical hermeneutic of the ancient Carthagenian school of biblical interpretation. They typically failed, however, to employ fully both their mottos and their own hermeneutic. Scripture continued to be interpreted in the light of their own cultural biases rather than on its Hebrew grammar and the Jewish history and culture in which it had been written. The results for the Jewish people continued to be tragic as most reformed traditions perpetuated the Judaeophobia, anti-Judaism, and anti-Semitism that they inherited from Rome. This was manifest in the demonic doctrine of supersessionism (replacement theology) and other anti-Judaic teaching.

While the father of the Reformation, Martin Luther, was initially philo-Judaic, the failure of Jews to convert *en masse* to Christianity (as part of Luther's eschatological expectations of the imminent return of Jesus) prompted him to become virulently anti-Semitic and to write some of history's most vitriolic diatribes against the Jews, documents which were used four centuries later by Hitler and the Nazis to authenticate and justify their attempt at a "final solution" to the Jewish "problem." Other reformers held similar views, and the denominations that have been built on their names and teachings have been inherently opposed to Judaism. So, until recently, Christianity–whether Orthodoxy, Romanism, or Protestantism–has remained essentially anti-Semitic, for it has expressed disdain for both Jews and for things Jewish.

From 1933 until 1945 the Holocaust, or *Shoah*, became the greatest single concentration of brutal and violent anti-Semitism in history. "Christian" Germans blindly followed Adolph Hitler's quest to establish the Third

Reich, the kingdom of God on earth. Part of this grand scheme to elevate the German people to supremacy over the rest of the world included the need to rid the earth of Jewish "vermin." Europe was to experience *Judenrein*, cleansing from Jews. Early in this process, Jews were shot by the thousands and buried in mass graves. This method proved inefficient because of the thousands of decomposing bodies became a threat to public health; therefore, more efficient processes were devised in which the Jews were herded into cattle cars and transported by rail to carefully planned killing centers where they were murdered with lethal cyanide gas. Then their corpses were plundered of anything of value (gold teeth, hair, and even skin!), and they were cremated. Names like Auschwitz, Buchenwald, Dachau, and others still ring across the pages of history with disgusting horror to civilized men of conscience. Six million Jews, including more than a million children, were slaughtered there.

The Holocaust with all of its horror decimated two-thirds of the Jewish population in Europe; however, Satan's genocidal plot was foiled. Subsequently, the corporate conscience of the free world was pricked with sympathy for the plight of the Jewish people, allowing God to turn evil for good by effecting the restoration of the State of Israel, preparing the way for the prophetic return of the Jews to their land in their last great *aliyah*. Though certain segments of the church continue to be anti-Semitic and anti-Zionist, most of the church has affirmed the right of Jews to live as Jews with self-determination. Most denominations have repudiated historical Christian anti-Semitism, and many have repented before God for their complicity in the persecution of the Jewish people or their silence when persecution was occurring. While Christian positions on the State of Israel remain varied, most organizations affirm the right of Jews to self determination, free from persecution, intimidation, and coercion. Mainline denominations generally are supportive of the Jewish community and Judaism while demonstrating apathy and even occasional antipathy toward the State of Israel. Evangelical denominations, on the other hand, are generally supportive of Israel while being apathetic toward the international Jewish community and even inimical toward Judaism.

REAWAKENING TO CHRISTIANITY'S JEWISH HERITAGE

Many Christian leaders have erroneously supposed that the New Testament writers' warnings against the dangers of legalism were a blanket indictment against Judaism; however, this could certainly not be the case, for we find these same writers practicing various elements of Judaism. While there is a danger in Judaism of looking to the ritual of the Old Covenant either for total justification or for a completion of the atonement of Jesus, there are many potential blessings in Judaism and secrets to carrying out the kind of praise and worship which God desires.

Today, the Holy Spirit is moving among people of all denominational backgrounds to awaken them to their heritage in Judaism. Thousands are throwing off the old anti-Semitic spirit and are taking an objective look into the blessings and advantages of Judaism in its New Testament order. While remaining ever on guard against legalism, they are, nevertheless, rejecting the spirit of anti-Semitism that has robbed thousands of Christians in the past of the opportunity to have a greater understanding of the eternal God. They are beginning to realize that true Christianity is Jewish, a fact which even the atheist Sigmund Freud recognized when he said, "Hatred for Judaism is at bottom hatred for Christianity." Love for Christianity necessarily implies love for Judaism.

ESCAPING THE NEW WAVE OF ANTI-SEMITISM

New waves of overt anti-Semitism continue to stir in various countries and to sweep over others. Israel's staunch and valiant defense of its right to existence and the accompanying turmoil in the oil-rich Arab nations have brought about a revival of popularity for anti-Semitism. Islamic anti-Semitism is excused and condoned by the Western news media which is essentially anti-Semitic, anti-Zionist, and anti-Christian (once again a manifestation of hatred against the God of the Bible and his restrictions against hedonism). Much of Latin America is filled with the spirit of anti-Semitism as Jews are persecuted and synagogues and businesses are targeted by terrorists' bombs. The old "blame-the-Jews" attitude continues to gain adherents whenever problems arise in the world.

Even in the United States and other "enlightened" Western societies, neo-Nazi elements are becoming more and more vocal and open with their anti-Semitism. Jews are not the only the objects of the anti-Semitic spirit. Those who will practice anything revealed in Judaism also find themselves targeted for persecution and violence. The powers of evil are gearing up for one final massive assault against God's chosen people, the Jews, and against his chosen system of religion. Eventually, however, the nations of the world will be judged on the basis of their actions toward Israel and the Jewish people.

God has determined that anti-Semitism is dangerous both to your spiritual and physical well-being. This truth applies to both nations and individuals. God will simply bless those who bless the Jewish people and curse those who curse them. This was his promise to Abraham (Genesis 12:3), and this promise is just as sure as God's promise of eternal life for those who believe. The fortunes of nations have risen and fallen in direct proportion to their posture toward the Jewish people. And, individuals have been blessed and cursed in like manner.

So, be careful! Don't let anti-Semitism poison your relationship with God and with the Jewish people. There is so much in Judaism that can make you a better Christian. Don't let Judaeophobia, anti-Judaism, and anti-Semitism keep you from it.

Bringing Back the Ark:
A Restoration Strategy

Chapter 23
BRINGING BACK THE ARK
A RESTORATION STRATEGY

The renewed interest in the Hebrew roots of the Christian faith is one of the greatest and most universal works that the Holy Spirit is producing in the church in this generation. After being marred for nearly two millennia by Judaeophobia and anti-Semitism, Christianity is experiencing what is only the beginning of a reawakening that has scholars, ministers, leaders, and laymen in virtually every denomination of the body of Christ engaged in the quest to reclaim the church's Judaic heritage.

Christians are changing the way they think about themselves and about the world around them. The traditional dualistic world view that the church has inherited from the Greco-Roman mind-set is gradually being replaced by the holistic world view of Judaism by which Jesus and the apostles lived and expressed their faith. This is affecting the way more and more Christians throughout the world are thinking and acting about their families, their community life, their church relationships, and–most importantly–their relationship with the God of the Bible.

The reawakening that is occurring independently in lives of believers throughout the world is a sovereign work of God, for its universal manifestation in isolated places cannot be traced to any single identifiable human source. The Holy Spirit is at work leading individuals, Bible study groups, local congregations, fellowship groups, and even organizational structures into various elements of restoration truth. The wave of spiritual renewal that has penetrated virtually every denomination has prepared the hearts of God's people for the final restoration, the restoration of the church to its biblical heritage in preparation for the return of its *Jewish* Messiah.

The question that confronts those who have a burning passion for the restoration of Christianity's Jewish roots is this: How can we promote and sustain this growing phenomenon? Or, put another way: How can we keep this work from becoming another passing fancy of a fad-conscious society and see to it that it makes a profound and lasting impact upon the lifestyle of a large segment of the Christian community and changes forever their thinking with regard to Israel, the Jewish people, and Judaism?

A MODEL FOR RESTORATION

The answer to these questions is found in the strategy which King David employed in restoring the ark of the covenant to a place of prominence and honor among Israel. Listen to 1 Chronicles 13:1-4's account of this event: "Then David consulted with the captains of thousands and hundreds, and with every leader. And David said to all the congregation of Israel, 'If it seems good to you, and if it is of the Lord our God, let us send out to our brethren everywhere who are left in all the land of Israel, and with them to the priests and Levites who are in their cities and their common-lands, that they may gather together to us; and let us bring the ark of our God back to us, for we have not inquired at it since the days of Saul. Then all the congregation said that they would do so, *for the thing was right in the eyes of all the people*." The parallel between the restoration of the ark to Israel and the restoration of the Judaic heritage to the church is striking, indeed.

When the people of Israel chose Saul as king, they abandoned God's system in favor of a man of their own choosing. "They have not rejected you, but they have rejected me, that I should not reign over them," God told Samuel (1 Samuel 8:7). The ark of the covenant and its attendant service were abandoned in favor of a cult of personality worship, and Israel became like every other nation. The parallel with the church could not be more! Concurrent with its rejection of its Jewish roots, the church also abandoned its spirituality in favor of a cult of personality and power. Instead of a living experience, religion became a ritualistic performance for the masses. Finally, in the Middle Ages, the church's Judaic heritage was all but obliterated, and the church became a Gentile institution governed more by Hellenic philosophy than by biblical faith.

The Protestant Reformation and the counter reformation within the Roman Catholic Church made significant steps in the direction of restoration; however, they stopped far short of fully restoring the faith once delivered to the saints (Jude 3). Progressively over the ensuing centuries, God has continued his restoration. Now, at the beginning of the twenty-first century, this work has been accelerated, with significant numbers of people around the world committed to restoring the foundations of Christian faith that were laid by Jesus and the apostles on the bedrock of biblical Judaism.

Now the spirit of Messiah is calling the leaders of the universal church to consider whether it is appropriate to restore the New Testament order of God's Judaic system of praise, worship, and service. Leaders from various denominations and fellowships are hearing the call to come together for dialogue about the foundations of our faith. Leaders of every calling, from priests and pastors, to educators and writers, to captains of industry and political leaders are hearing God's call: "If it seems good to you, and if it is from the Lord our God, let us send everywhere to our kinsmen . . . that they may meet with us," and let us collectively discover and restore the Judaeo-Christianity that the apostles practiced.

INTERACTIVE MINISTRY ON LEADERSHIP LEVEL

We must recognize that God's work is too great for any one man or any single organization; therefore, it is vital that we serve as catalysts for interactive ministry on a leadership level. David's strategy was to bring leaders together to analyze the challenge for restoration in his day to see if it was an imperative from God.

We must understand that networking is the focus of God's designs for our time. Leaders must abandon their proclivities toward self-aggrandizement and turf-protection to become mutually submitted to one another in the fear of the Lord and for the welfare of the body of Christ. We must learn to work together as a team with each member's talents and otherness respected and honored. We must stop trying to build up our own ministries and concentrate on helping one another build up the kingdom of God. We must affirm daily our unity in the Messiah, seeking by example and word to bring to completion our Lord's prayer that we "all may be one."

One means of achieving this goal is by adopting a true servant-leadership model. Again, David is the prime example. Knowing that his authority came from God, David neither fought to gain power nor struggled to maintain power. While Saul became insane trying to protect his power and Absalom lost his life trying to seize it, David was content to be a servant of God and of the people and leave the question of who was in authority over the people in the hands of God. For this reason, he was a man after God's own heart, a shepherd and a servant of Israel.

Jesus said, "He that is greatest among you, let him be your servant." God is not looking for lords; he is looking for servants. This concept runs cross-current with the world's models of leadership, where power is grabbed by the heaviest hand and maintained with murderous efficiency. Our model must be the yeshivas of the rabbis, where every man was "greenlighted" to express his own views on every issue but where all issues were decided in the multitude of counsellors.

UNITY IN DIVERSITY

Because of its emphasis on orthodoxy and credalism, Christianity has sought to establish unity through uniformity. If some could not subscribe to the majority's belief system, they were anathematized and ostracized. This approach to the issue of unity has produced a fragmented Christianity more often than not engaged in internecine strife with more energies expended upon exchanges of polemic pyrotechnics than upon engaging the enemy of men's souls. Denominationalism's quest for purity of doctrine has produced impurity of the soul in far too many of its adherents.

The Judaic model of unity, on the other hand, is one of unity in diversity, with each person's distinctives respected. Regardless as to what their views may be, the total Jewishness of each person is affirmed. Christians could well learn from this Jewish idea. We can affirm our total brotherhood either in Adam or in Christ, a concept that can help us with the Christ-mandated task of loving all mankind. We can honor the diversity in the body of Christ and not seek to make every member a hand or an eye (1 Corinthians 12). We can be our brother's brother regardless as to his ethnic, racial, cultural, or denominational background.

We can place greater attention on the Judaic concept of orthopraxy rather than on our Christian concepts of orthodoxy. Someone has said that many Jews do not believe anything but they do everything that their Scriptures require while Christians believe everything and do nothing. Perhaps this statement is a bit extreme; however, it does illustrate a point. Christians are far too concerned about beliefs and ideas (a Greek concept) and give too little attention to practicing their faith (a Jewish concept).

TOGETHER WE CAN

If the cause of restoring the church's Judaic heritage is to succeed in changing the face of Christianity in this generation, it will do so only because those who have this vision come together in truly Judaic fashion to promote and sustain this cause. We must reach out with compassion to all of our fellow citizens of the kingdom of God to invite their involvement in the research, analysis, and development of the concepts of restoration. We must dare to be inclusive. When others draw a circle that excludes us, we must have the wit and wisdom to draw a bigger circle that includes them and their circle. Every Christian body is included in this word, for every communion has faith and practice that is rooted in the Judaic heritage of Jesus and the apostles. When we include everyone in this restoration, we are not perceived as elitist purveyors of some strange, foreign teaching. Though it may seem idealistic, if we present this message with the proper attitude of love and inclusion, it will be accepted for the truth that it is and for the blessing that it will bring the body of Christ. It will be said that "the thing was right in the eyes of all the people."

Restoring Christianity's Judaic Heritage

Chapter 24
RESTORING CHRISTIANITY'S JUDAIC HERITAGE

When nearly a century ago Julius Wellhausen boldly proclaimed that Jesus was a Jew, not a Christian, the cause of prophetic restoration received a dramatic boost from a very unlikely source. While Wellhausen's motive for his statement was the promotion of his anti-revelational liberalism that sought to "demythologize" the Bible by taking God and spiritual things out of it, his statement sent shock waves through academic circles. While some saw this statement as an opportunity to further their assault on the revelational authority of the Bible, others were burdened with the quest of searching for the historical Jesus.

Around the turn of the twentieth century, a few scholars began to consider what had been unthinkable for centuries–the fact that Jesus was a Jew and the religion which he practiced throughout his lifetime was biblical Judaism. The church, including Catholic, Orthodox, and Protestant traditions, had long enshrined Jesus as the cosmic Christ to such a degree that his Jewish humanity was all but forgotten. While in dogma and creed it had maintained that he had been very God and very man, for all practical purposes the humanity of Jesus had been lost, including his identification as a Jew among his Jewish brethren.

The church's denial of the Jewishness of Jesus has represented a revival of the ancient heresy of docetism, which utterly denied the humanity of Jesus, calling his physical appearance merely an apparition used to disguise his absolute deity. Monophysitism declared that Jesus had only one nature, the divine. Jesus came to be portrayed as a Western European with blond hair and blue eyes and of such obvious divinity that a nimbus always appeared around his head. The truth is that the absolute humanity of Jesus was a precondition to his prophetic office: he could not have redeemed man without becoming man, living as man, overcoming all sin as man, and dying as man (Romans 8:3; Hebrews 2:9, 10, 14). This he did as a Jew. While the ecumenical council of Chalcedon in 451 C.E. established the doctrine of the contemporaneous total deity and total humanity of Jesus in his incarnation, the church since that time has largely denied the most basic fact of his humanity–that Jesus was a Jew. Robert T. Osborn has called this Christian rejection of the Jewishness of Jesus the "Christian blasphemy," a willful prevarication to support its continuing anti-Judaism.

With the rediscovery of the Jewishness of Jesus has come a growing interest in studying the influence of Judaism upon Jesus and upon the nascent church. For centuries, most of the church had believed that Jesus as the Christ had brought an entirely new religion which replaced Judaism–that he brought totally new ideas theretofore unknown to man. Despite the fact that the Scriptures themselves declare that Jesus grew in wisdom and stature as a part of the normal process of human maturation (Luke 2:52), the church denied the influence of his Jewish family and environment upon Jesus and his human spiritual and intellectual life.

CHRISTIAN FOUNDATIONS IN JUDAISM

The truth is that Jesus borrowed eclectically from all of the various Judaisms that were a part of first century Israel, just as he addressed himself to those traditions of the various Jewish sects that contravened the Word of God (*Tanakh*). Since there was no monolithic Judaism in the first century, Jesus came into contact with, and was influenced by, the various expressions of Jewish faith. The "Golden Rule," the origination of which the church has attributed to Jesus, is in reality an adaptation of a statement that Hillel made a generation earlier. It can be readily demonstrated that most of the teachings of Jesus were antedated in the messages of the prophets and sages of Israel, including those of what has been called the intertestamental period and of the great rabbinical schools in the decades before and during the time of his ministry. He also can be seen to disagree in some way with each of the first century Judaisms, including the Sadducees, the Pharisees, the Essenes, the Qumran community, the Zealots, the Herodians, and others. The church has done itself and the Jewish people a great disservice by ascribing originality of concepts and statements to Jesus which he quoted and/or adapted from those before his time. Of course, as the person of the Word (*Memra* or *Logos*) of God, Jesus gave all the Word to the prophets; however, in the voluntary limitation of his humanity, he grew in wisdom by assimilating teaching of Torah in home, synagogue, and temple.

As understanding of the interrelationship between biblical Judaism and the gospel of Jesus has continued to unfold, more and more scholars have begun to recognize that the religion which Jesus practiced was Judaism, the same religion that he as the *Logos* theophany at Sinai had delivered to the Jewish people. The practice of Judaism was not optional to Jesus, for it was also a precondition to his prophetic office. He was born of woman, under the Torah, under the obligation to observe the entire law of Yahweh (Galatians 4:4). He was an observant Jew, very orthodox in fulfilling the requirements of the law to the letter. It was in this way that it could be said of him that he knew no sin, for if he had violated the law, he would have been a sinner (1 John 3:4; 1 Peter 2:22). In this way he established the perfect righteousness that made him a perfect sacrifice for the sins of the whole world (Hebrews 2:10). His observance of the law established the righteousness that is credited to the believer instead of his faith in Jesus so that the believer who is cleansed from sin through the blood of Jesus is justified by the imputed righteousness of Christ (2 Corinthians 5:21; Romans 3:21, 22). While Jesus was often in conflict with the oral Torah or the tradition which was later codified in the *Mishnah* and the *Gemara* of the Talmud, he in no way violated the commandments of God in the written Torah, nor did he renounce all of the tradition of the sages. Jesus simply practiced biblical Judaism.

As knowledge of the Jewishness of Jesus and of his observance of Judaism has expanded both in the academic community and elsewhere, more and more scholars have come to understand that Jesus simply did not come to establish a new religion called Christianity. He did not come to replace an old religion with a new one. He did not come to replace a bad religion with a good one. He came only to reform what he had authored at Sinai by perfecting it through his death at Calvary (Hebrews 12:2). Christianity as we know it is the product of well-intended men's efforts to make the gospel relative to their Gentile cultures, efforts which resulted, however, in a system that was divorced from its heritage.

THE TIME OF REFORMATION

The ministry of Jesus could be encapsulated in one word–reformation (Hebrews 9:10). Jesus was a reformer, not an innovator. His whole purpose was to reform Judaism, taking the eternal principles of that system and making them applicable to and liveable in the entire world. His reformation was actually a *restoration*, a returning of the Torah to its original intent and purpose. His fundamental position with regard to Judaism was stated in Matthew 5:17: "Do not think that I came to destroy the Law or the Prophets. I did not come to destroy but to fulfill." It was never the intention, design, or will of Jesus to abrogate the law and destroy Judaism, replacing it with a new religion. And, he was not forced to do so because of the unbelief of Israel's leadership (Romans 3:3, 4). He maintained his own personal faithfulness to the religion which he, himself, had authored, and he encouraged the Jews, including his own disciples, to be faithful to the fundamental principles of that religion, reformed and perfected only by his own death and resurrection (Matthew 5:19, 20; Luke 18:18-22).

The major areas of reform that Jesus brought to Judaism were in its sacrificial and ceremonial systems. Jesus fulfilled once and for all the sacrificial system as it related to offerings for sin when he became the one and only sacrifice for sin on the cross of Calvary (Hebrews 9:25-28). When the blood of Jesus was shed, the atonement for the sins of all mankind was made; therefore, the ongoing system of animal sacrifices for sin became superfluous. It is important to note, however, that the system of sacrifice for sin was not destroyed. It was only reformed with a new and better sacrifice, the perfect sacrifice of the body and blood of Jesus. The remainder of the sacrificial system took on a new dimension in the church that was manifest in sacrifices of praise (Hebrews 13:15), prayer (Revelation 5:8), and of living bodies submitted to the will of God (Romans 12:1).

Much of what was done in Judaism's ceremonial system was also rendered superfluous by the life, death, resurrection, and ascension of Jesus. What had been an agrarian, natural society was transformed by Jesus into a spiritual society, the church. While many of the Judaisms of Jesus' time had come to emphasize the fact that the spiritual applications of the eternal principles of the Torah were more important than mere slavish devotion to its external ritual, Jesus developed this idea further, reforming the entire ceremonial system of Judaism. The Sabbath and the agricultural festivals took on spiritual significance. First of all, Jesus became the Sabbath for the believer (Hebrews 4:1-11). He also became the Passover to those who received him (1 Corinthians 5:7). Pentecost became a time for celebrating the giving of the Holy Spirit as well as the giving of the Torah. The ceremonial ablutions were fulfilled in spiritual washings of regeneration and sanctification (1 Corinthians 6:11). Again, however, the system of Judaism was not destroyed: it was merely reformed. Celebration of the Sabbath and of the festivals continued in remembrance of the Lord of the Sabbath and of his works of redemption (Passover) and empowerment (Pentecost). Without exception, the work of Jesus was one of reformation of the existing system of Judaism, not of its abrogation and replacement with a completely new system called Christianity.

THE NASCENT CHURCH AND JUDAISM

There is ample evidence in the Apostolic Writings that the first century church continued in the teachings of Jesus and remained inherently Jewish. The church of Jesus Christ, like its Lord and namesake, was Jewish and continued to function within Judaism as a reformed sect (Acts 24:14). The apostles did not seek to divorce the church from Judaism. They rather sought to make their views regarding the Messiahship and eternal redemptive work of Jesus normative for all of their Jewish brethren. They continued daily in the temple as loyal parts of the worshipping community of Israel (Acts 2:46), even submitting themselves to temple ritual that could in no way be demanded of them by the reformed Judaism of Jesus (Acts 21:23-27). Even the requirements that the church enjoined upon the Gentiles were taken directly from Judaism (Acts 15:19, 20).

Though Paul has been accused by the Jewish people of being an apostate from Judaism and has been hailed by many Gentile Christians as being the one who dealt the theological death blow to Judaism, replacing it with a Gentilized Christianity, the truth is that there was no one more faithful to Judaism than Paul. Throughout his life he maintained his status as a Pharisee, a disciple of Gamliel (Acts 23:3; 22:6). Though he reasoned and taught the truth of Jesus' reformation of Judaism, he continued to encourage both Gentiles and Jews alike to maintain the New Testament order for the observance of God's ancient religion (1 Corinthians 5:8). Like Jesus and other Jewish leaders before him (especially the Diaspora Jews), Paul recognized that the ritual, external observances of the system of the law were not to be equated with the internal, spiritual relationship with God through the eternal principles on which the law and Judaism were founded and of which those external observances were temporal manifestations. This is why Paul willingly submitted to rites of temple purification (Acts 21:24-27) and encouraged the Gentile churches to observe the festival of Passover with its New Testament celebration in the communion of the body and blood of Christ (1 Corinthians 5:7, 8). What Paul consistently taught was not a new way of salvation. According to him, men must attain a right relationship with God in the same manner in which Abraham did, by faith (Romans 4:16; Galatians 3:5-29). Paul patterned Christian life after Judaism as interpreted by his Jewish Lord, not after Platonism or Gentile mystery religions, as some Christian theologians have asserted.

INDIGINIZATION BRINGS DE-JUDAIZATION

The church, however, failed to hear the warnings of Paul in Romans 11:18-20 that the Gentile branches not boast against Israel and the exhortations of Jude that it earnestly contend for the faith once delivered to the saints (Jude 3). Indeed, as Paul had predicted, after his departing, grievous wolves entered in who did not spare the flock of God (Acts 20:28, 29). The door that God opened to the Gentile nations swung both ways, letting in the traditions and concepts of the non-Jewish world, as well as opening the faith of God to the nations. Just as there can be no doubt about the intention of God to bring the Gentiles into the household of faith, so there can be no doubt that his Spirit sought to insulate the church from the concepts of the Hellenistic world. The church, however, rapidly lost its legacy in Judaism and was overpowered by corrupted ideas of the pagan cultures into which it was called to minister.

In their attempt at indiginization or contextualization of the gospel so that the Hellenistic world could receive it, the Greek fathers of the church succumbed to the process of syncretism in which Platonic philosophy and Greek religious ideas were added to the Judaic teachings of the church. From the time of Justin Martyr attempts were made to reconcile Platonism with Christian teaching, a process which reached its zenith in Clement of Alexandria and Origen, who believed that Plato had been a Christian even though he was not aware of it. Such attempts at syncretism between Platonism and Christianity were well intended but ill advised. Eventually these accretions so overwhelmed the heritage of the church in the Hebrew faith that Christianity became a Gentilized movement, both in demographics and in theology and polity. What began in the good intentions of the apostolic fathers, the apologists, and the polemicists of the first four centuries to make their faith relevant and appealing to the sophisticated intelligentsia of Greek society actually led the church down the road to compromise with philosophies and religious ideas that were foreign to the faith of Jesus Christ.

This compromise produced a Gentilized gospel that was divorced from its Jewish matrix, a gospel that alienated the church from the commonwealth of Israel. While it is true that the parting of the ways between Judaism and Christianity was by mutual agreement and was facilitated by the Jewish community as well as by the church, the church must bear the greater share of responsibility for renouncing its heritage and separating itself from Israel. Eventually the church came to ignore and in many cases even to repudiate the Jewishness of the Jesus of the gospel in favor of the Christianized and Gentilized Christ of the church, in whose name it spewed forth centuries of venomous boastings against the natural branches of God's olive tree. Those initial polemic pyrotechnics escalated into the conflagration of the pogroms and the inquisition and ended in the Holocaust of the twentieth century, with wave after wave of the anti-Semitism which still remains a grave disfigurement on the face of the church.

RESTORING THE CHURCH'S JUDAIC HERITAGE

The Reformation of the sixteenth century began to restore the light of faith to the Christian church; however, it stopped far short of what God had intended, became steeped in nationalism, and perpetuated the anti-Judaism which had been part of its spiritual heritage for some fourteen centuries.

Gradually, however, God has brought about a greater awareness of the truth about the apostolic church and its inherent Jewishness. Initially in the minds of scholars, many of whom were considered eccentric by their peers, the responsibility of honoring the Jewish people for the heritage of the church came to the fore. Then with the tragic events of the twentieth century, the plight of the Jewish people was emblazoned inescapably on the corporate consciousness of the Christian church.

The result has been that in some circles the historical church doctrine of supersession or replacement theology has been abandoned in favor of a revisionist theology which argues for the continuing validity of two parallel and equal covenants and religions–Judaism for the Jews and Christianity for the Gentiles. Though well intended, this doctrine flies in the face of the clear statement of Scripture, which unequivocally declares that there is "one Lord and one faith" (Ephesians 4:5).

On the other hand, however, there have been many who have realized that for Christianity to be a truly authentic expression of the religion which Jesus practiced and taught, it must return to its Judaic roots and restore its essential Jewishness. These believers realize that the only way in which the biblical mission of the church can be fulfilled is for the church to recognize and repent of its own sins of Judaeophobia, anti-Judaism, and anti-Semitism and to restore its inherent Jewishness, thereby facilitating among the Jewish people a more accurate perception of Jesus as the Jewish Messiah, not just the Christian Christ. The Christian church must take responsibility for its role in feeding the fires of anti-Semitism. It must repent fully for its sin either of actively persecuting the ancient people of the Bible or quietly countenancing the overt actions of others against the Jews. It must realize that its attitudes are the result of its denial of its own essential Jewishness as well as that of Jesus, himself. When the church becomes more Jewish in content and expression, the Jewish people will be able to come to an accurate perception of biblical Christianity, as opposed to its historical perversion as Christendom.

For nearly nineteen centuries, the church has been spinning out of control in a vortex of lost identity, wrenched from its biblical moorings, denying what it was designed by its Founder to be. Now, like a child snatched as a newborn from its birth parents, it is crying out, searching for its roots, its self identity. And many are awakening to the realization that Judaism is the parent of Christianity. This great awakening is already beginning, and it will only increase throughout the world as the Holy Spirit moves on the hearts of believers of all denominational persuasions to recognize and re-establish the Jewishness of their faith through Jesus, their Jewish Lord.

This is not a call for Christians simply to become more Jewish by practicing the cultural elements of modern Judaism. It is not a call to major in minutiae or to collect artifacts. It is a call for Christians to be more in love with their Jewish Lord. It is a call to have a right relationship with God by having a right understanding of the Jewish Book and a right experience with the Jewish Lord. The time is now for those who truly love the Word of God to search the Scriptures diligently to see the truths which have been kept from them and to begin the process of restoration.

The many believers throughout the world who are searching for orthodoxy in Christianity need to take one step further. The answers are not to be found in England, or in Italy, or in Greece. The answers are in Israel. The church must look beyond the Reformers, the Thomist theologians, the influences of Plato and the philosophers, and even beyond the Greek and Latin fathers. It must return to the Hebrew faith of old if it is to find the orthopraxy that will enable it to be the light of the world and show mercy to Israel.

After being characterized for nearly nineteen centuries by Judaeophobia at best and by overt anti-Semitism at worst, the Christian church is beginning to receive what will become a miraculous healing. The Holy Spirit is awakening a hunger in people in nearly every segment of Christianity for a restoration of the Judaic heritage of the first century church. Edward Flannery encapsulated what God is doing when he called for an "over-Hellenized, over-Latinized Christianity" to experience a "re-Judaizing process to restore it to its inherent Judaic ideal." That this work is a product of the agency of the Holy Spirit is underscored by the fact that no one individual, denomination, or group of people can claim responsibility for this widespread and growing phenomenon.

Could it be that a renewal of the Judaic heritage of the gospel of Jesus Christ is the next great awakening of the Holy Spirit in the ongoing fulfillment of the restoration of all things that Peter predicted in Acts 3:20, 21 would precede the *parousia* of our Lord? Is it possible that Christians everywhere could soon reclaim their lost legacy in Judaism? Will God finally and irrevocably expose the Hellenization and Latinization of the gospel and restore his church to its rightful Judaic heritage? With the growing emphasis on this biblical and prophetic truth, it would seem that at long last the answer to these questions is a resounding, Yes!

PERSONAL REFLECTIONS

Much can be gained from understanding the Jewish Scriptures, the Jewish law, and the Jewish faith (Romans 3:1). With such an understanding one has an expanded awareness of God's omniscience in authoring a plan of salvation for mankind that has been in operation since the creation of the world. One also gains a new appreciation for the continuity of the Holy Scriptures and of God's plan that has unfolded from generation to generation. In addition, one acquires a more complete understanding of the incarnation, life, death, and resurrection of the only begotten Son of God.

Among the great works which the Holy Spirit is bringing to pass in our generation are a revived commitment to the survival of the Jewish people and their religion and a revolutionary awakening of Christians of various communions to their heritage in biblical Judaism. This awareness is expanding in most, if not all, denominations of Christianity. It is a healthy sign of spiritual maturity when men are able to conquer their prejudices and traditions to recognize the roots from which their faith has grown. And, it is a healthy sign of spiritual revival when such an awakening is taking place across denominational lines and throughout the world.

Restoration of Christianity's Hebrew foundations is an expansive effort which touches on every area of Christian life and worship. Many scholars throughout the world are researching various aspects of this idea, documenting the historical correlation of Judaism, the faith of the First Covenant, and Christianity, the faith of the New Covenant.

Efforts such as these will produce an appreciation for the Hebrew faith. As we gain a clearer insight into the inherent Jewishness of Jesus and of the gospel, we also receive a greater appreciation and love for those ancient people, his kinsmen according to the flesh.

This is the *raison d'être* of Restoration Foundation. There are thousands of people throughout the world who share a common burden for Judaic restoration and the salvation of Israel. They are, however, fragmented and isolated, a fact which has kept their efforts minimized both in their own eyes and in the eyes of the world. It is time, however, for those whom God has given this vision to network together to share ideas and resources in the interest of impacting all of Christianity with this message of restoration.

For forty years, the major focus of my own academic and ministerial career has been a systematic study of Christianity's Hebraic heritage. This ministry of restoration has burned into my heart a vision to share the inherent Jewishness of the Christian faith with all believers throughout the world.

I began to envision a networking organization that would bring together biblical scholars, church leaders, and other persons interested in Judaic restoration in a forum free of denominational agendas to do research and development into the restoration of the Judaic heritage of the Christian church and to devise means of marketing this concept the Christian community. Restoration Foundation was the product of this vision.

Restoration Foundation is a nonprofit educational and publishing resource to the body of Christ. The vision of Restoration Foundation is to promote the restoration of the Christian church's Judaic heritage by researching the historical and theological understanding of the Hebrew foundations of the gospel of Jesus Christ, developing the concept and its practical applications, and encouraging its implementation in the church.

The foundation is transdenominational. Its integrity is protected from either direct or indirect denominational or organizational influence or manipulation. It seeks to bring together leaders in the field of Judaic restoration to pool their resources for research, development, and promotion of this important part of the prophetic restoration ministry.

Restoration Foundation seeks to maintain of a network of individuals, ministries, and organizations that share a common interest in promoting Christianity's Jewish roots. It is designed to provide a vehicle for interfaith and inter-organizational fellowship, dialogue, and cooperation. It establishes retreat forums to provide intense and interactive Bible study, private and corporate prayer, personal interaction and fellowship, and dialogue that promotes idea exchange and concept testing among peers in a nonthreatening atmosphere free from hidden agendas and denominational/organizational objectives. This forum has been and will continue to be one of the most important parts of the Restoration Foundation agenda.

The foundation also focuses on a very vital aspect of Judaic restoration–the promotion of this concept to a Christian church whose traditional Judaeophobia causes it to be biased against Judaism and the Jewish people and to be predisposed not to receive this message. The foundation is careful that its language communicates truths in a way that is non-threatening and non-judgmental way, free of legalism.

Restoration Foundation organizes, produces, and promotes seminars and other teaching forums for instruction in Judaism's legacy to the Christian church. There is room in the field of this ministry for many specialists, each of whom can make invaluable contributions to the overall understanding of the Christian church and its constituent congregations and ministries. The foundation, therefore, does not seek to control its members, nor does it attempt to establish an orthodoxy. Instead, it promotes the Judaic concept of unity in diversity in contrast with the traditional Christian concept of unity through uniformity which has produced nothing but division.

Development, production, and marketing of materials for educating families in the Judaeo-Christian faith as it is confirmed in both the Hebrew Scriptures and the Apostolic Writings are a featured and important part of Restoration Foundation. Works that constituent members of the foundation are doing in this area of ministry are promoted by the foundation.

Through its Golden Key Books, Restoration Foundation seeks to publish materials and to produce audio and video presentations of seminars and other instructional and promotional materials that facilitate understanding of the interrelationship of Christianity and Judaism.

Restoration Foundation also publishes *Restore!* magazine, a high-quality journal that is helping Christians around the world recover the Hebrew foundations of their faith. The name *Restore!* is an imperative to all believers in the Christian church, for everyone must restore the Jewish roots of his faith. *Restore!* presents theologically sound, methodologically practical teachings on the church's Judaic heritage.

An important underlying work of Restoration Foundation is its use of every means possible, including prayer, education, and promotion, to eradicate Judaeophobia and anti-Semitism from the entire Christian church and from the world at large. In aid of this effort Restoration Foundation works to minister love, commitment, and assistance to the nation of Israel and to all Jewish people.

The Restoration Foundation vision is admittedly expansive; however, we believe it is biblically based. We pray that Restoration Foundation will be empowered to take the message of Judaic restoration into the entire Christian community worldwide so that the body of Christ can be prepared to receive the returning Jewish Messiah, Yeshua HaMashiach, Jesus Christ.

We welcome your comments, criticism, and advice. We also invite you to join Restoration Foundation as a Golden Key Partner. Let us hear from you!

John D. Garr, Ph.D.
President

INDEX